PAUL AND THE PERSON

Paul and the Person

Reframing Paul's Anthropology

Susan Grove Eastman

WILLIAM B. EERDMANS PUBLISHING COMPANY
GRAND RAPIDS, MICHIGAN

Wm. B. Eerdmans Publishing Co.
2140 Oak Industrial Drive NE, Grand Rapids, Michigan 49505
www.eerdmans.com

26 25 24 23 22 21 20 19 18 17   1 2 3 4 5 6 7 8 9 10

ISBN 978-0-8028-6896-1

Library of Congress Cataloging-in-Publication Data

Names: Eastman, Susan Grove, 1952– author.
Title: Paul and the person : reframing Paul's anthropology / Susan Grove Eastman.
Description: Grand Rapids : Eerdmans Publishing Co., 2017. | Includes bibliographical references
  and index.
Identifiers: LCCN 2017014597 | ISBN 9780802868961 (pbk. : alk. paper)
Subjects: LCSH: Theological anthropology—Christianity. | Bible. Epistles of Paul—Theology. |
  Bible. Epistles of Paul—Criticism, interpretation, etc.
Classification: LCC BS2655.A58 E26 2017 | DDC 233.092—dc23
  LC record available at https://lccn.loc.gov/2017014597

For Eddie

Contents

Foreword

Susan Eastman is an intellectual explorer. From the familiar terrain of Paul's statements about humanity she has gone in search of concepts, frames of reference, and models of personhood that could help us make sense of Paul. She has traveled far, into philosophy (ancient and modern), neuroscience, and experimental psychology—mostly territory unknown to biblical scholars—and she has returned in triumph. The book before you offers genuinely fresh insights into some of the most difficult material in Paul's letters, while giving us new ways of conceiving what it might mean in contemporary terms.

Paul's complex anthropological terminology (flesh, body, spirit, mind), his unique configuration of the human condition (as both sinners and under Sin), and his innovative language of participation (in Christ, Christ in me) have drawn his interpreters into a long and deep conversation with his letters. Platonist, Stoic, Aristotelian, and existentialist philosophies have all been deployed as intellectual frames in which to make sense of Paul's anthropology, some more successfully than others. The truth is that, without a conceptual framework that makes some sense *to us*, we end up merely repeating Paul's language without understanding it. Rudolf Bultmann's brilliant attempt in the mid-twentieth century to interpret Paul's anthropology in Lutheran-existentialist terms now feels outdated, not least since its individualist assumptions clash with more recent relational understandings of the self. Ernst Käsemann was already moving in a promising direction, with his understanding of the body as the self-in-relation, but what has been lacking for some forty years has been a coherent, well-researched reading of Paul's anthropology that draws on contemporary insights into what constitutes us as persons and what shapes our identities as embodied agents. Eastman has now filled this significant gap.

Of course there is no single contemporary understanding of the human being, and within each disciplinary field there are strong disagreements and multiple points of difference. What Eastman has discerned, however, is a significant convergence in key aspects of contemporary research, a convergence sufficiently close to core features of Paul's language to provide exciting new possibilities for interpretation. Through her explorations of developmental psychology, neuroscience, and the philosophy of personhood, she has identified common, or at least overlapping, insights into the self as irreducibly embodied and socially formed. In what she labels the "second-person perspective," the self is formed not alone in self-referential cognition (a first-person "I"), nor in objective knowledge of things beyond oneself (a third-person "he/she," "it," or "they"), but in encounter with others, in the "I-you" address where relationships are not additional to the already-formed individual but are constitutive of the person. In other words, old models of individual autonomy are defunct, even if they persist in the popular imagination of the West; we become individuals only *in and from* relationships, good or bad.

Can this perspective help us make better sense of the way Paul talks of sin as not just something we do but something that shapes us (as in Romans 7)? Can it shed light on Paul's perplexing language of participation in Christ (as in Galatians 2)? Can it draw Pauline studies into better dialogue with contemporary theology, which is already in interdisciplinary conversation along the lines explored here? As the following pages show, the answer to all these questions is a resounding Yes! What Eastman offers here is not an *explanation* of Paul's anthropology, as if what he wrote is *nothing other* than what contemporary psychologists or philosophers are saying about the human person. Nor is it an anachronistic *imposition* on the Pauline texts, since she is careful to give those texts their own voice and to place them also in illuminating comparison with ancient philosophy, in the person of Epictetus. Rather, Eastman stages what she terms a *conversation* between Paul and contemporary perspectives on the person, a dialogue that helps us identify *contemporary models or metaphors* that fit both the Pauline texts and our own best understandings of who we are as embodied, relational creatures.

The "fit" does not require complete similarity, and it retains the integrity of Paul's God-talk. But it sheds significant new light on puzzling Pauline texts, and—this is rightly of importance to Eastman—it enables us to communicate this element of Paul's gospel in terms that resonate with the thought and experience of our contemporaries. There never will be a "last word" on Paul's anthropology, because the task of interpretation is fresh in each generation and in each new context. But this book does give us rich new insight into Paul and well-conceived language with which to communicate his theology effectively today. That is a precious gift indeed.

JOHN M. G. BARCLAY
Lightfoot Professor of Divinity
Durham University

Preface

The writing of this book has been a long journey, with many twists and turns along the way. It reflects a persistent fascination with the question of how Paul's gospel intersects with the vicissitudes of daily life, a fascination that brings me back again and again to questions about Paul's understanding of personhood—in short, his anthropology. My interest in what I might call "participatory identity" grew out of an earlier project on imitation language in Galatians.[1] I began to consider ways in which mimesis was related to participation in the ancient world, and to mull over the nonvolitional aspects of mimesis in human experience. That curiosity about imitation and participation took me considerably beyond the bounds of New Testament scholarship, first into studies of imitation in infants, and eventually into the fascinating discoveries of "mirror neurons" in a research lab in Parma, Italy. I began to see imitation as a largely unconscious medium of exchange through which we take parts of people into ourselves via a process of mimetic internalization, and they return the favor. This process happens between parents and children, but not only there. Indeed, as my students often tell me, once we have been alerted to the human propensity to imitate others and the neurological underpinnings of that propensity, we see it everywhere.

At the same time, I noticed the strong links between mimesis and participation in the ancient world, beginning with Plato and Aristotle but finding distinctive articulation in the first century in the Stoic philosophers. I began to suspect that my real topic was the language of participation in Paul, particularly the way in which a participatory account of human personhood might

---

1. *Recovering Paul's Mother Tongue: Language and Theology in Galatians* (Grand Rapids: Eerdmans, 2007).

help make sense of Paul's puzzling use of the prepositions "in" and "with." Hence my turn to the topic of Paul's anthropology, including his assumed understanding of what it is to be a human being, what makes for suffering, what makes for flourishing, and how people change completely and yet remain "themselves." My wrestling with these questions juxtaposes Paul, his ancient context, and contemporary theorists of the person in philosophy and the cognitive sciences.

Although such interlocutors may seem far afield for many New Testament scholars, I have come to believe that such boundary-crossing conversation is crucial if we want to read Paul in ways that are both accessible and compelling beyond the limits of the guild of Pauline studies. From outside the guild, and even in private conversations with other New Testament colleagues, Pauline scholarship is not infrequently characterized as—dare I say it?—boring. Or if not boring, at the least somewhat arcane and distant from life in any broader sense. There are very many exceptions to this judgment, among which I note excellent recent volumes bringing theologians and biblical scholars together on central topics in Pauline exegesis.[2] Other scholars are working at the interface of scientific studies and Pauline interpretation.[3] I want to push us further along that road toward meeting points with other conversation partners as well, precisely in the service of a theological interpretation of Paul's letters that takes them seriously as a word of address to contemporary readers.

I am well aware of many lacunae in this study, which I offer as a prompt

2. See, e.g., Mark Elliott et al., eds., *Galatians and Christian Theology: Justification, the Gospel, and Ethics* (Grand Rapids: Baker Academic, 2014); Kevin J. Vanhoozer, Constantine R. Campbell, and Michael J. Thate, eds., *"In Christ" in Paul: Explorations in Paul's Theology of Union and Participation*, WUNT 2.384 (Tübingen: Mohr Siebeck, 2014); and Joshua B. Davis and Douglas Harink, eds., *Apocalyptic and the Future of Theology: With and Beyond J. Louis Martyn* (Eugene, OR: Cascade, 2012).

3. Joel Green has written on biblical studies and neuroscience but not specifically on Paul's letters. See, for example, his *Body, Soul, and Human Life: The Nature of Humanity in the Bible* (Grand Rapids: Baker Academic, 2008). Note also Colleen Shantz, *Paul in Ecstasy: The Neurobiology of Paul's Life and Thought* (Cambridge: Cambridge University Press, 2009). Recently Matthew Croasmun has investigated emergence theory in relationship to Paul's notion of sin; see his "'Real Participation': The Body of Christ and the Body of Sin in Evolutionary Perspective," in Vanhoozer, Campbell, and Thate, *"In Christ" in Paul*; and his book *The Emergence of Sin* (Oxford: Oxford University Press, 2017). Craig S. Keener's magisterial new work, *The Mind of the Spirit: Paul's Approach to Transformed Thinking* (Grand Rapids: Baker Academic, 2016), came out just as this book was on its way to press. For an excellent study of Paul's account of the role of the Spirit in human transformation, with some reference to psychoanalytic theories, see Volker Rabens, *The Holy Spirit and Ethics in Paul: Transformation and Empowering for Religious-Ethical Life*, 2nd ed. (Minneapolis: Fortress, 2014).

to a further exchange of ideas, not as the final word on Paul's anthropology. In particular, I have not engaged with notions of the person as a self-in-relation, as found in Second Temple Jewish texts, for three reasons. In the first place, I have chosen to shine the spotlight on the Stoics, not because they are closer to Paul's thought than are his Jewish contemporaries (they are not), but because their natural theology lends itself particularly well to comparison with the naturalistic methodologies of scientific investigations. For the same reason, I have limited my ancient interlocutors primarily to Epictetus as a spokesperson for a particular brand of Stoicism, because Epictetus's thought intersects in such intriguing ways with current work in the cognitive sciences. Such limitation in breadth allows more engagement in depth with Epictetus's robust, witty, and provocative personal voice.

Second, to bring Second Temple Jewish texts into the conversation adequately would require the equivalent of a second volume, doubling the size of this book. Rather, the topic deserves a separate, in-depth exploration that would build on excellent existing studies of Paul's anthropology in its Jewish context and bring them into dialogue with contemporary second-person perspectives on human identity.[4] Third, therefore, I reiterate that I consider this book an invitation to further work, not the final word on Paul's anthropology in either ancient or current contexts. My hope is that the relatively narrow scope of the book makes possible a sharply delineated model of a new kind of conversation between specific ancient and contemporary voices, including early Jewish texts and potentially modern Jewish philosophers of the self.[5]

I also have not engaged with social-scientific studies of the Pauline literature. There already are many such studies available, as this is now a well-

4. Considerable groundwork for such an interdisciplinary project already exists; I note in particular John M. G. Barclay and Simon Gathercole, eds., *Divine and Human Agency in Paul and His Cultural Environment* (London: T&T Clark, 2006); Kyle B. Wells, *Grace and Agency in Paul and Second Temple Judaism: Interpreting the Transformation of the Heart* (Leiden: Brill, 2014); and Rabens, *The Holy Spirit and Ethics in Paul*, 147–67, 247–48. Seminal work on Jewish texts and the construction of the self includes Jacqueline E. Lapsley, *Can These Bones Live? The Problem of the Moral Self in the Book of Ezekiel* (Berlin: de Gruyter, 2000); Carol A. Newsom, *The Self as Symbolic Space: Constructing Identity and Community at Qumran* (Leiden: Brill, 2004); and Armin Lange and Eric M. Meyers, eds., *Light against Darkness: Dualism in Ancient Mediterranean Religion and the Contemporary World* (Göttingen: Vandenhoeck & Ruprecht, 2011).

5. For example, Martin Buber, *I and Thou*, trans. Walter Kaufmann (New York: Touchstone, 1971), and Emmanuel Levinas, *Totality and Infinity: An Essay on Exteriority*, trans. Alphonso Lingus (Dordrecht: Kluwer Academic, 1991), exercise considerable influence on philosophers and scientists who adopt a second-person standpoint for their work.

established field of research. I am asking different but related questions: how are the human agents within Paul's communities constituted? May we speak of such agents in individual as well as corporate terms, moving beyond what I consider to be a false dichotomy between singular and plural notions of agency "in Christ"? And how might Paul's view of persons be reframed in fresh, contemporary terms?

This last question naturally leads to further questions about ways in which Paul's anthropology may be deployed as a resource for understanding and caring for people in extreme situations, situations that appear to threaten their very integration or status as a person. I have in mind conditions such as autism, dementia, extreme trauma, comas, and ultimately death itself. But these are not the only areas calling for further exploration; Paul's voice needs to be added to contemporary philosophical debates about the category "person," particularly in an age when human beings are frequently depicted as undifferentiated from other animals, on the one hand, and as potentially replaceable by intelligent machines, on the other hand. Furthermore, in an age of identity politics and persistent social inequalities, the interpersonal constitution of the self has significant implications for ways in which the church engages with questions of social justice. There are urgent issues involved in these debates; Paul, I think, has something constructive and liberating to say to them. But these matters exceed the scope of this book; indeed, I plan to discuss many of them in a subsequent volume. Here I have attempted to demonstrate a way of framing Paul's anthropology in conversation with ancient and contemporary voices, as an impetus to bringing his voice to bear in contemporary questions about human identity.

In writing a book structured as a complex conversation, I have relied necessarily on many others. I am grateful to all those willing to share in the journey and clarify my thinking, and grateful to God, who moves in and among such connections. The genesis of this project traces back to many exchanges with J. Louis and Dorothy Martyn; like very many others, I suspect, I have experienced their friendship as an incarnation of grace. Their combined influence deeply shapes my reading of Paul, through Lou's apocalyptic interpretation of Paul's gospel and Dorothy's remarkable integration of psychoanalysis and theology. My debt to both is immeasurable and joyful. Although Lou eschewed the language of debt and obligation, and Dorothy would agree with him, the present study is part of my attempt to "pay it forward."

Along with the Martyns, many other friends and colleagues have contributed to the writing of this book. John Barclay, Kavin Rowe, and John Swinton all read earlier drafts of chapters and generously gave valuable feedback.

Along the way, other friends as well have been tremendous encouragers and occasional guides for the perplexed. The list is long, and doubtless incomplete: Esther Acolatse, Alexandra Brown, Douglas Campbell, Liz Dowling-Sendor, Craig Dykstra, Beverly Gaventa, Paul Griffiths, Richard Hays, George and Deborah Hunsinger, L. Ann Jervis, Joel Marcus, Fleming Rutledge, Love Sechrest, Alan Torrance, J. Ross Wagner, Brittany Wilson, and Lauren Winner. In struggling with the interdisciplinary nature of this project, I have gained insight from my colleagues in the Duke Divinity School Initiative for Theology, Medicine, and Culture: Warren Kinghorn, Farr Curlin, and Ray Barfield. The students in my course "Paul and the Person" contributed in ways they may not know, as did doctoral students Aminah Al-Attas Bradford, Hans Arneson, Jody Belcher, Joe Longarino, Emily Peck-McClain, and Philip Porter.

Andrew Pinsent, director of the Ian Ramsey Centre for Science and Religion at Oxford University, has been a tremendous supporter since we met at an Oxford conference on the second-person perspective in science and religion. He subsequently invited me to present papers at two other conferences sponsored by the Ian Ramsey Centre; I am the happy beneficiary of these conversations bringing together scientists, philosophers, and theologians around questions of divine and human action. Here at Duke I have learned much from participation in the Neurohumanities Research Group of the Duke Institute for Brain Sciences, under the gracious leadership of Deborah Jenson and Len White.

My heartfelt thanks go to my editor at Eerdmans, Michael Thomson, who has been a wise and very patient guide from the first idea of this book to its completion. The inimitable Judith Heyhoe, faculty editor at Duke Divinity School, read through the completed manuscript with a fine-toothed comb; Michael Burns read most of the manuscript as well, and the anonymous reviewer at Eerdmans offered pertinent suggestions to improve the manuscript. Together they saved me from many errors; any that remain are of course my own.

Portions of the book were written during a sabbatical made possible by the Issachar Fund. My thanks go to the Issachar Fund and to Deans Richard Hays and Ellen Davis for the generous gift of time. Without that gift the book would still be half-written.

My husband, Eddie, has given his unflagging support to this project from beginning to end, through difficult times and good times. He knows what this means. I dedicate this book to him.

Introduction

The Puzzle of Pauline Anthropology

> The tension between cosmology and anthropology characterizes
> the whole of Paul's theology.
>
> —Ernst Käsemann, *Commentary on Romans*

> Existence is always fundamentally conceived from the angle of the
> world to which one belongs.
>
> —Ernst Käsemann, "On Paul's Anthropology"

> If we are to understand mind as the locus of intelligence, we can-
> not follow Descartes in regarding it as separable in principle from
> the body and the world. . . . Mind, therefore, is not incidentally
> but intimately embodied and intimately embedded in its world.
>
> —John Haugeland, "Mind Embodied and Embedded"

With notable exceptions, the topic of Paul's anthropology has not received
much attention in recent years. Reasons for this neglect may range from a
theological aversion to anthropocentric approaches to Pauline theology, to
a wariness of reductionist readings of Paul, to a turn from seeing Paul as the
champion of the individual to seeing him as concerned primarily, or perhaps
only, with the community. This chapter begins with a quote from Ernst Käsemann, whose own work displays this tension and movement, as he himself
acknowledged: "We started from the position that Paul, more than any other
New Testament writer, viewed man as an individual. We went on from this to

call anthropology crystallized cosmology and to term every person the projection of his respective world and that world's Lord. How is this antithesis to be bridged?"[1] Indeed, whether Paul even thought in terms of persons is a debated question.[2] I think that he did, but not with an abstract or individualistic concept "person." Rather, he displays a functional understanding of human beings as relationally constituted agents who are both embodied and embedded in their world. Exploring that understanding is basic to the purpose of this book.

In my judgment, the time is right for rethinking such a notion of the person in Paul's thought. In the first place, we are witnessing a widespread, multipronged surge of interest in the topics of personhood, human cognition, and relatedness, fueled in part by advances in neuroscience and experimental psychology, but also by current concerns in philosophy and theology.[3] To

---

1. Ernst Käsemann, "On Paul's Anthropology," in *Perspectives on Paul*, trans. M. Kohl (Mifflintown, PA: Sigler, 1996 [1969]), 29.

2. Many scholars assume that Paul did not think in terms of individuals or selves at all. See, e.g., Dale Martin, *The Corinthian Body* (New Haven: Yale University Press, 1995), 25; Robert Jewett, *Romans*, Hermeneia (Minneapolis: Fortress, 2007), 733; James D. G. Dunn, *Romans 9–16*, Word Biblical Commentary 38B (Dallas: Word, 1988), 715. J. Louis Martyn speaks of the "newly competent human agent" in Paul almost exclusively in corporate terms as the church: "The identity, then, of the morally competent agent is clear. That agent is itself the new creation, the new *community*, the *corpus Christi*, the body of Christ that is daily brought newly into being by God's own participation in the moral drama, as he places that drama under the liberating Lordship of Christ" ("Afterword: The Human Moral Drama," in *Apocalyptic Paul: Cosmos and Anthropos in Romans 5–8*, ed. Beverly R. Gaventa [Waco, TX: Baylor University Press, 2013], 165). For a fresh interpretation of Paul's understanding of human transformation that pushes across the individual/collective divide, see Volker Rabens, *The Holy Spirit and Ethics in Paul: Transformation and Empowerment for Religious-Ethical Life* (Minneapolis: Fortress, 2014).

3. The literature is vast, cutting across many disciplines. In experimental psychology, see, e.g., Peter Hobson, *The Cradle of Thought: Exploring the Origins of Thinking* (Oxford: Oxford University Press, 2004); Vasudevi Reddy, *How Infants Know Minds* (Cambridge, MA: Harvard University Press, 2008); Axel Seemann, ed., *Joint Attention: New Developments in Psychology, Philosophy of Mind, and Social Neuroscience* (Cambridge, MA: MIT Press, 2011); for an overview of developments in neuroscience, see Nikolas S. Rose and Joelle M. Abi-Rached, *Neuro: The New Brain Sciences and the Management of the Mind* (Princeton: Princeton University Press, 2013); Giacomo Rizzolatti and Carrado Sinigaglia, *Mirrors in the Brain: How Our Minds Share Actions and Emotions* (Oxford: Oxford University Press, 2006). The work of Shaun Gallagher provides a particularly helpful overview of the issues in science and philosophy in *How the Body Shapes the Mind* (Oxford: Oxford University Press, 2005). Studies of the person in ancient thought, bridging classics and philosophy, include Christopher Gill, *The Structured Self in Hellenistic and Roman Thought* (Oxford: Oxford University Press, 2006); Pauliina Remes and Juha Sihvola, eds., *Ancient Philosophy of the Self* (New York: Springer, 2008); Stephen Everson, ed., *Psychology*, Companions to Ancient Thought 2 (Cambridge: Cambridge University Press, 1991). Perspectives bridging science and theology appear in Malcolm A. Jeeves, ed., *From*

a large extent, biblical scholarship has been absent from these debates, and certainly Paul's voice has been on the margins at best.[4] That absence marks a missed opportunity, because reframing matters of Pauline anthropology in conversation with contemporary theories of the self opens up new angles of vision, particularly in regard to the participatory aspects of Paul's thought. These angles promise a way past the impasses created by attempting to squeeze Paul into dualistic and individualistic frameworks. We have the opportunity to rethink the ways in which we understand as well as appropriate Paul's understanding of what it means to be a person.

Cells to Souls—and Beyond: Changing Portraits of Human Nature (Grand Rapids: Eerdmans, 2004), and Michael Welker, ed., *The Depth of the Human Person: A Multidisciplinary Approach* (Grand Rapids: Eerdmans, 2014). This list is but a sampling of the literature.

4. Hans Dieter Betz called for renewed attention to Paul's anthropology in "The Concept of the 'Inner Human Being' (*ho esō anthrōpos*) in the Anthropology of Paul," *New Testament Studies* 46 (2000), rightly noting, "The ever increasing emphasis on the body and its physiological and social complexities seems to drive an 'internal', non-physical human world out of existence. Yet, as long as ordinary people continue to have 'internal' experiences and take these notions as reflecting reality, it is difficult to imagine that they would readily change their popular acceptance of what in origin are Platonic notions about the external body and the internal soul. An operative question is: do people's experiences grow out of realities in human nature, or are such experiences ideological constructs imposed on people's minds?" (322). Betz's questions are prescient; his article nonetheless focuses primarily on Paul's adaptations of classical Platonic motifs, not on conversation with contemporary science. One New Testament scholar attempting to bridge the gap is Joel Green. See his *Body, Soul, and Human Life: The Nature of Humanity in the Bible* (Grand Rapids: Baker Academic, 2008), and edited volumes *What about the Soul? Neuroscience and Christian Anthropology* (Louisville: Abingdon, 2004) and *In Search of the Soul: Perspectives on the Mind-Body Problem*, 2nd ed. (Eugene, OR: Wipf & Stock, 2010), which engages philosophical debates around substance dualism and emergence theory. Green's work is groundbreaking, but it does not deal in any depth with the letters of Paul. Colleen Shantz attempts a neurobiological explanation of Paul's ecstatic experiences in *Paul in Ecstasy: The Neurobiology of the Apostle's Life and Thought* (Cambridge: Cambridge University Press, 2009), which operates within a primarily individualistic framework. Recently Matthew Croasmun has investigated emergence theory in relationship to Paul's notion of sin; see his " 'Real Participation': The Body of Christ and the Body of Sin in Evolutionary Perspective," in *"In Christ" in Paul: Explorations in Paul's Theology of Union and Participation*, ed. Kevin J. Vanhoozer, Constantine R. Campbell, and Michael J. Thate, WUNT 2.384 (Tübingen: Mohr Siebeck, 2014), and *The Emergence of Sin: The Cosmic Tyrant in Romans* (Oxford: Oxford University Press, 2017). As this book was going to press, two more promising new works were published: Craig S. Keener, *The Mind of the Spirit: Paul's Approach to Transformed Thinking* (Grand Rapids: Baker Academic, 2016), and Frederick S. Tappenden, *Resurrection in Paul: Cognition, Metaphor, and Transformation* (Atlanta: SBL Press, 2016). Rabens, *The Holy Spirit and Ethics in Paul*, focuses on Paul's teaching about the Spirit but in many ways anticipates the relational understanding of Pauline anthropology that I will espouse in this book.

Furthermore, this reframing need not be either anachronistic or reductionist. It need not be anachronistic because an in-depth look at ancient as well as current pictures of personhood reveals intriguing points of convergence as well as difference in the functional sense of the self, or the human agent. This is not to say that there are not profound underlying differences between apparently similar claims in, for example, Epictetus, Paul, and a contemporary neuroscientist such as Vittorio Gallese. It is to say, however, that all three are concerned with questions of human agency, development, and flourishing, with enough commonality to allow an enriching and enlightening mutual conversation. If I were to say that neuroscience *explains* what Paul was talking about when he said, for example, "It is no longer I who lives but Christ lives in me," I would indeed be imposing an anachronistic framework on Paul's thought. Rather, I want to say that some current theories in neuroscience and other experimental cognitive sciences disclose a constitution of personhood that is amenable to Pauline thought in ways that individualistic and autonomous understandings of the self are not. The goal is not explanation, in terms of either historical or scientific causality; the goal is to find new ways of pointing to and expressing Paul's meaning and, along the way, find that the pointers look intriguingly similar to some other expressions of the self in the ancient world.

Reframing Pauline anthropology in conversation with ancient voices as well as contemporary theorists in science and philosophy also need not be reductionist. This further claim will be strongly contested by scholars who think that, in order to bring Paul's thought (or any theistic faith) into conversation with "modern" science and philosophy, it is necessary to shear it of any transcendent, divine causality.[5] Many philosophers and scientists today, however, reject such an a priori commitment to a closed universe and indeed are part of

5. I have in mind the work of Troels Engberg-Pedersen, who repeatedly frames his research project in terms of a reading of Paul that provides a real "option" for "we moderns." Engberg-Pedersen thinks that the way to do so in a nonanachronistic way is through the lens of Stoic thought. In his view, only purely naturalistic worldviews, such as that of the Stoics, are credible to contemporary scientists and philosophers, who are Engberg-Pedersen's target audience. He thus avoids anachronism while frankly embracing a form of reductionism that strips Paul's ethics of any apocalyptic worldview. See his *Paul and the Stoics* (Louisville: Westminster John Knox, 2000) and *Cosmology and Self in the Apostle Paul: The Material Spirit* (Oxford: Oxford University Press, 2010). Colleen Shantz seeks to explain Paul's thought by analyzing his experience in terms of neurobiological accounts of ecstatic experience, in *Paul in Ecstasy*. Notably, both Engberg-Pedersen and Shantz seem to operate with an a priori commitment to the idea of a freestanding individualistic self. Intrinsic to these debates are basic issues at the confluence of science and religion: questions of causality, materialism, and determinism.

a vigorous debate on the very question of whether the universe can be closed, or more precisely, whether a closed, purely materialistic account of the cosmos and of human consciousness can be adequate to the data.[6]

Again, the goal of juxtaposing Paul, ancient philosophy, and modern theorists of the person is not to gain explanatory power; it is to provoke a mutual conversation that may illuminate Paul's thought in new ways and, at the same time, bring Paul's voice into current debates about personhood. In the following pages I shall sketch out an interdisciplinary approach to Paul's anthropology that is grounded in Christology, takes seriously his conviction that the God revealed in Jesus Christ is both transcendently "other" and intimately involved in human history, and engages with contemporary as well as ancient depictions of what is intrinsic to being a person.

The word "sketch" in the last sentence is important. This is not a thorough survey of Paul's "anthropological terms," nor is it an exhaustive investigation of every possible aspect of Paul's view of the person.[7] This is not a theory of everything. It is, rather, an attempt to reframe an approach to Paul's anthropology by opening a discursive window between Pauline scholarship and current work in developmental psychology and neuroscience. When we also invite specific ancient understandings of the person into the conversation, the result is a rich interchange of ideas with surprising interfaces and differences. In generating such an interchange, my goal is to push the "reset" button on Paul's answer to an ancient question that never gets old: "What is man that Thou art mindful of him?" (Ps 8:4 RSV).

As we shall see, Paul's answer lives at the nexus of cosmology and anthropology—to echo the quote from Ernst Käsemann that begins this chapter. Utilizing the language of philosopher John Haugeland, we might say that Paul operates with an understanding of the mind as "intimately embodied

---

6. The literature is immense, and I can name only a few examples here. See, e.g., Thomas Nagel, *Mind and Cosmos: Why the Materialist Neo-Darwinian Conception of Nature Is Almost Certainly False* (Oxford: Oxford University Press, 2012). Nagel himself rejects a theistic view of the cosmos, while frankly acknowledging the deficits in "an axiomatic commitment to reductive materialism" (49). For a robust philosophical defense of a nonreductionist idea of the soul, see, among others, Lenn E. Goodman and D. Gregory Caramenico, *Coming to Mind: The Soul and Its Body* (Chicago: University of Chicago Press, 2014). For physicists' defense of transcendence, see Ian Hutchinson, *Monopolizing Knowledge* (Belmont, MA: Fias, 2011), and John Polkinghorne, *Quantum Physics and Theology: An Unexpected Kinship* (New Haven: Yale University Press, 2008) and *Science and Religion in Quest of Truth* (New Haven: Yale University Press, 2012).

7. Indeed, the very notion of isolating particular terms as "anthropological" betrays an a priori notion of what constitutes persons.

and intimately embedded in its world."[8] For the apostle, that world has cosmic as well as personal and social dimensions. Investigating this interrelationship between embodiment, cognition, and embedded participation in a larger matrix will require attention to key texts displaying what I call "participatory identity," as well as to Paul's complex use of body language and his operative models of knowing and experiencing God, others, and oneself. I briefly introduce two such texts below and then discuss them in depth in subsequent chapters. But prior to such in-depth discussion of the Pauline texts, two intervening chapters will introduce the other partners in the conversation—Epictetus as one representative of an ancient view of the person, and the theories of some current philosophers, experimental psychologists, and neuroscientists. An overview of Paul's depictions of the body will then round out part 1 of the book, laying the groundwork for a close reading of key Pauline texts in part 2.

The remainder of this introductory chapter sketches out the puzzle of Pauline anthropology, methodological questions, and terminology.

The Puzzle of Paul's Understanding of the Person

Paul's anthropology is indeed puzzling. At two key places in his letters Paul uses an odd grammatical formulation to depict a kind of construction of the self. It goes as follows:

I no longer [verb] but [subject plus verb] in me.

This construction occurs in the following two passages:

> For through the law I died to the law, that I might live to God. I have been crucified with Christ; *I no longer live, but Christ lives in me*; and [the life] I now live in the flesh, I live in the faith which is of (or in) the Son of God, who loved me and gave himself for me. (Gal 2:19–20)[9]
>
> I do not know (or understand) what I'm doing. For I do not do what I want, but I do what I hate. Now if I do what I do not want, I agree that the law is good. So then *I no longer am doing it, but sin dwelling in me*, . . . that

8. John Haugeland, "Mind Embodied and Embedded," in *Having Thought: Essays in the Metaphysics of Mind*, ed. John Haugeland (Cambridge, MA: Harvard University Press, 1998), 37.
9. See chapter 6 for discussion of the grammar and translation of this verse.

is, in my flesh. . . . Now if I do what I do not want, *I no longer am doing it, but sin dwelling in me.* (Rom 7:15–18, 20)

Each of these passages is a crucial and influential statement of Pauline thought; each has received extensive commentary; each is full of puzzles for the serious reader. Yet their parallel structure is rarely noted.[10] In each case, the speaker says, "I no longer am acting, but someone or something else inhabits my person as the subject of my actions." The difference between the constructions of the self in the two passages consists in the difference between distinctly other and yet personally indwelling actors—in the first case, "Christ who lives in me," and in the second, personified "Sin that dwells in me." These two actors could not be more opposed to one another. Yet the *structure* of these opposing constructions of the self is remarkably similar. In both cases the self is a self-in-relation-to-another, suggesting that it is not only "in Christ," but also in the realm of sin and death, that the person is shaped in relationship to a separate entity that is both external and indwelling.

A closer look will reveal three further striking points of contact between both passages. First, in both texts the law impinges on the self, albeit in distinctive ways that relate to the very different contexts of the letters.[11] In Galatians, Paul astonishingly says that he has died *to* the law *through* the law, so that he might live to God. In Romans the speaker affirms the goodness of the law and wants to do the good, which means to "live to God" in line with the intent of the law, but sin intervenes between that wish for the good and its outcome and uses the law to deceive and to work death (Rom 7:11).

---

10. There are many good reasons for this general neglect. These passages occur in different letters, in vastly different contexts within the letters, and they address different circumstances. The identity of the rhetorical "I" in Rom 7 is hotly debated, whereas few doubt that Paul is speaking personally in Galatians, even if he is also using himself as an example of everyone and anyone who is made right by the faith of Jesus Christ and not by the law (Gal 2:16). To many interpreters, if not to all, it seems impossible that the anguished self in Rom 7 could be the same person as the confident speaker in Gal 2:20. In fact, they seem antithetical to one another: one is full of confidence, the other of despair. One paradoxically "lives" even after "cocrucifixion" with Christ, while the other will shortly cry out for deliverance from "this body of death" (Rom 7:24). One New Testament scholar who does discuss the parallel construction of the self in Rom 7 and Gal 2 is Troels Engberg-Pedersen, "Philosophy of the Self in the Apostle Paul," in Remes and Juha Sihvola, *Ancient Philosophy of the Self*, 179–94. See also Robert Tannehill, *Dying and Rising with Christ: A Study in Pauline Theology* (Eugene, OR: Wipf & Stock, 2006), 59.

11. The meaning of "law" in both passages is debated; with the majority of scholars, I take it to refer to the law of Moses in both texts. For further discussion, see below, chapters 4 and 6.

Second, in both passages the self exists in relationship to "the flesh [*sarx*]" or "my flesh," albeit also in quite different ways: in Galatians 2:20 Paul simultaneously lives "in the [realm of the] flesh" and "in the [realm of the] faith"; in Romans 7:18 the speaker says, "I know that nothing good dwells *in me, that is, in my flesh.*" In Galatians, "flesh" thus appears to denote a realm of existence; in Romans, it seems to denote the speaker's bodily, singular self. Clearly, "flesh" is a complex word with a variety of possible meanings, and its interpretation requires close attention to the contexts in which it occurs.

Third, in both instances the "I" that appears to be replaced by an indwelling agent continues as the subject of active verbs. The "I" that has been "crucified with Christ" and "no longer lives" in Galatians 2:20a appears twice thereafter as the subject of the verb "to live" (2:20b)! And the "I" indwelt by "sin" that accomplishes evil contrary to the self's wishes nonetheless wants (*thelō*), acts (*prassō*), agrees (*symphēmi*), finds (*heuriskō*), delights (*synēdomai*), and sees (*blepō*) in the midst of the anguish it expresses (Rom 7:15–23).

These two structurally parallel and substantively contrasting texts serve to introduce the puzzle of Pauline participation and identity. Taken together, they suggest a pattern of talking about persons in which the self is never on its own but always socially and cosmically constructed in relationship to external realities that operate internally as well. Ernst Käsemann put this point trenchantly: "Man is always himself in his particular world; his being is open towards all sides and is always set in a structure of solidarity."[12] As Käsemann well knew, such a "structure of solidarity" extends in all directions, for ill as well as for good. It entails breathtaking susceptibility to one's environment and therefore to destructive as well as life-giving connections with realities beyond the boundaries of the self—if there are indeed boundaries, which is contested.[13] I shall argue that these realities may be personal, in an "I-Thou" relationship, such as that between Paul and Christ, or they may be impersonal and indeed depersonalizing, as in the "I-It" relationship between the self and "sin" in Romans 7:17–20. For Paul, these opposing relational loci are the only

---

12. Käsemann, "On Paul's Anthropology," 22.

13. See Käsemann, "On Paul's Anthropology": "Paul is apparently able to disregard the human person when he speaks of the power of sin which is in our members and which works through them. . . . We ourselves do not determine who we are" (28). For a discussion of this relational model of the person in regard to divine agency and grace, see John M. G. Barclay, "'By the Grace of God I Am What I Am': Grace and Agency in Philo and Paul," in *Divine and Human Agency in Paul and His Cultural Environment*, ed. John M. G. Barclay and Simon J. Gathercole (London: T&T Clark, 2008), 151–56.

alternatives in human existence; there is no place where an autonomous "individual" can stand aside and evaluate, let alone choose, between different possible identities. There is no freestanding "self" in Paul's cosmos, nor is there a neutral environment within which human beings may act out their personal lives. Rather, Paul's anthropology is participatory all the way down. It does not mean, however, that there is no "self."

This is a deceptively simple claim with profound and far-reaching implications for both the interpretation of thorny issues in Paul's letters and the deployment of a Pauline voice in contemporary debates about personhood. The claim that for Paul the self is always a self-in-relation-to-others raises further questions: what kind of agency is implied and exercised by a self that is not solely self-determining? What happens to both freedom and responsibility? In simple terms, when "I, yet not I, but another" describes a person's experience, who is doing the talking? What is the role of the body—both individual and social—in each account of the self? How are Paul's accounts of the person as self-in-relation to "sin," on the one hand, and to Christ, on the other, mutually related? Are they sequential or simultaneous? That is, do human beings move from being constituted in relationship to "sin" to being constituted in relationship to Christ, or may they be both at the same time? If human beings are always connected to, and profoundly shaped by, entities that are both external and internal, what does this interconnection mean for human thought processes? How do human beings know God, themselves, and others—or do they? How do people change—or do they? And if people are not self-directing, autonomous beings, what makes them distinctly human? What does it mean to talk about freedom? And what, if anything, is distinctive about being a person?

As we shall see, these were questions of vital importance in Paul's day, and they remain so in ours, as discoveries in neuroscience and experimental psychology call into question long-standing Enlightenment assumptions about human freedom, rationality, and autonomy. I shall argue that Paul's voice can provide a bracing, constructive contribution to such debates and can simultaneously find fresh expression when liberated from modern individualistic and cognitivist presuppositions. Reading Paul's participatory language of the self in the context of ancient and contemporary conversations about human flourishing can cast fresh light on key themes in Paul's thought regarding the human predicament and the good news of God in Christ.

In a sense, then, this project takes up the gauntlet thrown down by John Barclay in a discussion of Bultmann's theological project as "interpretation, not repetition":

Bultmann was surely entitled to press for an *explanation* of what it means for persons or groups to belong to a person (Christ) or to an event (the Christ-event) outside (before and beyond) themselves, in a way that simultaneously transforms their being. In other words, he was justified in seeking concepts of the self, of being, of identity, and of meaning that we can understand ourselves, and can spell out, at least partly, in contemporary terms. Bultmann knew that he needed such foundational concepts if he was to make sense of anything Paul said. We may not now choose the existentialist concepts he then found helpful, but we cannot pretend to *understand* Paul unless we have some comprehensible conceptual frame in which to place them. Otherwise, we are merely parroting his language.[14]

Such indeed is the goal of this book: to put forth "concepts of the self, of being, of identity, and of meaning that we can understand ourselves, and can spell out, at least partly, in contemporary terms" as a "comprehensible conceptual frame" for interpreting Paul's participatory logic. Specifically, I seek to reimagine Pauline anthropology within a framework shaped by juxtaposing specific ancient and modern notions of personhood. Because Paul's understanding of persons cannot be separated from his convictions about God, Christ, and the Spirit, along the way I will talk about divine action as well, from the participatory character of Christ's saving action to its effects in the constitution of persons. Thus I will explore three aspects of Paul's participatory logic: human involvement in the realm of sin and death, Christ's participation in that realm of human bondage, and human involvement in a new interpersonal regime inaugurated and indwelt by Christ. All three aspects of Paul's logic involve profoundly constitutive interpersonal bonds between people, whether for good or for ill. All three occur in a fully embodied and socially embedded existence that shapes our cognitive capacities as well.

Terminology

There was no abstract concept of the person in the first-century Hellenistic world; indeed, if we adopt post-Enlightenment assumptions about the individ-

14. John M. G. Barclay, "Interpretation, Not Repetition: Reflections on Bultmann as a Theological Reader of Paul," *Journal of Theological Interpretation* 9.2 (2015): 204; emphasis original. As discussed above, I am not so confident about *explanations* as a mode of appropriating Pauline thought in a contemporary context; I prefer to speak of finding contemporary *expressions* of that thought.

ual as autonomous, discrete, and self-determining, it is questionable whether such an "individual" existed in Paul's day. But the absence of a concept in modern guise does not mean the absence of personal agents in the ancient world. To the contrary, a look at actual self- and other-referential language as used by Paul and his contemporaries finds no lack of robust first and second person singular pronouns.[15] Neither Paul nor other first-century authors worry about *defining* "personhood" as a concept, but they have strong depictions of how human agents are constituted and how they act, and of what makes for suffering and what makes for flourishing.

That is, ancient authors, including Paul, did not operate out of an individualistic, post-Cartesian mind-set. Rather, in varying ways, when they spoke in the singular, it was also, always, to invoke the ways in which human agents are shaped by and intimately related to their social environments. But it does not mean there was no self. The difference lies between abstract conceptualities and immediate experience. Seneca invokes just such a difference to explain to his pupil Lucillus why he can talk confidently about every newborn having "a sense of its own composition." Anticipating Lucillus's objection, he states the counterargument:

"How does an infant understand this complicated and subtle relationship which is somehow beyond even your explanation? All creatures have to be born capable of argument in order to understand this definition which is impenetrable to most citizens in their togas." But there would have been an objection you can make, if I had said that animals could understand the definition of their composition, instead of their composition itself. Nature is more easily understood than described. So that infant does not know what his composition is, but he knows his composition, and an animal doesn't know what it is, but feels it is an animal. (Seneca, *Ep.* 121.9–13)[16]

The baby needs no definition but can rely on its own experience, thereby "understanding" without needing an "explanation" that relies on a capacity for abstract thought.[17] In this sense I find abundant evidence of personhood

15. For further discussion of the person in Epictetus, see chapter 1 below.
16. Translation from Elaine Fantham, *Seneca: Selected Letters* (Oxford: Oxford University Press, 2010).
17. Similarly, twentieth-century theorists of infant development assumed children could not imitate until they had the capacity to conceptualize others as separate from themselves. But the work of Andrew Meltzoff definitively demonstrates neonate imitation of faces within an hour of birth. Infant experience and awareness precede rather than follow the capacity for

in Paul's day and seek to form a framework for understanding Paul's anthropology in our day.

A similar caveat arises in regard to the term "self," which I will use interchangeably with the language of person. As I have noted above, many scholars would say that the first-century Mediterranean world had no notion of the self. Dale Martin articulates this view memorably when he asks us to "try to imagine how ancient Greeks and Romans could see as 'natural' what seems to us bizarre: the nonexistence of the 'individual,' the fluidity of the elements that make up the 'self,' and the essential continuity of the human body with its surroundings."[18] A great deal turns on the description of the individual as assumed in different scholarly works. In this case one may grant the continuity of the body with its surroundings yet resist the claim that therefore there is no self. To the contrary, A. A. Long argues for a strong idea of the self in Stoicism: "The self in this sense is something essentially individual—a uniquely positioned viewer and interlocutor, a being who has interior access of a kind that is not available to anyone else."[19] The self may be porous, inextricably enmeshed in a greater continuum of being, and intensely vulnerable to and shaped by its environment, but still there is something or someone that can act as the subject of active verbs. The question is how that actor is constituted.

As will be obvious, Paul himself, despite describing himself as inhabited by other active agents, nonetheless continues to speak in the first person singular. In addition to the speeches of Romans 7:7–25 and Galatians 2:18–21, which function in specific ways in his rhetoric, there are many other examples of Paul speaking freely and easily as the subject of his own actions. He thanks, he serves, he wants, he prays, he longs to visit his auditors, he is eager

---

conceptual understanding. For the seminal study of neonate imitation, see Andrew N. Meltzoff and M. Keith Moore, "Imitation of Facial and Manual Gestures by Human Neonates," *Science* 198.4312 (1977): 75–78. See further discussion in chapter 2 below.

18. Martin, *Corinthian Body*, 21.

19. A. A. Long, *Stoic Studies* (Cambridge: Cambridge University Press, 1996), 265. Whether the Stoics had a notion of the self and, if so, in what way are hotly debated topics among classicists. Long and Troels Engberg-Pedersen argue for a strong sense of a self-determining individual, and Christopher Gill argues for a more participatory, porous, and embedded self. See, e.g., A. A. Long, *Epictetus: A Stoic and Socratic Guide to Life* (Oxford: Oxford University Press, 2002), 28: for Epictetus, "volition [*proairesis*] is the self . . . as abstracted from the body"; Engberg-Pedersen, "A Stoic Concept of the Person in Paul? From Galatians 5:17 to Romans 7:14–25," in *Christian Body, Christian Self: Concepts of Early Christian Personhood*, ed. Clare K. Rothschild and Trevor W. Thompson (Tübingen: Mohr Siebeck, 2011), 85–89; Gill, *Structured Self*, 359–91. See further discussion in chapter 1.

to preach the gospel, he writes boldly, he confidently records all the places that he has preached, even as he talks of "what Christ has accomplished through me" (Rom 15:18–19).[20] And these are examples drawn only from Romans! Numerous illustrations could be drawn from his other letters as well. No one could accuse Paul of lacking a robust sense of himself, whether or not he had a "theory of the self." Similarly, despite the preponderance of second person plural pronouns in his letters, he also uses the singular at key points, particularly when exhorting or encouraging his auditors (Rom 14:2–9; 1 Thess 2:11) and when speaking about divine judgment (Rom 14:10–12; Gal 6:3–5; 1 Cor 4:5). The question is not whether Paul speaks as a robust "self" addressing other "selves" as well as communities, but how that personal agency and speech are qualified by participation in a larger relational environment and by indwelling agents. Recognizing the difficulty of finding language that avoids anachronistic modern individualism, I will speak of "person" and "self" as pointers to this somewhat mysterious, variously qualified and defined human agent.

One further matter remains regarding the terminology of the person, namely, the criteria by which "person" is defined or delimited. In contemporary parlance, person is often limited to some but not all members of the species *Homo sapiens*.[21] For example, questions about the boundaries of personhood arise in matters concerning the legal status of the unborn, or of people pronounced brain-dead or in a coma. When do living entities become persons, some may ask, or is there a time when they cease to be persons? Are there innate criteria by which to define or describe "personhood," such as self-awareness, rationality, mobility, free will, and so forth? Does being a person consist simply in being a member of the human race or in some subset of humanity, say, one's own religious or kinship group? The question is fraught, not least because of the way in which the ascription of personhood—and its obverse, the withholding of status as persons—justified genocide in the last century and may continue to do so today.

I raise this question concerning criteria because it is philosophically and theologically compelling, and because it resonates with Paul as well. I will argue that Paul constitutes all humanity, what now would be called *Homo sapiens*, as Adam's heirs and as those for whom Christ died; there is no innate

---

20. Rom 1:8–15; 15:15, 18–19.

21. I use the term *Homo sapiens* as a generic term to designate the only extant human species, while recognizing that other subspecies of the genus *Homo*, including Neanderthals and Denisovans, now are recognized as part of the human race as it has evolved over time.

or individual criterion by which some might be included and others excluded from this capacious embrace. There is no spark of divine reason that sets some humans apart from others, or adults apart from children. There is no social status that marks some, such as slaves, as having liminal standing with regard to human worth. Sometimes Paul distinguishes between groups such as Jews and Gentiles, but then he subverts the distinction elsewhere. On a deeper level his language is global and totalizing: "all have sinned" (Rom 3:23); "as in Adam all [*pantes*] die, so also in Christ shall all [*pantes*] be made alive" (1 Cor 15:22); "God has consigned all to disobedience, that he might have mercy upon all" (Rom 11:32); "[Christ] died for all [*hyper pantōn apethanen*]" (2 Cor 5:14-15). A great deal could be said about all of these verses, but my point here is straightforward: all humanity is included in Adam's heirs and in those for whom Christ died. If there were a working denotation of "person" here, it would be "one for whom Christ died," thereby including the entire human race.[22] And if this is the case, then it is also the case that for Paul, regardless of personal beliefs or "self-understandings," the person always and already exists in the presence of another; personhood is constituted in the self-donation of Christ for all humanity. It is grounded in gift, regardless of criteria. Such, in any case, will be my argument in the following pages.

Methodology: Second-Person Hermeneutics

A serious attempt to understand personhood in relational terms mandates an approach to understanding texts in ways that are embedded in actual existence. This perspective can be seen in a variety of scholarly fields. As Vasudevi Reddy puts it, speaking as an experimental psychologist: "Who is the expert when it comes to understanding people—the detached scientist or the ordinary person in everyday life?"[23] From a very different vantage point, Rudolf

---

22. Theological debates about personhood often focus on the notion of creation in the image of God. While the *imago Dei* is foundational for such accounts, in Paul's argumentation Christology is the lens through which to view the *imago Dei*. Put differently, in Paul's hands, the creation narrative limns humanity's fall more than its divine likeness; rather, Adam is primarily the representative figure through whom sin and death entered the world (Rom 5:14-19; 1 Cor 15:47-49). There is a mimetic likeness between human beings and God, but it is fully instantiated through Christ's mimetic assimilation to human dereliction (Phil 2:7). See Susan Grove Eastman, "Philippians 2:7-11: Incarnation as Mimetic Participation," *Journal for the Study of Paul and His Letters* 1.1 (2010): 1-22, and discussion in chapter 5 below.

23. Reddy, *How Infants Know Minds*, 5.

Bultmann claims: "Existential understanding of oneself . . . is real only in the act of existing and not in the isolated reflection of thought."[24]

Because this book reframes Paul's anthropology in conversation with both ancient and contemporary debates about the relational construction of the person, it is an experiment in what I shall call "second-person perspective hermeneutics." The term "second-person perspective" refers to a standpoint for intellectual inquiry in a variety of subjects including philosophy, psychology, and sociology.[25] This standpoint is disclosed by the grammar of second-person address more than either first-person, self-referential modes of knowledge or third-person, objectifying and distancing modes of knowledge. The other to be known is a "Thou," who addresses and knows the inquirer also as a "Thou." The self therefore always also exists as the recipient of an address, in the presence of an interlocutor.

It is difficult to describe this perspective without distorting it, not least because philosophical inquiry and biblical studies have been so dominated by third-person discourse.[26] Drawing on the philosophies of Martin Buber and Emmanuel Levinas, the second-person approach argues that persons begin with and in the encounter with others, in what Levinas calls "the face

24. Rudolf Bultmann, *Theology of the New Testament*, trans. Kendrick Grobel, 2 vols. (Waco, TX: Baylor University Press, 2007), 2:241.

25. In philosophy, see the work of Stephen Darwall, *The Second-Person Standpoint: Morality, Respect, and Accountability* (Cambridge, MA: Harvard University Press, 2006); Timothy Chappell, "Knowledge of Persons," *European Journal for Philosophy of Religion* 5.4 (2013): 3–28; Shaun Gallagher, *Phenomenology* (New York: Palgrave Macmillan, 2012); Eleanore Stump, *Wandering in Darkness: Narrative and the Problem of Suffering* (Oxford: Oxford University Press, 2010). In cognitive science and experimental psychology, see, e.g., Peter Hobson, *The Cradle of Thought: Exploring the Origins of Thinking* (Oxford: Oxford University Press, 2004), and Reddy, *How Infants Know Minds*. A good example of theological inquiry from an explicitly second-person perspective is Andrew Pinsent, *The Second-Person Perspective in Aquinas's Ethics: Virtues and Gifts* (New York: Routledge, 2012). Charles Taylor anticipates this turn to the second-person perspective in his history of the self as moving from a dialogical stance to an interiorization of the self, but in need of reclaiming the understanding that "we are human only in conversation" ("The Person," in *The Category of the Person: Anthropology, Philosophy, History*, ed. Michael Carrithers, Steven Collins, and Steven Lukes [Cambridge: Cambridge University Press, 1985], 278).

26. For a rich overview of second-person perspectives in the philosophy of religion, see the special issue of the *European Journal for Philosophy of Religion* 5.4 (2013), entitled *The Second-Personal in the Philosophy of Religion*, ed. Andrew Pinsent and Eleanore Stump. The editors support a "symbiotic" understanding of the first- and second-person perspectives; the "I" is always a self in relationship, a self in the presence of another. As will become clear below, I wish to push for a more precise differentiation between first- and second-person perspectives.

to face."[27] Philosopher Timothy Chappell puts the claim clearly in comments on John Donne's famous line "no man is an island": "No human *starts out* as an island. Each of us at least begins as a piece of the continent, a part of the main. Insofar as we ever come to be anything like 'entire of ourselves,' this is a learned and socialized achievement; an achievement, moreover, which is necessarily built upon our prior status as parts of the main. In a word, *individuality presupposes relationality*."[28]

Chappell describes the opposing point of view, which has long been dominant in Western philosophical tradition and often is attributed to René Descartes, as "individualism about persons" in which "relationality presupposes individuality." Chappell rightly questions the widespread attribution of individualism about persons to Descartes by exploring Descartes's debt to Augustine, who demonstrably operated within a second-person framework: "For Augustine to be an *I* to himself already presupposes that God is a *You* to him, and indeed that Augustine is a *You* to God."[29]

To say that second-person encounter is the foundation of personhood is both a psychological and a philosophical claim. As the references to Buber and to Augustine make clear, it also is a theological claim, one that has ancient roots in Jewish and Christian thought. Furthermore, this relational constitution of persons has implications for modes of knowledge. It suggests that knowledge, at least knowledge of self and of other people, begins interpersonally and not primarily within isolated individuals as knowing subjects. It suggests that cognition happens in the face-to-face, not simply or even primarily within the self; at its base, knowledge is conversational and dialogical, not monological.[30]

What might it mean to take this claim seriously as a hermeneutical guide to the interpretation of Paul's letters and particularly of Paul's anthropology? The question can be addressed from at least three angles.

---

27. Emmanuel Levinas, *Totality and Infinity: An Essay on Exteriority*, trans. Alphonso Lingus (Dordrecht: Kluwer Academic, 1991), 227–28.

28. Chappell, "Knowledge of Persons," 3–4.

29. Chappell, "Knowledge of Persons," 15.

30. See Charles Taylor, *The Ethics of Authenticity* (Cambridge, MA: Harvard University Press, 1991), 34–35: "We become full human agents, capable of understanding ourselves, and hence of defining an identity, through our acquisition of rich human languages of expression . . . including the 'languages' of art, of gesture, of love, and the like. But we are inducted into these in exchange with others. No one acquires the languages needed for self-definition on their own. . . . The genesis of the human mind is in this sense not 'monological,' not something each accomplishes on his or her own, but dialogical."

In the first place, the second-person perspective furthers my earlier questions about the construction of the self in Paul's thought. Does Paul himself presume an individualistic notion of persons, or does "individuality presuppose relationality" for him? And might such a way of thinking through personal identity move beyond dichotomous interpretations of Paul as either "the champion of the individual" or as having no concept of the self at all? Engagement with these questions is intrinsic to the basic aims of this book.

Second, the second-person perspective raises questions about the identity of contemporary readers of Paul. If we are who we are in social, interpersonal networks that shape our modes of vision, cognition, and even the questions we ask, then full interpretation of Paul's anthropological thought requires attention to our contemporary horizons, as well as consideration of Paul's first-century world. There are many ways to do this; in this book I engage philosophical and scientific debates about the constitution of the person as a self-in-relationship. Such a conversation describes my methodological approach to the puzzle of Paul's anthropology. As such, it is an exercise in "interpretation, not repetition," and an heir to Bultmann's interpretive project.[31]

Third, grammatically speaking, Paul's letters are second-person communications to particular communities. They are words of address through which a long tradition of ecclesial interpretation has expected the divine Word to speak to Paul's hearers in every generation in their concrete situations. That is, to read his letters as second-person communications is also to expect the divine Word to speak to contemporary readers in their time and place. Rudolf Bultmann stated such an expectation very clearly in his reflections on the differing goals of historically situated New Testament interpretation: historical reconstruction of the New Testament context is "in the service of the interpretation of the New Testament writings under the presupposition that they have something to say to the present."[32] Precisely in service of this second-person goal of encounter between God and human beings, Bultmann read Paul's thought through an anthropological lens, as do I. Whether Bultmann's philosophical presuppositions served his hermeneutical goals is another question. In what follows I embrace his goals, but with different presuppositions.

A concise sketch of work on Paul's anthropology illustrates differences between second-person hermeneutics and first- or third-person approaches to questions of interpretation. I begin with a brief comparison of Bultmann and his student and critic Ernst Käsemann, first noting what they have in

---

31. Barclay, "Interpretation, not Repetition."
32. Rudolf Bultmann, "Epilogue," in *Theology of the New Testament*, 2:251.

common.[33] For both, Paul highlights the individual, although the notion of what "individual" means differs significantly. At one point Käsemann explicitly cites his agreement with Bultmann on this matter: "Bultmann rightly draws attention to the importance which Paul assigns to the individual. . . . With unusual emphasis and by no means paraenetically, he brings the individual, as believer or unbeliever, into prominence."[34] Furthermore, for both Käsemann and Bultmann, fully theological interpretation of Scripture must bring the subject matter of the text into conversation with its present readers in all the particularities of their experience so that they hear God's word addressing them. Bultmann puts it as follows: "Faith can be nothing else but the response to the kerygma, and . . . the kerygma is nothing else than God's word addressing man as a questioning and promising word, a condemning and forgiving word. As such a word it does not offer itself to critical thought but speaks into one's concrete existence."[35] Käsemann elaborates the same point: "As Bultmann rightly points out, the primary concern of [Paul's teaching about the Word of God] is not to convey dogmatic information, nor even to give an elevating account of salvation history, although both these things are necessary and have their proper place. Paul's real concern is with address."[36]

Both Bultmann and Käsemann are passionately committed to an interpretation of the biblical text with life-changing traction in personal human life. In Bultmann's terms, the subject matter (*die Sache*) of the text is the kerygma, the gospel proclamation that comes to human beings not as "universal truths" or as historical observations but as "personal address in a concrete situation" that demands an individual decision in response.[37] Above all, Bultmann wants

33. For a more extended comparison of Bultmann and Käsemann on the Pauline notion of the body (*sōma*), see chapter 3 below.

34. Käsemann, "On Paul's Anthropology," 2.

35. Bultmann, *Theology of the New Testament*, 2:240.

36. Käsemann, "On Paul's Anthropology," 4.

37. Bultmann, *Theology of the New Testament*, 2:240. Karl Barth shared this understanding of the goals, if not the methods, of theological interpretation. He introduced the first edition of his monumental commentary on Romans with the bold claim, "Paul, as a child of his age, addressed his contemporaries. It is, however, far more important that, as Prophet and Apostle of the Kingdom of God, he veritably speaks to all men of every age" (*The Epistle to the Romans*, trans. E. C. Hoskyns [Oxford: Oxford University Press, 1977 (1933)], 1). Barth repeatedly told his readers that his goal was to "explain" Paul's letter to the Romans, and he clearly thought that a historical reconstruction of the text in its context was necessary but inadequate to that task. As he put it in the preface to the second edition: "Moreover, judged by what seems to me to be the fundamental principle of true exegesis, I entirely fail to see why parallels drawn from the ancient world—and with such parallels modern commentators are chiefly

to avoid interpreting biblical texts as "an objectifying kind of thought cut loose from the act of living"; he wants interpretation whose goal is a self-understanding that "is real only in the act of existing and not in the isolated reflection of thought."[38] Barclay restates Bultmann's goal succinctly: "The task of theological interpretation of the New Testament is not to repeat its time-bound and often mythological expressions but to unfold, in contemporary terms, the meaning of the early Christian faith response to the gospel."[39]

For the reception history of Bultmann's project, the key phrase in Barclay's summary is "in contemporary terms." For Bultmann those terms were the individualistic existentialist philosophy of his times.[40] By the late 1960s, times had changed, such that Käsemann argued, "we must draw attention to the change in our horizon," which emphasizes "the interdependence of all mankind," not isolated individuals.[41] Käsemann was extraordinarily prescient in his understanding of Paul's anthropology. In 2014 Wayne Meeks said of Bultmann's project, "The fundamental issue turns on the question of how we

---

concerned—should be of more value for an understanding of the Epistle than the situation in which we ourselves actually are, and to which we can therefore bear witness" (*Romans*, 11). In this opinion Barth differed from Bultmann, but as David Congdon points out, they shared the same "missionary starting point" (*The Mission of Demythologizing: Rudolf Bultmann's Dialectical Theology* [Minneapolis: Fortress, 2015], xxvi). Congdon quotes Bultmann's letter to Karl Jaspers that explained his goal of demythologizing: not "to make the faith acceptable to modern people, but rather to make clear what the Christian faith is" ("Antwort an Karl Jaspers [1953]," in *Kerygma und Mythos*, vol. 3, *Das Gespräch mit der Philosophie*, ed. Hans-Werner Bartsch [Hamburg-Volksdorf: Reich, 1954], 50), quoted in Congdon, xxvi. See also David Congdon, "The Word as Event: Barth and Bultmann on Scripture," in *The Sacred Text: Excavating the Texts, Exploring the Interpretations, and Engaging the Theologies of the Christian Scriptures*, ed. Michael Bird and Michael Pahl (Piscataway, NJ: Gorgias Press, 2010), 253–54: "True exegesis for both Barth and Bultmann requires instead an existential participation in the *Sache*—the 'subject matter' or 'object'—of the text." Congdon calls this approach "participatory exegesis," a term that well describes my project as well.

38. Bultmann, *Theology of the New Testament*, 2:241.

39. John M. G. Barclay, "Humanity under Faith," in *Beyond Bultmann: Reckoning a New Testament Theology*, ed. Bruce W. Longenecker and Mikeal C. Parsons (Waco, TX: Baylor University Press, 2014), 90. See again also Barth: "The matter contained in the text cannot be released save by a creative straining of the sinews, by a relentless, elastic application of the 'dialectical' method" (*Romans*, 7).

40. See, however, the appropriate caution urged by Schubert Ogden, who argues that Bultmann's hermeneutic is shaped only secondarily by his concern to address an existentialist worldview. Bultmann's demythologizing program arises primarily from his conviction of God's qualitative difference from the world ("Introduction," in *Existence and Faith: Shorter Writings of Rudolf Bultmann*, ed. Schubert Ogden [New York: Meridian, 1960], 18).

41. Käsemann, "On Paul's Anthropology," 11.

construe personal identity." He added, "The most interesting turn in moral philosophy of the past several decades is the growing persuasion, from a variety of quarters, that the modern individualist self is an illusion."[42] Indeed.

As I have noted, Käsemann agreed with Bultmann about Paul's teaching on the Word of God, as well as on the importance of the individual. This Word is a word of address to every person in his or her distinctive gifts and calling "to be in his own station in life a banner of victory uplifted for Christ." This means that the person "is a created being in that he experiences the divine address, which compels him to earthly pilgrimage. This fact makes him a historical being: he stands beneath the sign of exodus and his horizon is hope."[43] Käsemann went beyond his teacher, however, in two important respects, which already receive emphasis in this quote. First, he argued that for Paul the person is never freestanding but always exists in the mode of belonging to cosmic and corporate powers that are greater than the individual: "The terms used in Pauline anthropology all undoubtedly refer to the whole man in the varying bearings and capacities of his existence; but they do not apply to what we call the individual at all. Here existence is always fundamentally conceived from the angle of the world to which one belongs. . . . Man is a being who cannot be determined solely in the light of his own self. His existence stems from outside himself."[44]

This participatory mode of existence means, second, that Paul's conception of the person, both as unbeliever and as believer, is public and involved in history. There is no room for Christian spirituality as a matter of private, inward reflection withdrawn from the world. Indeed, there is no room for the church as an insular community set apart from the rest of society; rather, Christians in all the diversity of their God-given gifts are to cross any boundaries set by the church or the world and to live in service to God through the grand multiplicity of human beings in all corners of the world. Nothing less is demanded by the apostle's "apocalyptic" framework of thought, for which the basic question is, "who owns the earth?"[45]

In short, Käsemann shares Bultmann's urgent concern for hearing the gospel as a word of address to Paul's contemporary readers and not simply as a record of past events or as a propositional compendium of timeless truths. And he agrees that an account of Paul's anthropology is necessary for such

42. Wayne Meeks, "The Problem of Christian Living," in Longenecker and Parsons, *Beyond Bultmann*, 222.
43. Käsemann, "On Paul's Anthropology," 4, 5.
44. Käsemann, "On Paul's Anthropology," 26, 28.
45. Käsemann, "On Paul's Anthropology," 30, 25.

hearing, although he surely would not consider it adequate to Paul's theology. But he reads Paul within a different framework, one dominated by the action of God breaking into human history rather than by an emphasis on the sheer transcendence and qualitative otherness of God. For this reason he parts company with Bultmann's individualistic and ultimately docetic anthropology.[46]

My project has affinities with both Bultmann's and Käsemann's approaches to Paul's anthropology. Like both, I want to read Paul through a second-person hermeneutical lens in which Paul's letters are a word of address to contemporary readers. Like Bultmann, I want to address the current situation, while reckoning that the horizon within which we read and interpret and receive Paul's letters changes, just as the particular situations to which Paul wrote changed. This recognition requires a nimble hermeneutic that is attentive both to Paul's day and to ours. Insofar as philosophy and developments in psychology and neuroscience in the last few decades frequently have questioned the individualistic assumptions that formerly dominated our view of both Paul and his first-century context, the way is opened for a new approach to Paul's participatory thought.

Ironically, however, such an approach deeply undercuts Bultmann's own individualistic presuppositions, finding common ground instead with Käsemann's understanding of the person as "a projection of his respective world and that world's Lord."[47] Käsemann's reading of Paul is thus more amenable to a second-person methodology that emphasizes divine action in this world; furthermore, his insistence on the importance of physical existence as God's "handle" on human participation in Christ is deeply consonant with contemporary emphases on bodies as the source of cognition and as the medium of interpersonal connection and influence. Käsemann's own cosmic language, however, can itself become abstract. It is difficult to find traction in daily life for his emphasis on God's lordship and human obedience; what does such obedience look like in the concrete shared life of the community in the world?

More recently, Pauline scholarship has addressed this question through the application of social-scientific methodologies to Pauline studies. Valuable as these studies are, they do not address the question of the self; to put it baldly, how is the agency of persons constituted in the midst of the community? One contemporary Pauline scholar who does attempt to address this question is

---

46. Meeks: "Barth puts his finger on an essential weakness when he suggests that Bultmann's attempt to purge the New Testament kerygma of all 'objectifying' talk about God leads finally to a new Docetism" ("The Problem of Christian Living," 220–21).

47. Käsemann, "On Paul's Anthropology," 29.

Troels Engberg-Pedersen.[48] Engberg-Pedersen's work is self-consciously Bultmannian in its goals, which I share. He explicitly parts company with Bultmann in one key respect: whereas Bultmann's existentialist interpretation was anachronistic in regard to first-century worldviews, Engberg-Pedersen finds in Stoicism a historically credible, appropriate vehicle for reading Paul in a way that accords with "modern" thought. To be sure, Engberg-Pedersen (ostensibly) does not think that Paul was a Stoic; he recognizes the differences between Stoic cosmology and Paul's metaphysical claims and indeed apocalyptic worldview. But because he does not think such claims and worldview are amenable to modern philosophical and scientific thought, he argues that any credible live options for a modern appropriation of Paul's thought must be necessarily naturalistic; they must fit within a purely nonsupernatural framework of cause and effect in a bounded universe. For this reason, in Engberg-Pedersen's view, theological interpretations of Paul such as those of Käsemann and J. Louis Martyn are simply incommensurate with a credible modern worldview.

Because he also puts Stoic thought in conversation with Paul, Engberg-Pedersen will be an important interlocutor in the following pages. As will become clear, however, I do not share his presumptions about the necessity of excising "supernatural" elements from Paul's thought in order to render it a "live option" for "we moderns." Nor, as noted above, do all scientists and philosophers. But that is a topic for the rest of the book.

Rationale: The Promise and Limits of Conversation

Conversations are bound to be suggestive, fragmentary, and incomplete. I make no apologies for these limitations and take comfort in Bultmann's recognition that theological interpretation "permits only ever-repeated solutions, or attempts at solution, each in its particular historical situation."[49] Such interpretation requires not only analysis of Paul's letters but also a sustained engagement with contemporary frameworks of thought. Such engagement in turn will make demands on my readers. I ask for patience and a willingness to step out of particular disciplinary comfort zones in order to foster a genuine conversation across the boundaries that separate distinct fields of inquiry.

It is important to be clear at the outset about what I am *not* attempting or claiming here. I am not claiming to trace lines of influence between Paul's

48. See Engberg-Pedersen, *Cosmology and Self.*
49. Bultmann, *Theology of the New Testament*, 2:237.

anthropology and the thought or actions of his contemporaries, or ours. I am not claiming that they say the same things underneath different vocabularies or ways of life; such a claim would be untenable, in my view. I am not giving a comprehensive overview of either ancient or current views of the person; such a project would far exceed my expertise and the limits of this book and indeed would be historically questionable. I am not comparing patterns of thought; the mere idea of doing so would contradict the embodied, socially embedded understanding of persons that I will discuss in Paul and other ancient and contemporary thinkers. Finally, I am not claiming that contemporary discoveries in psychology and neuroscience, or theories about such discoveries, *explain* Paul's understanding of persons, whether in a reductionist way ("explaining away") or in an attempt to prove or corroborate Paul.

My project is therefore more limited in its goals: I aim to read specific, embodied, and historically embedded voices alongside each other in a mutually illuminating conversation. In order to do so, rather than attempting a wide-ranging survey of ancient and contemporary notions of the self, I have chosen very particular voices that may speak in more depth. My choice is based on interesting points of convergence as well as difference with Paul's conception of participation and personhood. Our first-century interlocutor is Epictetus, whose writings are frequently aligned with those of Paul and whose form of Stoicism seems in some ways most amenable to Cartesian notions of the self. For an introduction to issues in contemporary understandings of the person, I have chosen to use the work of Shaun Gallagher and Vasudevi Reddy, with side glances at other theorists and scientists as well. Gallagher is a philosopher who works in cognitive science; Reddy is an experimental psychologist who interacts with philosophy of mind. Both operate from a second-person standpoint in their methods and theories. Paul's letters provide the third conversation partner. But along the way I also engage with some influential readings of Paul's letters, which not only add insights into Paul's anthropology but also reveal the philosophical commitments and presuppositions of the interpreters.

I thus am inviting my readers into a complex interchange of ideas. One overarching heuristic question will guide the conversation: is the person foundationally, essentially a bounded, discrete being who exists primarily in the form of self-relation, such that self-relation mediates and grounds other-relation? Or is the person primarily constituted in a relational exchange, such that other-relation mediates and grounds the person's self-relation? Other questions will follow: what difference does it make whether self or other comes first in the constitution of the self? What are the implications and effects of each identity structure? The goal of this hermeneutical framework of inquiry is not to solve all problems in Pauline anthropology; it is to kick-start a kind of inquiry that can shed fresh light on Paul and provide a way of letting Paul shed new light on urgent questions about personhood in a contemporary context.

In a genuine conversation the participants have to bracket their own views temporarily as they attempt to understand each other, but they do not pretend or assume to be in underlying agreement. I will articulate the voices of my interlocutors as fairly and clearly as possible and then locate points of agreement as well as difference between them. It is by listening to others who think differently that we sharpen our understanding of our own views, commitments, and experience. Listening to Epictetus and Paul together with current voices in science and philosophy will raise old questions in new ways, as well as altogether new questions. Along the way, I hope to discover fresh, sharpened articulations of Paul's own theological claims in contemporary terms.

In my view, Paul himself mandates a theological interpretation of his letters that engages deeply and creatively with issues in today's world. He crossed religious and cultural boundaries to articulate his gospel for an audience that did not share his worldview. In a word, he improvised on the gospel: he knew the language and culture of his auditors so well, and he knew the message of the gospel so well, that he could speak the latter to the former in modes that communicated its power. My reading of Paul's understanding of personhood attempts to improvise on Paul's gospel for twenty-first-century readers.[50] Such improvisation works at the boundary between Paul's language and current traditions and languages—in this book, the languages of philosophical and scientific debate about what makes us human and how we know ourselves and others. At this particular boundary, it wrestles not only with what can be improvised or "translated" but with what cannot. For example, can Paul's "metaphysical dualism" be translated or improvised in naturalistic scientific idioms? I suspect not. But are second-person theories of mind, for instance, amenable to Paul's picture of God as both other and immanent, and of human beings as fundamentally constituted in relation to God and to each other? Yes, I think they are.

The difficulties of what cannot be improvised or translated can lead to a refusal to attempt any bridging of the gaps between Paul's world and ours, for

---

50. The language of improvisation here comes from Alasdair MacIntyre, *Whose Justice? Which Rationality?* (South Bend, IN: University of Notre Dame Press, 1989), 382–83. See discussion by Kavin Rowe, *One True Life: The Stoics and Early Christians as Rival Traditions* (New Haven: Yale University Press, 2016).

fear of reductionism. According to such a view, we can only repeat Paul's language and trust God to make the word plain. But such fear of reducing Paul's cosmic worldview or of mistranslating it into a false idiom runs the equal if not greater risk of rendering Paul irrelevant for contemporary readers. Paul himself took radical risks in reformulating the news of Jesus the Messiah of Israel to speak to his Gentile auditors. He would expect no less from us.

The Structure of the Argument

The book is structured in two parts. Part 1 reframes an approach to Paul's anthropology by introducing the partners in a three-way conversation, attempting to let them speak in their own words as much as possible. A chapter on Epictetus traces out his ways of talking about the self as both self-relation and other-relation. The next chapter introduces some recent work on the self as both embodied and socially embedded, primarily through the work of Shaun Gallagher, a current philosopher of science who engages in-depth with neuroscience and experimental psychology, and Vasudevi Reddy, who has written on the development of infant cognition.[51] Along the way I interact with other theorists as well, from neuroscientist Vittorio Gallese to experimental psychologists Andrew Meltzoff and Peter Hobson. At the end of the chapter I reflect on the work of these theorists in conversation with Epictetus.

Chapter 3 introduces Paul's discourse about the body through a brief overview of key verses, situating Paul's thought in relation to Greco-Roman practices of the body. Those practices assume the porosity and malleability of the body, as well as the connectivity between embodied existence and the surrounding environment. I then trace two influential interpretations of Paul's body language, examining the work of Rudolf Bultmann and Ernst Käsemann. Bultmann sees Paul's notion of the body as signifying the whole person in the capacity for self-relation; his depiction of the body is theoretically holistic but functionally dualistic, insofar as the person is split into the self as observing subject and the self as the object of observation. Käsemann emphasizes the physicality of the body and its role in connecting the self to its environment, so that the body is inextricably embedded in its world. Although Käsemann does not draw parallels between this notion of the body and its depiction elsewhere in Greco-Roman practices, the connections are there to be made. This complex discourse about Paul's body language then

---

51. Gallagher, *How the Body Shapes the Mind*; Reddy, *How Infants Know Minds*.

provides numerous points of contact for conversation with the thought of both Epictetus and current theorists.

After part 1 sets the stage, part 2 focuses on three key Pauline texts as exemplars of Paul's participatory anthropology: Paul's portrayal of sin as an oppressive, indwelling power in Romans 7:7–25; Christ's mimetic participation in human bondage and death, in Philippians 2:1–13; and Paul's claim, "I have been crucified with Christ; it is no longer I who lives, but Christ lives in me," in Galatians 2:20. Along the way I juxtapose these texts, including their christologically shaped understandings of the cosmos, with the conversation partners introduced in part 1. The conclusion will draw together these different strands of thought, with suggestions for future work building on a deeply participatory reading of Paul's anthropology in relationship to contemporary theories of the person.

PART ONE

A Three-Way Conversation

CHAPTER ONE

The Way to Freedom

Epictetus on the Person

> I want to be the purple, that small and brilliant portion which causes the rest to appear comely and beautiful. Why then do you say to me, "Be like the majority of people"? If I do that, how shall I any longer be the purple?
>
> —Epictetus, *Discourses*

Consider the following excerpt from an opinion piece in the *New York Times* entitled "Lent: It's Not Just for Catholics."[1] The author, Arthur Brooks, begins with a celebration of nonconformist individualism and then claims, "A true individualist—a nonconformist to his or her own natural impulses—consciously accepts suffering for the benefit it brings." The true nonconformist, that is, pushes against inner boundaries and fears, which ultimately boil down to the fear of death. Lent, it turns out, is the chance to embrace suffering and "stare down death" in such a way that suffering and pain are no longer experienced as such, but simply as opportunities for growth. According to Brooks, such pushing against one's own fears and embracing suffering can happen through any number of practices, from Lent to Buddhist contemplation of corpses. The point is the inner independence thus gained:

> But the spirit of these practices is open to everyone, religious or not. Think of it as a personal declaration of independence. The objective is not to cause yourself damage, but to accept the pain and fear that are a natural

---

1. http://www.nytimes.com/2015/03/12/opinion/arthur-c-brooks-lent-its-not-just-for-catholics.html?emc=eta1.

part of life, and to embrace them as a valuable source of lessons to learn and tests to pass.

So to all the nonconformists in business, politics and art: more power to you. But that's child's play. To say, "I am dust, and to dust I shall return": Now that's rebellion for grown-ups.[2]

Epictetus couldn't have said it better. Facing death, training oneself in a stance of inner freedom and detachment, resisting and controlling impulses, treating the challenges of pain and potential sources of fear as opportunities for a kind of education that renarrates them as practice in character—such choices appear to be Stoic through and through. Indeed, in *some* ways this is a Stoic interpretation of a Christian practice, but it has been transferred from the framework of Christian theology and practice into the realm of American individualism.

In another sense, therefore, Brooks's essay is neither Stoic nor Christian, but rather an instance of modern atomistic thinking. The tip-off is the little line, "the spirit of these practices is open to everyone, religious or not." Such a claim is nonsensical from the perspective of Lent as a journey toward the crucifixion and resurrection of Jesus Christ. But the claim is also incoherent from a Stoic perspective. For the Stoics taught that getting one's thinking right was completely tied to getting one's understanding of the cosmos in line with God's immanent guidance of the entire universe, in which social, natural, and divine realities are part of a continuum of being. Theirs was a practical natural theology, which funded the self-help advice they gave out so freely. To say that one could engage in practices of embracing suffering and death without a corresponding understanding of the order of the universe would be unintelligible to them. "The way things are" and "the way we should be" go hand in glove. In this sense Stoic thought is decidedly remote from a modern utilitarian individualism that says that everyone has "their personal truth" and is content with "whatever works," without regard to any "objective" reality. Stoic thought is too unified and comprehensive to allow such personal relativism.[3]

---

2. http://www.nytimes.com/2015/03/12/opinion/arthur-c-brooks-lent-its-not-just-for-catholics.html?emc=eta1.

3. Christopher Gill provides extensive and nuanced discussion of the difference between Stoic conceptions of the self and modern "subjectivist" conceptions. See, e.g., *The Structured Self in Hellenistic and Roman Thought* (Oxford: Oxford University Press, 2006), 328–44, 359–70. A. A. Long disagrees with Gill on the Stoic notion of the individual, but he agrees in arguing that the good for all human beings is not subjectively determined, but rather is determined by "Nature" as "a supreme providential power whose right-reasoning is manifested by events and

I start out with this excerpt from a recent op-ed because it shows how much modern misconceptions of Stoic thought may pervade and distort common understandings of Christian practices. The practice of Lent is not an invitation to nonconformity and individualistic freedom; rather, it is a shared reflection on the crucifixion and resurrection of Jesus Christ. Ashes on the forehead and the solemn declaration "Remember that you are dust and to dust you shall return" are not "staring down death" but a sharing in the death of Jesus. In the article, both Christian practice and Stoic ideas are unmoored from their respective worldviews and ways of life, rendering each incoherent.

So Brooks's invitation to a "Stoic Lent" provides a cautionary tale, a warning of what *not* to do, as I begin to introduce different ways of construing the self, both past and present. My focus here is Epictetus, whose rich, sophisticated, and brilliant advice for a life of freedom and integrity can hardly be adequately traced in this short chapter. Epictetus, born around 55 CE, was at one time a slave of Epaphroditus, who himself was a freed slave in the household of Emperor Nero. Consequently, Epictetus experienced firsthand the vagaries and instabilities of life close to power. Allowed to study philosophy under the great Stoic teacher Musonius Rufus, Epictetus eventually received his freedom and gained a reputation as a philosopher. When Domitian came to power and banished the philosophers from Rome late in the first century, Epictetus was among that number. He fled to Greece and set up a philosophical school in the relative obscurity of the Roman colony of Nicopolis, where he remained until his death in roughly 135. His student Flavius Arrian recorded his lectures and published them as the *Discourses*, along with a compendium of Epictetus's thought called the *Encheiridion*.[4]

Among the many philosophers in Paul's day, all of whom claimed to guide the seeker to a wise and happy life, I have chosen Epictetus for several reasons.

the structure of the world" ("The Logical Basis of Stoic Ethics," in *Stoic Studies* [Cambridge: Cambridge University Press, 1996], 141). Neither Gill nor Long shares earlier assumptions that the first century was dominated by an anthropological dualism inherited from Plato. For an example of such an assumption, see Hans Dieter Betz, "The Concept of the 'Inner Human Being' (*ho esō anthrōpos*) in the Anthropology of Paul," *New Testament Studies* 46 (2000): 315–41. Betz argues that Paul's anthropological constructs arise out of a need to formulate "a Christian alternative to the predominant religio-philosophical dualistic anthropology of body and soul" in the first century (315). I agree with many of Betz's conclusions about the holistic character of Paul's conception of the person, but I see the first-century context as far more nuanced in terms of the concept of the person.

4. Luke T. Johnson, *Among the Gentiles: Greco-Roman Religion and Christianity* (New Haven: Yale University Press, 2009), 65–67; A. A. Long, *Epictetus: A Stoic and Socratic Guide to Life* (Oxford: Oxford University Press, 2002), 10–12.

First, the arm of his influence is long, reaching down to the present day. Origen praised Epictetus as "admired by ordinary people who have the urge to be benefited, and who perceive improvement from his words" (*Against Celsus* 6.2). Pascal said of Epictetus that he "understood the individual's duty so well. I'm tempted to say he would deserve adoration, if he had also realized the individual's powerlessness."[5] Descartes self-consciously embraced Stoic ideals and formulated maxims for life very like those of the Stoics, even though his cosmology differed significantly from that of Epictetus. In the eighteenth century, Anglican bishop Joseph Butler credited Epictetus with providing a basis for morality without requiring revelation, through the idea of an inborn sense of right and wrong: "We naturally and unavoidably approve some actions, under the peculiar view of their being virtuous and of good desert; and disapprove of others."[6] Praised by Thomas Jefferson and Walt Whitman, the philosopher continues to appear in contemporary culture in a variety of ways. James Stockdale, an American pilot who spent over seven years as a prisoner of war in North Vietnam, subsequently wrote a book about Epictetus as the resource that kept him going during that time. Tom Wolfe's novel *A Man in Full* features a protagonist who is deeply influenced by Epictetus.[7] A perusal of Epictetus's works quickly demonstrates his enduring appeal; at times he seems strikingly contemporary in his astute observations concerning human relationships and society.

Second, no other Hellenistic philosopher has so frequently been associated with Paul himself. This association has a long lineage; there are three extant adaptations of Epictetus's *Encheiridion* for use by Christian monks, dating back to at least the tenth century.[8] In one instance, a Christian adaptation of the *Encheiridion* substitutes the name of Paul for that of Socrates.[9] Given such precedents, perhaps it is understandable that the great scholar of Epictetus, A. A. Long, simply claims without comment that Stoic ideas appear frequently in Paul's letters.[10] As noted in the introduction, Troels Engberg-Pedersen has argued strongly and

5. Blaise Pascal, "Discussion with Monsieur de Sacy," in *Pensées and Other Writings*, trans. H. Levi (Oxford: Oxford University Press, 2008 [1995]), 183.

6. Long, *Epictetus*, 264–66.

7. Long, *Epictetus*, 268–70.

8. Gerard Boter, *The* Enchiridion *of Epictetus and Its Three Christian Adaptations: Transmission and Critical Editions* (Leiden: Brill, 1999).

9. "This is the way of Paul because of what he was, in everything persuading himself to pay attention to nothing but reason; and even if you are not yet a Paul you must live as if you wish to become a Paul" (*Ench.* 51.3), ascribed to St. Nilus (*Nil* 71 *ad fin*) (Boter, *The* Enchiridion *of Epictetus*, 159, 367).

10. Long, *Epictetus*, 259.

provocatively that Stoic ethics provide historical corollaries and compelling access to Paul's thought for contemporary readers, whom he calls "we moderns."[11] Whether Engberg-Pedersen is correct in this assessment is a matter for further discussion; in my view, as will become clear later, there are ground-level differences between Paul's view of the world and that of Epictetus, and these cosmological differences cannot be set aside in a quest for a common ethics, let alone a shared notion of the person.[12] Nonetheless, juxtaposing Epictetus, Paul, and modern theories of the self provides a way to sharpen understanding of Paul's theology and of what is at stake in his peculiar and puzzling anthropology.

Third, Epictetus has a particularly supple, richly developed discussion of aspects of human identity and flourishing, including agency, self-perception, rationality, embodiment, and social relations, which is distinctively amenable to exploring the notion of the person.[13] Among the Stoics, Epictetus comes closest to contemporary ideas of persons as autonomous, self-contained individuals, although his underlying cosmology subverts the similarities. Although he had no word that translates "person" (nor did Paul), it would appear that Epictetus had a working model of what it means to be a human being.

Whether in fact Epictetus had a theory of the self, however, is a debated topic. A lot depends on how both "theory" and "self" are defined. Does Epictetus have to have an abstract and developed concept of the self in order to have a working understanding of what it means to be a person? And does there have to be a discrete, autonomous, freestanding, and bounded individual for there to be a "self"? Or can there be a person existing on a continuum of being and interaction with continuous give-and-take between what's "internal" and what's "external"? And which of these pictures more accurately fits Epictetus's teachings? Among modern classicists, A. A. Long sees in Epictetus the harbingers of individual identity, autonomy, and free will; Christopher Gill disagrees and emphasizes instead continuity with Greek philosophical concepts of the person as communally constructed.[14] Both scholars consider the points of

11. Troels Engberg-Pedersen, *Paul and the Stoics* (Louisville: Westminster John Knox, 2000) and *Cosmology and Self in the Apostle Paul: The Material Spirit* (Oxford: Oxford University Press, 2010).

12. On this point, see in particular the review by J. Louis Martyn, "De-apocalypticizing Paul: An Essay Focused on *Paul and the Stoics* by Troels Engberg-Pederson," *Journal for the Study of the New Testament* 24.4 (2002): 61–102.

13. Engberg-Pedersen focuses on Epictetus in his discussion of Stoic conceptions of the self in *Cosmology and Self*, 109–21.

14. Long, *Epictetus*, 207–30; Long, "Representation and the Self in Stoicism," in *Stoic Studies*, 264–85; Gill, *Structured Self*, 375–79.

contact between Epictetus and contemporary theories of the self, but they differ as to which contemporary theories provide the best analogues: Long assumes a Cartesian picture of the self and sees in Epictetus the precursors of individualistic notions of free will, whereas Gill sees intriguing analogies with more recent theories of the person as embodied and socially embedded. This debate has affinities with distinctions between the body as "self-relation" and as "other-relation," which I have proposed as a heuristic framework for this investigation: both are to be found in the copious and compelling advice that Epictetus gave to his followers.

Individualism: The Self as Self-Relation

Like other Hellenistic philosophers, Epictetus taught above all the way to a happy life, which for him meant inner freedom from compulsion and living in harmony with the divine order of the cosmos. His teaching thus emphasizes ad infinitum the principles of self-understanding that ground such freedom and harmony. First and most important is the distinction between what is under our control and what is not. His *Encheiridion* begins as follows: "Some things are under our control [*eph' hēmin*], while others are not under our control [*ouk eph' hēmin*]. Under our control are conception, choice, desire, aversion, and, in a word, everything that is our own doing; not under our control are our body [*to sōma*], our property, reputation, office, and, in a word, everything that is not our own doing" (*Ench.* 1).

What is in our power as human beings, says Epictetus, is simply this: conception, and the way we evaluate all the data of consciousness, whether that be events that happen to us or even thoughts that arise in us.[15] This data is named collectively by the term *phantasia*, usually translated "impressions" or "representations."[16] The latter translation conveys the idea that what concerns Epictetus is the way we represent events to ourselves—the way we narrate them and evaluate them in relationship to what truly concerns us. And it turns out that what truly concerns us or, in Stoic terms, "belongs to us" (what is proper to who and what we are as rational human beings) is very limited indeed. It is the capacity to accept, and thereby "to choose," to live in harmony with the way

15. The term "data of consciousness" comes from P. E. Matheson, trans., *Epictetus: The Discourses and Manual*, vol. 2 (Oxford: Oxford University Press, 1916), 239.

16. For the translation "representations," see Long, "Representation and the Self in Stoicism."

things are and to dismiss everything else as irrelevant to our well-being. What is in our power therefore includes (1) our choice of attitudes and consequent actions that are true to who we are and (2) our refusal to become subject to passions or false understandings of events. These attitudes are "internals"; everything else, including our body, is "external."

The first book of Epictetus's discourses expounds on the same theme of what is and is not in our power: "Among the arts and faculties [*dynameis*] in general you will find none that is self-contemplative [*theōrētikēn*], and therefore none that is either self-approving or self-disapproving" (*Disc.* 1.1.1).[17] In fact, only one faculty can tell us what to do in any given situation:

> That one which contemplates both itself and everything else. And what is this? The reasoning faculty [*hē dynamis hē logikē*]; for this is the only one we have inherited which will take knowledge both of itself—what it is, and of what it is capable, and how valuable a gift it is to us—and likewise of all the other faculties. For what else is it that tells us gold is beautiful? For the gold itself does not tell us. Clearly it is the faculty which makes use of external impressions [*phantasiais*]. . . .
>
> As was fitting, therefore, the gods have put under our control only the most excellent faculty of all and that which dominates the rest, namely, the power to make correct use of external impressions, but all the rest they have not put under our control. (*Disc.* 1.1.4–8)

This faculty, the power to make correct use of external impressions, is the power to choose or to refuse, to desire or to avoid (*Disc.* 1.1.12). It is the only thing deserving of our attention, the one thing that makes us what we are. Absolutely everything else—from property to reputation to relationships to our physical bodies—is outside our control and therefore does not really belong to us: "We must make the best of what is under our control, and take the rest as its nature is. 'How then, is its nature?' As God wills" (*Disc.* 1.1.17).

In other words, go with the flow, accept what comes your way, and keep a good attitude. This advice sounds just fine, until we realize how extreme Epictetus's advice can get. What if I'm to be beheaded, Epictetus? Should I accept that prospect as God's will also? The answer is yes—why should you think you are a special case, an exception to the events that can happen to

---

17. *Epictetus: The Discourses as Reported by Arrian, the Manual, and Fragments*, trans. W. A. Oldfather, vol. 1 (London: William Heinemann; New York: G. P. Putnam's Sons, 1926); all translations of Epictetus hereafter are from Oldfather, unless otherwise noted.

anyone? In any circumstance, the only thing we need is the knowledge of what is ours and what is not ours. If we must die, we don't need to die groaning. If we must go into exile, we have the choice of going with serenity and a smile on our face. We may be chained, but nothing can chain our choice, our will, our moral purpose: "My leg you will fetter, but my moral purpose [*proairesis*] not even Zeus is able to overcome. 'I will throw you into prison.' My paltry body, rather!" (*Disc.* 1.1.23).

Translated as "will," "volition," or "choice," *proairesis* is the central faculty for human identity and freedom. A. A. Long calls it "Epictetus's favorite name for the purposive and self-conscious center of a person."[18] More than "God-given," it is in fact a portion of divinity, a share in the divine nature (*Disc.* 1.1.12); at the same time, it signifies autonomy because once given, such "choice" is beyond the control even of Zeus. Above all, *proairesis* signifies freedom; "free by nature from hindrances and constraint" (*Disc.* 1.17.21), it is "an inalienably free space within the human being."[19] This faculty exercises its freedom in the sphere of assent to truth and rejection of falsehood. Indeed, only *proairesis* can compel *proairesis*: "For if God had so constructed that part of his own being which he has taken from himself and bestowed upon us, that it could be subjected to hindrance or constraint either from Himself or from some other, He were no longer God, nor would He be caring for us as He ought" (*Disc.* 1.17.26–27).

Long glosses this desiderative power as "the only faculty we have that can have cognizance of itself as well as everything else . . . our desiderative and impulsive faculty . . . our capacity to give or withhold assent. It is our *proairesis*, our moral character." This *proairesis* is not the same as the governing faculty (*hēgemōn*) of the soul. Rather, it is the rational exercise of the soul's commanding part. It is the capacity to choose whether to welcome or whether to avoid all that is not in our control, all that does not "belong" to us. And as Epictetus's remarks about the body show, when we learn to reason rightly, we realize that the only thing that truly belongs to us, that truly is in our power, is the right exercise of *proairesis*. This capacity, says Long, "is the essential self, as Epictetus conceives of this, the bearer of personal identity."[20] Moreover, through the rational exercise of choice, the individual gains both autonomy and responsibility, demonstrating the existence of a self that is "essentially personal and individualized."[21]

18. Long, *Epictetus*, 207.

19. Kavin Rowe, *One True Life: The Stoics and Early Christians as Rival Traditions* (New Haven: Yale University Press, 2016).

20. Long, "Representation and the Self in Stoicism," 217.

21. Charles Kahn, "Discovering the Will: From Aristotle to Augustine," in *The Question*

If there is such an essentially personal and individual self, how is it structured? How is it related to itself, and how is it related to others? And at the end of the day, just how autonomous is it? One way to address these questions is through two lenses: self-perception, and the relationship between *proairesis* and the body.

Self-Perception

As we have seen, Epictetus's first *Discourse* begins with a discussion of self-perception: "Among the arts and faculties [*dynameis*] in general you will find none that is self-contemplative, and therefore none that is either self-approving or self-disapproving." Epictetus then lists the limits of grammatical and musical faculties. The only faculty that can "study itself" (Long's translation) is "that one which contemplates both itself and everything else. And what is this? The reasoning faculty; for this is the only one we have inherited which will take knowledge both of itself—what it is, and of what it is capable, and how valuable a gift it is to us—and likewise of all the other faculties" (*Disc.* 1.1.4).

This is Epictetus's take on the widespread Stoic claim that human beings are born with a capacity for self-perception. Epictetus uniquely identifies this capacity with reason itself as an innate, inborn gift: "our birth involves the blending of these two things—the body, on the one hand, that we share with animals, and, on the other hand, rationality and intelligence, that we share with the gods" (*Disc.* 1.3.3).[22] Other Stoics also speak about self-perception, but not as the exercise of reason. Rather, they describe it as something characteristic of nonrational animals and children, as well as adults; reason is limited to human adults, who alone are rational animals. Indeed, all Stoics hold that every animal, including humans, is born with self-awareness and an innate knowledge of what is proper to its own particular constitution or sentient life. The first aspect of Stoic self-relation is this first-personal self-awareness, or as Cato puts it in Cicero's *On Ends*, a sense of oneself. For example:

> [The Stoics] hold that as soon as an animal is born—for this must be the starting point—it is appropriated to itself and led to preserve itself and to love its own constitution and those things which preserve its constitution,

of "Eclecticism": Studies in Later Greek Philosophy, ed. John Dillon and Anthony Long (Berkeley: University of California Press, 1988), 253, quoted in Long, "Representation," 276.

22. Trans. Matheson.

and to be alienated from its death and from those things that seem to lead to death. They prove that this is so from the fact that, before either pleasure or pain has affected them, infants seek what preserves them and reject the opposite, something which would not happen unless they loved their constitution and feared death. But it cannot be the case that they desire anything unless they have a sense of themselves and therefore love themselves. Hence it must be realized that the principle has been drawn from self-love. (3.16)[23]

Writing much later, in a summary of early Stoic doctrine, Diogenes Laertius finds the same idea in Chrysippus: "They [the Stoics] say that an animal has self-preservation as the object of its first impulse, since nature from the beginning appropriates it, as Chrysippus says in his *On Ends* book I. The first thing appropriate [*oikeios*] to every animal, he says, is its own constitution [*systasis*] and the consciousness [*syneidēsis*] of this" (Diogenes Laertius 7.85).[24] And from Hierocles, writing about 200 CE, we hear the following: "We should realize that as soon as an animal is born it perceives itself. . . . The first thing that animals perceive is their own parts . . . both that they have them and for what purpose they have them. . . . Therefore the first proof of every animal's perceiving itself is its consciousness of its parts and the function for which they were given. The second proof is the fact that animals are not unaware of their equipment for self-defense" (*Ethics* 1.37–38, 51, 64–65).[25]

Varied as these different statements are, they all begin with common-sense observations about animals and children: both seem to have a sense of themselves, an attachment to their bodies as belonging to themselves, an awareness of what will help and what will hurt them, and an impulse toward self-preservation and flourishing.[26] These observations imply some kind

---

23. Translation in Gill, *Structured Self*, 36. Gill sees this passage as indicative of a "psychophysical holism" in Stoicism, in which "Nature, taken collectively, is seen as one such whole, and this larger whole 'appropriates' the smaller one. It does so by bringing it about that the smaller one, the animal, 'appropriates itself' and thus expresses its own potential wholeness" (*Structured Self*, 37). That is, the animal's self-relation is mediated and facilitated by the larger encompassing medium of Nature.

24. Translation from A. A. Long and D. N. Sedley, *The Hellenistic Philosophers*, vol. 1 (Cambridge: Cambridge University Press, 1988), 57a.

25. Translation, Long and Sedley, 57c.

26. It is interesting to note how many of these statements start with the observation of infants and children. Piso, speaking about Antiochus of Ascalon, in Cicero, *On Ends* 5.55, says, "All the ancient philosophers, in particular those of our school, turn to cradles because it is in childhood that they think we can most easily recognize the will of nature." See discussion

of self-awareness that is fitting for each species: mouths are for eating and making noise; legs are for walking; eyes are for seeing. Coupled with this self-knowledge is an innate awareness of external phenomena in relation to the newborn: baby turtles head for water; mammals instinctively drink milk; chicks open their beaks wide to be fed.

Because these observations apply to nonrational animals and children as well as human adults, they cannot be taken to refer to some kind of mental self-consciousness as a distinctly human trait. Rather, in light of the holistic view of the self in Stoicism, they are suggestive of a psychophysical feedback loop that carries messages from the body to the governing faculty and back again in a thoroughly embodied way. Similarly, the evidence that self-perception can happen while animals and humans are asleep suggests that it is not necessarily a conscious process.[27] Thus it would be a mistake to interpret the language of "self-perception" in these texts in terms of Cartesian ideas of self-consciousness or a mental awareness of, and access to, an inner "core" or essential self in some conscious way. Rather, in these texts Stoic self-perception seems to be a process of information sharing between the body and the governing faculty, which also is embodied. This information sharing happens both in unconscious routine bodily processes and in the conscious recognition of one's bodily parts and their uses.

Seneca's letter 121 to Lucillus, quoted in the introduction, provides further correction of any attempt to see in the Stoics a modern Cartesian conception of personhood in abstract, mental terms. Claiming that all animals have an inborn knowledge of their "constitution," which he has defined as the relationship between the body and the governing faculty of the self, Seneca anticipates his reader's objection in a passage worth revisiting in its larger context:

> "How does an infant understand this complicated and subtle relationship which is somehow beyond even your explanation? All creatures have to be born capable of argument in order to understand this definition which is

---

in Jacques Brunschwig, "The Cradle Argument in Epicureanism and Stoicism," in *The Norms of Nature: Studies in Hellenistic Ethics,* ed. Malcolm Schofield and Gisela Striker (Cambridge: Cambridge University Press, 1986), 113–44, and Gill, *Structured Self,* 362–63. As we shall see in the next chapter, this is also where some recent studies of human cognition and the person begin; see, e.g., Alison Gopnik, Andrew N. Meltzoff, and Patricia K. Kuhl, *The Scientist in the Crib: What Early Learning Tells Us about the Mind* (New York: Harper, 2001), and Peter Hobson, *The Cradle of Thought: Exploring the Origins of Thinking* (Oxford: Oxford University Press, 2004).

27. See the discussion in Gill, *Structured Self,* 40–42.

impenetrable to most citizens in their togas." But there would have been an objection you can make, if I had said that animals could understand the definition of their composition, instead of their composition itself. Nature is more easily understood than described. So that infant does not know what his composition is, but he knows his composition, and an animal doesn't know what it is, but feels it is an animal.

Besides, he only understands his composition crudely and superficially and vaguely. We too know we have a mind, but we do not know what the mind is, where it is, what is its nature and from what source. Just as we are aware of our own mind, although we do not know its nature and place, so all animals are aware of their own composition. For they must necessarily feel the organ by which they feel all other things; they must necessarily have a feeling they obey and by which they are governed. No man among us fails to understand that there is something that stirs his impulses; but he doesn't know what it is. And he knows he has an impulse, but he does not know what it is or its origin. So infants too and animals have a perception of their governing part, but it is not yet sufficiently clear or articulate. (Seneca, *Ep.* 121.9–13)[28]

"How does an infant understand this complicated and subtle relationship which is somehow beyond even your explanation?" For anyone remotely familiar with twenty-first-century debates about human development and theories of mind, the question has a familiar ring. How can we talk about infants' awareness of themselves and others, prior to the development of a capacity for abstract thought? Modern theorists are divided on this question. Seneca, however, is very clear indeed: the "infant does not know what his composition is, but he knows his composition." Seneca thus neatly parses the distinction between abstract general theories and particular experiential knowledge. The child does not need a theory in order to have the experience of self-awareness. Conceptual understanding will come later.

Perhaps the closest contemporary analogue to Hierocles's and Seneca's descriptions of self-perception is the concept of proprioception in neuroscience.[29] Coined in 1906 by Charles Sherrington, the term "proprioception"

28. Elaine Fantham, trans., *Seneca: Selected Letters* (Oxford: Oxford University Press, 2010).

29. First suggested by Brunschwig, this connection between Stoic self-perception and proprioception is developed by Long in "Hierocles on *oikeiosis* and Self-Perception," in *Stoic Studies*, 257–60, and Gill, *Structured Self*, 41–42, 364. Long quotes Oliver Sacks, who suggestively describes the loss of proprioception as a "loss of the fundamental organic mooring of

denotes the neurological flow of information within the body, and between the body and the brain.[30] It is distinct from but interacts with "exteroception," the perception of external stimuli. The interaction between the two kinds of perception is similar to the way in which, in Stoic analysis, the awareness of what is proper to one's own constitution interacts with environmental stimuli such as particular foods or threatening behavior. There is an intimate relationship between such proprioceptive self-relation and exteroceptive other-awareness and relation, but according to these Stoic sources, human and animal development begins with self-perception and then moves out into perception of external objects. It would appear that self-perception is prior to and foundational for all other perception in all sentient beings.

The analogue of proprioception helps us keep in mind the embodied, holistic notion of the self that underlies these Stoic ideas of innate self-perception. Matters appear a bit differently in Epictetus, however. For Epictetus, self-perception is exercised by the faculty of reason and therefore is singularly human. Furthermore, Epictetus does not appear to distinguish between children and adults in this matter.[31] It is true that in the course of a life this capacity can be diminished and dulled by a false evaluation of impressions, but it is a given part of the human constitution, bestowed by a benevolent deity on all human beings, just as *proairesis* is given to all human beings and only to human beings. Simply by virtue of being human we thus are endowed with a rational capacity to study ourselves, to be students of our own impulses and actions, and to take responsibility for them. Such rational self-study then, in turn, divides the rational "subject" from the object of study, including the body.

Thus if self-perception is the function of our reasoning capacity, which is linked to the *proairesis* that Epictetus so emphatically distinguishes from the body, then it seems that there is an implicit dualism in the way we are structured. We can and do watch ourselves. In fact, much of Epictetus's advice might be summarized as "Watch yourself!"—"Watch what you think and what you do!" Does not this counsel imply an aspect or function of the self that watches,

---

identity" or loss of "our sense of *ourselves*; for it is only by courtesy of proprioception . . . that we feel our bodies as proper to us, as our 'property', as our own" (*The Man Who Mistook His Wife for a Hat* [New York: Perennial Library, 1987], 43).

30. This is a minimal definition of proprioception. For extended discussion of the term in relationship to body image and body schema, see the careful argument of Shaun Gallagher, *How the Body Shapes the Mind* (Oxford: Oxford University Press, 2005), 17–39.

31. See *Disc.* 1.6.12–22: human life begins in the same place as that of nonrational animals, but it ends with studying and attending, as nature does, to a life in harmony with nature. See discussion in Long, *Epictetus*, 173.

as well as an aspect of the self that is watched? To address this question, I turn next to Epictetus's distinctive language about the body and the implicit dualism in his account of the relationship between "body," "soul," and *proairesis.*

Self-Relation to the Body and to God Within

For Epictetus, right judgment begins with a right understanding of who we are: "If someone could only subscribe heart and soul, as is fitting, to this doctrine, that we are all primarily begotten of God, and that God is the father of human beings as well as of gods, I think that he will entertain no ignoble or mean thought about himself" (*Disc.* 1.3.1).[32] But what does it mean to be "begotten of God"? It means the following:

> Seeing that our birth involves the blending of these two things—the body, on the one hand, that we share with animals, and, on the other hand, rationality and intelligence, that we share with the gods—most of us incline to this former relationship, wretched and dead though it is, while only a few to the one that is divine and blessed. Since, then, every person necessarily handles each thing on the basis of his opinion of it, those few who think that they are born for integrity and security in their use of impressions, have no low or abject opinion of themselves, whereas the majority think the opposite. (*Disc.* 1.3.3–4)[33]

It appears that Epictetus inclines to a certain anthropological dualism. On the one hand, we are bodily creatures, which sets us in relationship with other animals; on the other, we are rational, which denotes our union with God. Long glosses this summary as "By virtue of our bodies, we are akin to the other animals, but by virtue of our minds, we are akin to God."[34] Epictetus thus implies a division within the person between "body" and "rationality." Although he subscribes to the basic Stoic conception of the corporeality of all things, including the mind, and he does talk about the mind as corporeal *pneuma* (*Disc.* 2.23.3; 3.3.22), such talk is infrequent. More often his language is quite dualistic in this respect, including a striking denigration of the body as "mud" and "chains," along with all other "externals" such as property and fam-

32. Oldfather trans., with minor changes.
33. Trans. Long, *Epictetus*, 157.
34. Trans. Long, *Epictetus*, 157.

ily relationships (see, e.g., *Disc.* 4.1.99–111). With regard to human rationality, Epictetus is "reticent" on the Stoic doctrine of the corporeality of all things, including God, as Long explains: "We should take his sharp contrast between the body and the mind to be Platonic in an ethical rather than a metaphysical sense. Just as he takes no interest in the exact composition of the world's elements, so he virtually ignores the mind's physical structure. What he wants to emphasize is a duality in our human constitution that gives us the option of deciding whether we shall be godlike (by identifying with our minds) or merely animal (by identifying with our bodies)."[35] In other words, the freedom of the self is at issue, and that freedom is intertwined with an inner sanctum that provides room for personal choice.

Second, then, Epictetus's language implies an ongoing discernment concerning the primary constitution of one's identity in two kinds of self-relation: a relationship to the "portion of divinity" within through the exercise of rational *proairesis*, or a relationship merely to one's physical, bodily self, the aspect of the self that we share with animals. And this duality in the self in turn implies that the decision to identify exclusively with the divine reason within would take us away from identification with bodily existence. Although Epictetus never says we should neglect our bodies, he does teach detachment from them: we should treat them as nature treats them, but in an indifferent sort of way, in accordance with their given constitution:

> Observe what Socrates says to Alcibiades, the most handsome and youthfully beautiful of men: "Try, then, to be beautiful." What does he tell him? "Dress your locks and pluck the hairs out of your legs?" God forbid! No, he says, "Make beautiful your moral purpose [*kosmei sou tēn proairesin*], eradicate your worthless opinions." How treat your paltry body [*sōmation*] then? As its nature is. This is the concern of Another; leave it to Him.— What then? Does the body have to be left unclean?—God forbid! But the man that you are and were born to be, keep that man clean, a man to be clean as a man, a woman as a woman, a child as a child. (*Disc.* 3.1.43–44)

Or as Epictetus says elsewhere, we take care of the body as something that does not belong to us; the body is like the room at an inn where we stay for a night and then move on (*Disc.* 1.25.13).

Third, one's evaluation of one's own worth is inseparable from recognizing and embracing the divinity within, which is one's own rationality. For

35. Trans. Long, *Epictetus*, 157.

example, a woman who acts like an animal of low worth—say, a fox, but certainly not a lordly lion—betrays a low opinion of herself. Most important, that low opinion is also a false opinion, because she has forgotten the fact that from birth she has an innate rationality, the God within. As Epictetus says elsewhere,

> You are bearing God about with you, you poor wretch, and know it not! Do you suppose I am speaking of some external god, made of silver or gold? It is within yourself that you bear him, and do not perceive that you are defiling him with impure thoughts and filthy actions. . . . He has delivered your own self into your keeping, saying: "I had no one more faithful than you; keep this person for me unchanged from the character with which nature endowed him—reverent, trustworthy, faithful, high-minded, undismayed, unimpassioned, unperturbed." (*Disc.* 2.8.13, 23)

On the one hand, then, human beings are bodily creatures in a relationship of continuity with all other animals; on the other hand, human beings are truly constituted as rational creatures in a relationship of continuity with the divine rationality within. But precisely because the divine is in both nature and the self, the constitutive relationship with divine rationality is also both self- and other-directed. It is not, however, mediated by the body.

Individualism

In Epictetus's teaching about relationships to the body and to the God within, the capacity to make correct use of impressions distinguishes rational, divinely constituted beings from nonrational animals. Such rational evaluation of impressions implies that "there must be a 'me' to which they appear and an 'I' which reacts to them."[36] This claim does not deny selfhood to nonrational animals: "By its reflexive formulation, 'self-belonging' [*oikeiōsis*] characterizes the disposition of care and ownership that an animal has in relation to itself."[37] But *proairesis* is more, for it supplies and requires self-understanding in relationship to the order of the cosmos, thus consciously choosing to think and therefore to act in accordance with what is reasonable in an objective, ordered sense.

36. Long, "Representation and the Self in Stoicism," 276.
37. Long, "Hierocles on *oikeiosis* and Self-Perception," 253.

What is reasonable is what accords with the divinely ordered flow of all that is, which is the same as the rational working of our own judgment:

> [Zeus] has presented to each person each person's own divine spirit [*daimōn*], as a guardian, and committed the person's safekeeping to this trustee, who does not sleep and who cannot be misled. To what better and more caring guardian could he have entrusted us? So when you close your doors and make it dark inside, remember never to say you are alone, because you are not; God is inside and your own divine spirit too. What need have they of light to see what you are doing? It is to this god that you should swear allegiance, as soldiers do to Caesar. . . . What, then, will you swear? Never to disobey, or press charges or complain about anything God has given you, or be reluctant in doing or suffering anything that is inevitable. Is this oath anything like that other one? There men swear to put no one ahead of Caesar. *But here we swear to put ourselves ahead of everything else.* (*Disc.* 1.14.12–17)[38]

Here again Epictetus appears to presume an "I" that is both the subject and the object of human loyalty. His conversational style and warm, personal account of the relation of the self to God may seem deceptively similar to Christian understandings of the relationship between God and human beings: the assurance of divine care on a personal level, the companionship and indwelling of God, the call for commitment to God above all else, and the implicit trust in the goodness of God. But the last line betrays a fundamental difference between the Stoic and the Christian worldview: "we swear to put *ourselves* ahead of everything else." There is no conflict between putting self and putting God ahead of everything else, because God is in the self and *is* the true self.

Implicit in this picture is a self-relation in which we become students of our own nature and place in the universe at the same time as we become students of the divine providence that orders and permeates all that is. As Epictetus puts it, nonrational animals instinctively avoid what is hurtful and seek what is good, but God gave human beings the capacity and requirement of understanding and choosing, along with the possibility of misusing, that faculty of reason. That faculty is indeed a portion of God within the self. "You will also find many things possessed by us in common with the irrational animals. Do they also, then, understand what happens? No! For use is one thing, and understanding another. God has need of the animals in that they

---

38. Trans. Long, *Epictetus*, 26.

make use of external impressions, and of us in that we understand the use of external impressions" (*Disc.* 1.6.12–13).

Such self-relation could easily be interpreted as denoting separation between the rational faculty and an irrational sensory self. But for Epictetus, as for all the Stoics, there is emphatically no such separation. The rational or correct use of impressions is a function of the person as a whole, not one rational part attempting to control irrational forces. Nonetheless, in this reasoning process a space opens up for self-examination, introversion, and evaluation; it becomes possible to put the brakes on the impulse to react to any event, to turn it over in one's mind, to consider whether or not to follow the impulse, and to renarrate it through a form of self-talk. Epictetus gives vivid examples of this method of self-talk:

> Today when I saw a good-looking boy or woman I did not say to myself: "If only I could have sex with her" and "Her husband is a happy man." For to call the husband happy is to say the same of the adulterer. And I don't draw a mental picture of what comes next—the woman with me, getting undressed, and lying down by my side. . . . You must want to be pleasing just to yourself, you must want to appear beautiful to God. Make it your passion to become pure in the presence of your pure self and in the presence of God. (*Disc.* 2.18.15–19)[39]

Notice how Epictetus refuses certain evaluative thoughts and substitutes others, and how he rewards himself with praise for doing so. Undergirding this process is a detachment from all opinions of himself apart from his own and that of God—which, as we know, amount to the same thing because the "pure self" is the portion of divinity within the self, wherein God dwells.

Here, it seems, is a picture of an "I" that stands apart: detached, evaluating, self-controlled. This is a self that can say to compelling thoughts or emotions, "Wait for me a bit, impression; let me take a look at you and what you are about, let me test you" (*Disc.* 2.18). This "I" talks to itself, controlling its relationship to external events by narrating them in positive ways rather than negative ones: "You say, 'I don't like leisure, it is a solitude.' 'I don't like a crowd, it is turmoil.' Say not so, but if circumstances bring you to spend your life alone or in the company of a few, call it peace, and utilize the condition for its proper end; converse with yourself [*lalei seautō*], exercise your sense-impressions [*gymnaze tas phantasias*], develop your preconceptions" (*Disc.* 4.4.26).

39. Trans. Long, *Epictetus*, 215.

Precisely this capacity for "self-talk" through propositional statements (*lekta*) that narrate experience in one way rather than another enacts the freedom of the individual. Long likens such propositional statements to a personal trainer who shows us a different way to think about something but doesn't actually move our limbs. Here, suggests Long, is the inner space where the individual finds freedom in the middle of a cosmos determined by divine order, or providence.[40]

Self-Perception, Inner Detachment, and Individual Freedom

To summarize thus far: at this point Epictetus appears to see human beings through a first-person perspective. Human cognition begins and ends with self-perception, so that all experience is known in relation to oneself and filtered through an inner evaluative faculty. In Long's view, Epictetus thus has a philosophy of the self as "representation," which is "the way in which individual human beings perceive themselves, or what it is for them to have a first-person outlook on the world or first-person experience. The self in this sense is something essentially individual—a uniquely positioned viewer and interlocutor, a being who has interior access of a kind that is not available to anyone else."[41] Here self-perception is a prerequisite for all other perception; recalling Timothy Chappell's language from the previous chapter, we might say, "relationality presupposes individuality." To be sure, Long clarifies that this individual, first-personal starting point does not imply some sort of free-floating ego in a modern, post-Cartesian sense; rather, it describes a faculty constituting "moral identity" and "character" formed by experience and narrative, which itself is instantiated by nature. Nonetheless, he insists on the persistence of a unique, discrete "I": "In order to be at all . . . we need a persisting view of ourselves, a bottom-line representation or narrative that is called into play whenever an 'I' is called upon."[42]

Long's emphasis on individualism, autonomy, and free will in the Stoics in general, and Epictetus in particular, is shared by Charles Kahn and Troels Engberg-Pedersen, all of whom see in the Stoics the forerunners of Cartesian understandings of the self.[43] Engberg-Pedersen, in fact, finds in the Stoics

---

40. Long, "Representation and the Self in Stoicism," 284.
41. Long, "Representation and the Self in Stoicism," 265.
42. Long, "Representation and the Self in Stoicism," 282.
43. See, e.g., Kahn, "Discovering the Will"; Troels Engberg-Pedersen, "Stoic Philosophy

the precursor of Boethius's famous definition of the person as "a rational substance of an individual nature."[44] But not all classicists agree; Christopher Gill in particular believes that the language of autonomy and individualism betrays a post-Cartesian worldview imposed on the first-century cosmos of the Stoics and basically alien to it.[45] Rather, he insists that the Stoics, including Epictetus, saw human beings as thoroughly participatory beings rather than as individuals in a modern sense. What evidence is there in Epictetus for this view?

The Constitution of the Self as Other-Relation

For all Stoics, including Epictetus, human beings do not exist in isolation from their environment but are deeply embedded in it. This embeddedness has naturalistic grounding and social force. Like everything in the cosmos, the self exists on a continuum with all of nature, which in turn is infused and in some way coterminous with divine reason—that is, with God. Epictetus repeatedly claims that to know oneself rightly is to know oneself as a part of this divinity, in continuity with the divine order that guides all nature. At the same time, every person is socially formed from birth, for good or for ill. For this reason, education in philosophy is necessary in order to recall us to ourselves, to our true divine identity, and to train us to resist false impressions of reality. These two factors—being a part of the whole cosmos and being a part of society such that we require education to regain our freedom—establish humans as participatory beings whose freedom consists in acting in accordance with nature. We are who we are by virtue of belonging to a greater reality, and that belonging happens on many levels.

---

and the Concept of the Person," in *The Person and the Human Mind: Issues in Ancient and Modern Philosophy*, ed. Christopher Gill (Oxford: Oxford University Press, 1990), 109–35.

44. "When around AD 520 the Christian philosopher Boethius defined the person (*persona*) as 'an individual substance of a rational nature', he was summing up the whole ancient tradition rather than being innovatory" (Engberg-Pederson, "Stoic Philosophy and the Concept of the Person," 110).

45. Gill's most extensive discussion is in *The Structured Self*, 325–407. He argues against first-person, "I"-centered subjective accounts of the person in ancient thought and finds analogies in some contemporary "third person" and "participatory" theories of mind, suggesting that "we should begin from modern non-Cartesian discussions of personhood or rationality, rather than from the 'I' centered or subjective definitions of personhood or personal identity that have played an important role in much modern thought" (336).

God, Nature, Providence

Whatever the words "God," "nature," "providence" might mean today, they surely had a distinctly different meaning for Epictetus. They cannot be understood apart from the cosmology that undergirds his teaching about the way to a good and happy life. So we start with a brief look at these three words. The first thing to note is that Epictetus uses these terms interchangeably.

First, "God." Epictetus stands out among the Stoics for the extraordinarily personal language he uses about and toward God. He addresses God, often through the name of Zeus, with great warmth and devotion. God is the "father" of all human beings, and while this divine paternity means that, in good Roman fashion, God rules like a king, it also means that God cares personally for each and every human being. Epictetus often speaks to God in prayer and exhorts his students to do the same, to make their lives a form of praise to God. God gives a portion of divine reason to every person, and this gift is proof of God's benevolent care for humanity.

But despite such personal language about God, God is not other than humanity. Underlying Epictetus's second-person discourse is the pantheism that is foundational for all Stoic ethics. God is not above or outside of the natural world, which is the corporeal cosmos. Rather, God is coextensive with nature as its ordering principle: God and nature are one. This is a thoroughly naturalistic cosmology and theology, such that there is no causality from outside of the material world. There is no Creator God who exists prior to or apart from the creation of the cosmos; there is no God outside of time; there is no God apart from nature. Conversely, there is no nature apart from God, and therefore there is no "self" apart from God. To act in accordance with nature is to act in accordance with God, which is also to act in line with one's own rational self. For this reason the recognition that God is "with us" leads to behavior that, above all, is true to ourselves.

Epictetus thus has a very strong view of providence. Nature operates as God ordains because nature is coextensive with God. Epictetus is an inveterate optimist. All things happen as God wills. There is no room here for social criticism or any attempt to change social ills such as slavery. Indeed, there is no room to identify slavery as a social ill. For Epictetus, the freed slave turned philosopher, freedom has nothing to do with ending slavery and everything to do with the inner disposition of the slave. Change is not up to us—in fact, there is nothing intrinsically desirable about social change. It is up to us to recognize that God orders all things well and to adjust our attitudes accordingly. Herein lies the secret of both Stoic fatalism and Stoic freedom. When we learn to embrace whatever circumstances we are in and to reject all complaining or fear or anxiety, we find true freedom: an inner, sovereign indifference and detachment that cannot be manipulated by fear or any other emotion.

The Social Cosmos: Roles, Relationships, Education

The participatory, interpersonal character of the Stoic social cosmos is evident in the importance assigned to the roles people are given to play in the social order, the ways in which relationships contribute to the formation of the self, and the importance of philosophical education as the primary way to attain inner freedom.

Roles

Since embracing the divine order of nature leads to freedom and happiness, that order obviously is not simply descriptive but prescriptive; it tells us how to direct our lives correctly. Furthermore, that order comes to us through the roles that society gives us, or more precisely, that God gives us through the instrumentality of social structures. Some of us are men, some are women; some are rich, some are poor; some are free, some are slaves; some are noble, some are ignoble, and so forth.[46] The important thing is to know what roles we have been assigned in life and to embrace them. "Remember that you are an actor in a play," says Epictetus, "the character of which is determined by the Playwright: if He wishes the play to be short, it is short; if long, it is long; if He wishes you to play the part of a beggar, remember to act even this role adroitly; and so if your role be that of a cripple, an official, or a layman. For this is your business, to play admirably the role assigned you; but the selection of that role is Another's" (*Ench.* 17). Therefore, any ideas of "freedom" and "autonomy" in Epictetus must be very different from modern uses of those words; they find their meaning in the way in which the individual realizes and accepts his or her place in the larger social cosmos. People are free by embracing their given

---

46. Epictetus thus at times emphasizes personal identity as shaped by participation in the *polis*, likened to a human body (*Disc.* 2.5.24–27; 10.5.4). See the discussion in Michelle Lee, *Paul, the Stoics, and the Body of Christ* (Cambridge: Cambridge University Press, 2006), 98–101. Nonetheless, even when exhorting his listeners to play their allotted roles in society, Epictetus emphasizes the sovereignty of their individual moral choice (*Disc.* 2.10.1).

role in society and their place in the cosmos, rather than by rebelling against it or trying to change it. But underlying this kind of "freedom" is the Stoic cosmos in which God interpenetrates and orders all of nature, including all of society, for the good.

When we situate the notion of the individual within this ordered world, it also takes on a distinctive meaning. This chapter began with a quote in which Epictetus says that, in the garment of society, he wants to be the purple thread that stands out from the white. This claim would seem to be highly individualistic, but behind it stands the notion that some people are meant to be distinctive and others to be run-of-the-mill. The point is to know what kind of person you are. Are you one of the crowd, or are you a wise person who stands out as an example to the rest? It all depends on how you see yourself; your choices and behavior will follow. Conversely, your choices and behavior reveal your estimate of yourself: " 'Unless I take part in the tragedy I shall be beheaded.' Go, then, and take a part, but I will not take a part. 'Why not?' Because you regard yourself as but a single thread of all that go to make up the garment. What follows, then? This, that *you* ought to take thought how you may resemble all other men, precisely as even the single thread wants to have no point of superiority in comparison with the other threads. But *I* want to be the purple" (*Disc.* 1.2.17–18, emphasis original).

Relationships

One of the primary arenas for learning inner detachment and the correct use of impressions is in personal relationships. Here the paradoxical blending of individualism and connection in Epictetus's thought becomes most acute. On the one hand, through the detachment that keeps the rational self from becoming subject to external impressions, the wise person builds a wall of self-sufficiency around his or her core; such a person can lose nothing because nothing in the way of possessions or relationships really belongs to that one in the sense of being constitutive of that one's own self. Such a person thus achieves a certain invulnerability by being self-contained.[47] On the other hand, precisely because of this invulnerability, that one is able to sustain relationships over against external threats.

47. For an insightful comparison between Epictetus and Paul on this topic, see John M. G. Barclay, "Security and Self-Sufficiency: A Comparison of Paul and Epictetus," *Ex Auditu* 24 (2008): 60–72.

To illustrate this paradoxical importance of detachment for relationships of integrity and permanence, Epictetus tells many stories. He talks about a man who left his sick daughter to the care of others because it was too painful to watch her suffer. The father's emotions got in the way of genuine help for his daughter, whereas Stoic detachment would have helped him to stay with her and do his duty better (*Disc.* 1.11.1–26). Or Epictetus counsels the dutiful fulfillment of social obligations that go with particular roles, not because of emotional attachment, but simply because those are the roles assigned to us:

> Our duties are in general measured by our social relationships. He is a father. One is called upon to take care of him, to give way to him in all things, to submit when he reviles or strikes you. "But he is a bad father." Did nature, then, bring you into relationship with a *good* father? No, but simply with a father. "My brother does me wrong." Very well, then, maintain the relation that you have toward him; and do not consider what he is doing, but what you will have to do, if your moral purpose is to be in harmony with nature. (*Ench.* 30)

Here one's primary relationship is not with one's father or brother, but rather with one's own moral choice. As Epictetus puts it elsewhere, "The good is preferred above every form of kinship. My father is nothing to me, but only the good" (*Disc.* 3.3.5).

In other words, relationships with other people are mediated by the primary allegiance to the individual's own moral purpose, one's commitment to the good for oneself. "To this topic you ought to devote yourself before every other, how, namely, you may avoid ever being so intimately associated with some one of your acquaintances or friends as to descend to the same level with him; otherwise you will ruin yourself" (*Disc.* 4.2.1). Paradoxically, however, the side effect of such loyalty to our own reason and choice is in fact a relationship characterized by faithfulness and integrity, made possible precisely because the self is not at risk. No one can take anything of value from us, including even our lives; we can therefore afford to be in relationship with anyone and everyone as long as our *proairesis* is intact: "Everything has two handles, by one of which it ought to be carried and by the other not. If your brother wrongs you, do not lay hold of the matter by the handle of the wrong ... but rather by the other handle—that he is your brother" (*Ench.* 43).

To modern eyes this seems an odd kind of nonempathetic relationship, but empathy is not a word in Epictetus's vocabulary; one suspects it would imply a slavish subjection to passions and lead to the incorrect judgment of impressions: "When you see someone weeping in sorrow, either because a child has gone on a journey, or because he has lost his property, beware that you be not carried away by the impression that the man is in the midst of external ills, but straightway keep before you this thought: 'It is not what has happened that distresses this man (for it does not distress another), but his judgment about it' " (*Ench.* 16). In such a case, says Epictetus, it is good to sympathize outwardly, but not in your innermost self! For every human encounter is an opportunity to practice right judgment:

> If we see an exile, "Poor fellow"; or a poverty-stricken person, "Wretched man, he has nothing with which to get a bite to eat." These, then, are the vicious judgments which we ought to eradicate, this is the subject upon which we ought to concentrate our efforts. Why, what is weeping and sighing? A judgment [*dogma*]. What is misfortune? A judgment. What are strife, disagreement, fault-finding, accusing, impiety, foolishness? They are all judgments and that, too, judgments about things that lie outside the province of moral purpose and are assumed to be good or evil. (*Disc.* 3.3.17–19)

In every judgment and every encounter, we are to seek the good of all, which is intertwined with the good for ourselves through our own correct use of impressions. The point is that such self-interest, which Epictetus takes as axiomatic and natural, is intertwined with doing our duty toward others. The good for ourselves requires doing the good for others, and the good for others requires prioritizing the good for ourselves (*Disc.* 1.19.11–15). A saying common in some Christian circles, "God first, others second, self last," would make no sense to a Stoic. Nonetheless, if we are to advance in the inner freedom that facilitates a life of integrity, we can do so only through the school of personal interaction.

Education

What is education for Epictetus? It is nothing other than training in philosophy. What is philosophy? It is nothing other than training in the right use of impressions. And what is the right use of impressions? It is inner detachment from all false judgments: "To accuse others for one's own misfortunes is a sign of want of education; to accuse oneself shows that one's education has begun; to accuse neither oneself nor others shows that one's education is complete"

(*Ench.* 5). Indeed, after vigorously depicting detachment from the threats of beheading, exile, and chains, Epictetus declares, "These are the lessons that philosophers ought to rehearse, these they ought to write down daily, in these they ought to exercise themselves" (*Disc.* 1.1.25). Education in such habits of thought is the way to freedom, not as a disembodied escape from the world or as mental exercises alone, but as a vigorous, daily training program in a wise and happy life.

Given Epictetus's strong belief in a providential ordering of all being, it is reasonable to wonder why philosophy is necessary. It is necessary because, over time, our innate and divinely given faculty of *proairesis* gets distorted. This distortion happens through being part of a society that gets off track and assigns value to things that do not really matter: status, reputation, property, attractiveness, and so forth. Society confuses appearances with reality, and our behavior follows suit. For example: "Immediately after they are fourteen, women are called 'ladies' by men. And so when they see that they have nothing else but only to be the bedfellows of men, they begin to beautify themselves, and put all their hopes in that" (*Ench.* 40). Note how the societal distortion of young women's identity then shapes and limits their behavior. How contemporary and relevant Epictetus's observations can be!

Furthermore, every time we do not rightly distinguish between what is in our control and what is not, our ability to choose rightly (i.e., rationally) gets scabbed over and desensitized. For this reason philosophy takes practice and hard work on a daily basis. As Epictetus says, with eminent common sense, "If you wish to be a good reader, read. If you wish to be a good writer, write. . . . The same principle holds true for affairs of the mind also; when you are angry, you may be sure, not merely that this evil has befallen you, but also that you have strengthened the habit and have, as it were, added fuel to the flame" (*Disc.* 2.18.2, 5–6).

When we repeatedly do something, it becomes easier and easier; in this way we become habituated to false judgments. Our governing faculty becomes habituated, so that "a callousness results and the infirmity strengthens the avarice" (*Disc.* 2.18.10). Epictetus likens this state of affairs to physical sickness: "For the man who has had a fever and then recovered is not the same as he was before the fever, unless he has experienced a complete cure. Something like this happens also with the affections of the mind. Certain imprints and weals are left behind on the mind, and unless a man erases them perfectly, the next time he is scourged upon the old scars, he has weals no longer but wounds" (*Disc.* 2.18.10–11). Philosophy is difficult! It requires hard work, repeated corrections, and habituation in right thinking. And for this reason it requires a teacher and lessons. Paradoxically, learning to be self-contained requires both living in relationship and resisting the dangers attendant on social ties.

What, then, is the goal of this challenging regime of philosophy? It is, as is evident by now, learning to will what God wills, which is the same as learning to live in line with nature, to align our reasoning faculty with a divinely ordered cosmos and society. This is the way of freedom.

In a lengthy discourse, Epictetus sets out step by step the training that leads to freedom. Paradoxically it begins with the recognition of our own enslavement to many masters. Epictetus draws heavily on his own observations as a slave growing up in Nero's household to describe with excruciating vividness the bondage of the upper classes—the "handsomest and sleekest slavery" of the senatorial class (*Disc.* 4.1.40). Reminding his audience of what every person really wants in life, which is "to live securely, to be happy, to do everything as he wishes to do, not to be hindered, not to be subject to compulsion" (*Disc.* 4.1.46), he calls as a witness one who has risen through the ranks to the status of a friend of Caesar. Such a one, surely, is free!

> Come into our midst and tell us. When did you sleep more peacefully, now or before you became Caesar's friend? Immediately the answer comes: "Stop, I implore you by the gods, and do not jest at my lot; you don't know what I suffer, miserable man that I am; no sleep visits me, but first one person comes in and then another and reports that Caesar is already awake, and is already coming; then troubles, then worries!" Come, when did you dine more pleasantly, now or formerly? Listen to him and to what he has to say on this topic. If he is not invited, he is hurt, and if he is invited, he dines like a slave at a master's table, all the time careful not to say or do something foolish. And what do you suppose he is afraid of? That he be scourged like a slave? How can he expect to get off as well as that? But as befits so great a man, a friend of Caesar, he is afraid he will lose his head. (*Disc.* 4.1.47–48)

The higher the rank, the greater the bondage. But there is another kind of slavery yet more insidious, and that is bondage to the passions. To the boastful young man who thinks he does whatever he wants, Epictetus says mockingly, "Were you never commanded by your sweetheart to do something you didn't wish to do? Did you never cozen your pet slave? Did you never kiss his feet?" (*Disc.* 4.1.17).

Only by recognizing the myriad ways in which we sell our dignity, as well as our inner freedom to act in accord with the divine order of things, do we learn our need of training in philosophy. We learn the ways in which we ourselves are "bad," and we learn that "no bad man is free" (*Disc.* 4.1.5). We learn that we have many "masters" in the form of circumstances; indeed, whatever we fear has power over us. So if we fear exile, death, pain, the loss of property or family or reputation, all of these things have power over us.

Epictetus then leads his audience in a careful examination of what, logically, is in our power. This is the educational task. It consists in ruthlessly paring down the sense of what belongs to the proper self, excising any concern for the "use of the body and its cooperation," and focusing exclusively on the choice of what to accept as true and what to reject, what to desire and what to avoid (*Disc.* 4.1.73). Once one has learned to distinguish the line between what lies within the sphere of *proairesis* and what does not, one has achieved freedom from fear and freedom from compulsion. One has learned, that is, to make correct judgments about impressions and thereby to keep one's inner citadel intact: "How then is a citadel [*akropolis*] destroyed? Not by iron, nor by fire, but by judgments. . . . But here is where we must begin, and it is from this side that we must seize the acropolis and cast out the tyrants; we must yield up the paltry body, its members, the faculties, property, reputation, offices, honours, children, brothers, friends—count all these things as alien to us" (*Disc.* 4.1.87).

Paradoxically, however, the way to such freedom is not simply through loyalty to one's own judgments. It requires a different step, which is the submission of one's will to God. How is it possible to be free from compulsion? "I have submitted my freedom of choice [*hormē*] unto God. He wills that I shall have a fever. It is my will too" (*Disc.* 4.1.89). The way to freedom is to want what God wants and nothing else. And what God wants is evident in the flow of events, no matter how extreme they seem by human judgments: "Therefore it is my will to die; therefore it is my will to be tortured on the rack" (*Disc.* 4.1.90).

How is it possible to attain such a state of mind? Well, says Epictetus, the wise traveler through life knows that he or she needs a companion, and the best companion, the only fully trustworthy companion, is God. So to travel safely, one must attach oneself to God. How to do so? Simply by submitting to God's will. And how to know the divine will? By observing the way things are. We are spectators for a time at the divine pageant of life, there to praise God by accepting all that God sends our way (*Disc.* 4.1.105). Epictetus is supremely optimistic about the course of this world as providentially arranged; for him there is no hostile fate because all is ordered well. Therefore:

> Instruction consists precisely in learning to desire each thing exactly as it happens. And how do they happen? As He that ordains them has ordained. . . .

Mindful, therefore, of this ordaining we should go to receive instruc-
tion not in order to change the constitution of things—for this is not
vouchsafed us nor is it better that it should be—but in order that, things
about us being as they are and as their nature is, we may, for our own part,
keep our wills in harmony with what happens. (*Disc.* 1.12.15, 17)

There is a paradox hidden in Epictetus's insistence on receiving instruc-
tion; after all, he himself was a teacher and made his living by instructing
others. On the one hand, Epictetus is confident that nature itself provides us
with all that we need to learn right judgment. God is the only companion we
need on our journey through life. Simple observation of the order of things
should alert us to the divine reason that governs all things well—telling us
how to distinguish between what is proper to our self and what is beyond
our control.

On the other hand, because our self-perception becomes distorted, we
forget we are children of God, and therefore our perception of everything
else is skewed as well. Like fourteen-year-old girls who realize that men see
them only as sex objects and act accordingly, we forget who we are when we
see ourselves through others' eyes. Apparently not all roles given by society
are also given by God. Apparently we need to see ourselves through the eyes
of a Stoic teacher and not just through anyone's eyes. To recover a correct
self-perception, therefore, we need education in philosophy, which above all
teaches us the right way to think about things. And for such education, we
need two things: a teacher and practice, practice, practice in correctly evaluating the data that come our way. In this sense, Epictetus utilizes a second-
person relationship, but all in the service of a first-person goal, namely, correct
self-relation, which is also correct God-relation.

The Constitution of the Self

I have divided this chapter into discussions of the self as self-relation and as
other-relation. But because in the Stoic cosmos everything is on a continuum
of being, such a distinction is artificial, just as distinctions between objective
and subjective perspectives, or indeed between first-person, second-person,
and third-person perspectives, are artificial on the Stoic spectrum of life. To
be related rightly to oneself is simultaneously to be related rightly to God and
to nature, which are so closely interpenetrating as to be almost equivalent.
For this reason Gill doubts that there is any modern concept of the self in an

individual, first-person, and "subjective" sense, and Engberg-Pedersen claims that "practical rationality and objectivity are conceived by the Stoics as being logically inseparable from individuality and as 'matching' it, so individuality and subjectivity are conceived as being logically inseparable from rationality and objectivity."[48] Such an exaltation of individual agency, which is paradoxically inseparable from the "objective" reality of the divinely ordered nature in which the person is embedded, is most acute in Epictetus.

Nonetheless, it makes a difference whether one starts with self-perception or with other-perception as the basis for ethics and for the constitution of a person. What, then, can we say about Epictetus's picture of personhood? Several themes have become clear.

First, human beings are innately self-aware and rational, having been given this faculty as a portion of divinity within them. That is, self-perception and the capacity to see oneself correctly are fundamental to the make-up of every human being. Central to Epictetus's program is a regime of self-talk, and therefore of self-relation. In this regard he starts and ends with a first-person perspective.

Second, therefore, all sense impressions, all data that come to us from outside this primary self-awareness, are filtered through our evaluative judgments and consequently through the ways we narrate impressions to ourselves.

Third, even though Epictetus never questions the Stoic doctrines of the corporeality of all things and the correlative psychophysical wholeness of human existence, in practical terms he talks dualistically. The "paltry body" is not a part of the person, any more than reputation or relationships are constitutive of the self. Thus in theory, philosophy is done by a fully embodied and whole person, but in practice it is done by a self that watches itself and relates to itself. There is a core identity, identified with *proairesis* as the free exercise of choice, around which the student in philosophy learns to build a fortress of correct judgments. This dualistic self-talk, in which there is an "I" that watches and narrates itself to itself, is the vehicle of inner detachment so central to Epictetus's notion of freedom. By constituting the self in this inner dialogue, his second-person conversational style and method are in service of a first-person self-relation.[49]

48. Engberg-Pedersen, "Stoic Philosophy and the Concept of the Person," 125. See Gill's appreciative and critical discussion of Engberg-Pedersen's position in *The Structured Self*, 359–70.

49. "Epictetus' *daimôn* is his and every person's normative self, the voice of correct reason that is available to everyone because it is, at the same time, reason as such and fully equivalent to God. Although Epictetus sometimes speaks as if the presence or availability of

Fourth, the network of human relationships within which Epictetus and his students exist is the arena for practice in making right judgments about impressions. It is a training ground for *proairesis*, nothing more and nothing less. As such, it is absolutely necessary to practice in doing one's duty by learning to behave with nobility, integrity, and freedom in accordance with nature. But essentially the goal is not the well-being of others—that is in God's hands, not ours—but our own inner good. Engberg-Pedersen characterizes Stoic ethics, including those of Epictetus, as moving "from self to shared."[50] That is, they move from the well-being of the self to the well-being of society through the recognition that the good of the whole is necessary for the good of the self. But to stop there is to miss the point. Rather, an appropriate slogan for the way in which Epictetus teaches his students might be "from self to shared to self."

Fifth, in one sense Epictetus's idea of what is necessary to the self is radically inclusive, particularly in the context of the first century. Social status and gender are irrelevant. Slaves are as much persons as are free people, women as much as men. In regard to contemporary questions about personhood, Epictetus would have no problem including people on the autistic spectrum; emotions and relationality understood in emotional terms have nothing to do with personhood or freedom in Stoic terms. Similarly, particularly for Epictetus, the state of the body—the little or paltry body—has nothing to do with one's status and freedom as an acting agent. In contrast, insofar as "rationality" is the center of the self, those apparently lacking in the capacity for rational thought have no personhood or agency in Epictetus's cosmos.[51]

Sixth, Epictetus never advocates "doing your own thing" in a modern sense; to the contrary, the free person is the one who submits to the divine order of things. We do not make up right and wrong; we discover it in submission to the will of God. Epictetus would never say, "It doesn't matter what

---

this voice pluralizes the person, or makes the person distinct from his *daimôn*, we should regard that language as metaphor or, better, as a way of articulating the idea that in listening to and obeying one's normative self one is at the same time in accordance with the divinity who administers the world" (Long, *Epictetus*, 166).

50. Engberg-Pedersen lays out his basic model in *Paul and the Stoics*, 33–36, 53–79.

51. Long discusses the idea of the "soul" as distinguishing "those vital functions which most sharply mark off animals from plants": "We may speak unkindly but correctly of someone who has sustained gross and irreversible brain damage, but whose bodily functions can continue to be made to work, as living the life of a vegetable. What we mean is that such a person cannot live a normal human life, and has perhaps, even, ceased to be a person" ("Soul and Body in Stoicism," in *Stoic Studies*, 240).

you believe as long as you're sincere." It matters completely whether we are aligned with the divine reality of which we are a part. As both Long and Gill insist, there is an "objective" basis for Stoic ethics in the order of nature.[52] Our self-relation is mediated and guided by the larger whole of which we are a part, which has an objective, third-person reality apart from us. There is no discrete and autonomous self in a post-Cartesian sense. Rather, Epictetus adopts a perspective that is both objective *and* participatory. As Gill puts it, in Stoicism there is

> a striking, even paradoxical, combination of a strongly naturalistic pic-
> ture of human beings as psychological and psychophysical wholes with
> certain radical ethical claims stemming from Socratic thought. The main
> ethical claims are these. (1) The achievement of happiness is "up to us"
> through virtue and rational reflection in a way that is not constrained
> by one's inborn nature or social situation. (2) Happiness involves a time-
> independent, invulnerable perfection of character, marked by freedom
> from distress or passion. (3) Only the fully rational and virtuous person
> is fully integrated and coherent while non-wise people are psychologically
> and ethically incoherent and live incoherent lives.[53]

Whereas Engberg-Pedersen and Long view this self as primarily subjective and self-referential in a first-person sense, Gill views it as structured in a third-person, objectivist way.

Finally, then, Epictetus's teaching, like that of Paul, cannot be excised from the cosmos he inhabits. That cosmos is one in which everything is on a continuum, from an inert rock to the divine Logos that coheres with nature and orders it from within. Human beings are a part of this continuum and find their freedom through embracing their place in it. The exercise of individual rationality is a participation in divine rationality. Conversely, access to divine rationality requires a self-directed focus on the one thing fully and irrevocably in our power—the correct, rational use of impressions.

---

52. Long, "The Logical Basis of Stoic Ethics," 150–51, 155. See also Gill's discussion of the difference between Stoic "objective" thought and post-Cartesian subjectivism, in *The Structured Self*, 359–70.

53. Christopher Gill, "The Ancient Self: Issues and Approaches," in *Ancient Philosophy of the Self*, ed. Pauliina Remes and Juha Sihvola (New York: Springer, 2008), 53.

Conclusion

We can find elements of both first-person and third-person perspectives in the structure of the person as taught by Epictetus. What is not possible is a genuinely second-person understanding of relationally constructed identity. This is because there is no genuine "other" in a cosmos in which everything is a part of the whole. God-relation *is* self-relation, and self-relation *is* God-relation. Epictetus operates with a naturalistic psychology and worldview, not a supernatural or transcendent worldview; in his cosmos, there is no outside causality. As Long states, he is a natural theologian, not a secularist, but neither does he subscribe to belief in a transcendent Creator who is qualitatively other than the created order.[54]

Thus it is very easy to see why Troels Engberg-Pedersen finds in the Stoics a key to appropriating Paul's ethics for "we moderns." But unlike Bultmann, Engberg-Pedersen does not embrace a second-person hermeneutical goal in which the reader is addressed existentially by the Word of God. Rather, like Epictetus, Engberg-Pedersen assumes a naturalistic worldview, or at least he assumes that such a worldview was the only option for contemporary readers of Paul. He rejects any conception of " 'God' as a 'supernatural' being, that is, as a separate, or an a-cosmic, higher being somehow 'added' to the universe," because he believes that "a classic-style theism is unconvincing in the light of today's scientific worldview and philosophical reflection." In this sense, then, his methodology and his hermeneutical goals are consistent; he embraces a naturalistic methodology in the name of historical criticism: "A methodological naturalism is the taken-for-granted view in historical theology. No serious church historian would attempt to explain, say, revivalist movements with reference to supernatural interventions. Historical and sociological factors would be assumed to do the job."[55]

Engberg-Pedersen spells out his naturalistic philosophical commitments, hermeneutical goals, and interpretive methods with admirable clarity.[56]

54. Long's comments on Epictetus's "theology" are particularly perceptive in this regard. See his *Epictetus*, 142–47.

55. Troels Engberg-Pedersen and Niels Henrik Gregersen, "Introduction," from the website for the Centre for Naturalism and Christian Semantics (CNCS) at the University of Copenhagen, http://teol.ku.dk/english/dept/cncs/dokumenter/cncs_project_description.pdf.

56. "*None of us finds it appropriate to define what is meant by 'God' in Christian semantics.* Supernaturalism may be one way of articulating the Christian view of God, as this was done under the influence of Middle Platonism, in the Aristotelian 'perfect-being'-theism of the Middle Ages, or in some Enlightenment traditions. But we share the historical assumption

Unlike those of Bultmann, they are thoroughly consistent in a nonanachronistic way. Their consistency, in turn, forces us to confront the inescapable link between worldviews, goals, and methods in any hermeneutical project. When the method excludes the possibility of divine causality, it presses for a naturalistic worldview. Consequently, when a naturalistic worldview is presumed, it insists on the limits of "historical and sociological factors" to the exclusion of all other possibilities.

We may ask what is at stake in this insistence on reading Paul's anthropology in light of Stoic thought, within the constraints of a monistic cosmos. For Engberg-Pedersen the issue is not an accurate understanding of Paul's own thought, which he in fact presumes to be inaccessible as a live option for contemporary readers. The goal, rather, is a framework for appropriating Paul within what Engberg-Pedersen presumes to be the "modern," philosophical, and scientific worldview of contemporary readers. In other words, to interpret Paul for today, we need to frame his thought in today's terms.

But just what are those terms? In the next chapter we look at contemporary theories of the self drawn from philosophy of science and experimental psychology. We will find that these theories differ significantly from the individualism and "autonomy" that Engberg-Pedersen finds in Epictetus and purports to find in Paul as a key to contemporary appropriations of Paul's anthropology. Rather, they testify to a shifting landscape of the self in contemporary scientific thought, in which the idea of a bounded, autonomous, and free individual has come under critical scrutiny, and embodied interaction is seen to be formative at the most basic levels of human development.

---

that Christian semantics has not always been bound to such a philosophical framework and *we believe that. Thus the historical work that is done at CNCS serves to counteract the imprisonment of theology within a supernaturalist framework, and the systematic endeavour is to articulate viable alternatives today*" (Engberg-Pedersen and Gregersen, "Introduction"; emphasis added).

CHAPTER TWO

"Who Are You?"

Contemporary Perspectives on the Person

What kind of beings do we think we are?

—Nikolas Rose and Joelle Abi-Rached, *Neuro*

Questions about human identity and personhood have entered the stream of public conversation in multiple ways over the last few decades. They appear in TED talks and almost weekly in op-eds in major newspapers, usually written by philosophers, psychiatrists, or neuroscientists. Much of this interest has been fueled by a meteoric rise of publications on neuroscientific discoveries about the brain, although the more cynical among us might also attribute it to sheer human narcissism. In 1958 there were about 650 scholarly papers published in the field of brain sciences. In 2008 there were more than 400 journals publishing more than 26,500 scholarly articles in the new field of neuroscience, a term that came into use as recently as 1962. In the United States, President George Bush designated the 1990s as "the decade of the brain." As Nikolas Rose and Joelle Abi-Rashed observe, "neuro" has become the new prefix for everything from pharmacology to economics to theology.[1]

The brain is a hot topic, and the heat is fueled in part by ancient and enduring questions about the nature of the self and the status of human beings as persons.[2] In the previous chapter we looked at Epictetus on the nature of

1. Nikolas S. Rose and Joelle M. Abi-Rached, *Neuro: The New Brain Sciences and the Management of the Mind* (Princeton: Princeton University Press, 2013), 5, 6–7.

2. For the role of pharmaceutical companies in funding neurobiological research aimed at new drugs for psychiatric and psychological conditions, see T. M. Luhrmann, *Of Two Minds: An Anthropologist Looks at American Psychiatry* (New York: Vintage, 2001), 55–56.

the self in self-perception, self-relation, and other-relation, and at differing theories about the manner in which Epictetus conceives of the individual. In contemporary terms, questions about the nature of the self and the status of persons include fundamental issues regarding whether human beings are responsible, self-directing, and discrete individuals; mere products of their environments or of unconscious neurobiological processes; or something more that is not captured by either of these extremes. In particular, research and theorizing in neuroscience, as well as in developmental psychology and philosophy of mind, now question two long-standing dualistic and individualistic assumptions about the self: that the essence of the self is in a nonmaterial "soul" that is separate from the body, and that the self is a freestanding, autonomous agent, fully conscious of and responsible for its thoughts, motivations, and actions. The more one delves into the vast literature on the construction of the self, the more complicated and entangled the arguments become, as scientists and philosophers seek to resist determinism, maintain human "freedom" and responsibility, and do justice to the data.[3] Furthermore, in reaction to the mushrooming interest in all things "neuro," there now is a burgeoning literature criticizing many of the claims made in the name of neuroscience.[4]

But the new emphasis on the self-in-relation-to-others predates the rise of neuroscience as a new discipline and finds strong support in other, less contentious fields. Indeed, over the last few decades, research in experimental psychology has explored similar questions about the development of persons. The study of infants and young children has proved particularly fruitful and in its own way has overturned many previous assumptions about human development. The use of video to enhance careful observation of infants and their caregivers has opened up more insights into the intricate dance be-

3. Many, if not most, of these discussions take place within an assumed naturalistic, purely materialistic framework. Whether it is possible to resist determinism within such a framework is another question; full discussion is beyond the scope of this book. See, e.g., Raymond Tallis, *Aping Mankind: Neuromania, Darwinitis, and the Misrepresentation of Humanity* (London: Routledge, 2014); Thomas Nagel, *Mind and Cosmos: Why the Materialist Neo-Darwinian Conception of Nature Is Almost Certainly False* (Oxford: Oxford University Press, 2012); Alvin Plantinga, *Where the Conflict Really Lies: Science, Religion, and Naturalism* (Oxford: Oxford University Press, 2011); Lenn E. Goodman and D. Gregory Caramenico, *Coming to Mind: The Soul and Its Body* (Chicago: University of Chicago Press, 2014).

4. See, e.g., Tallis, *Aping Mankind*; Robert A. Burton, *A Skeptic's Guide to the Mind: What Neuroscience Can and Cannot Tell Us about Ourselves* (New York: St. Martin's Press, 2013); Gregory Hickok, *The Myth of Mirror Neurons: The Real Neuroscience of Communication and Cognition* (New York: Norton, 2014).

tween very young infants and adults.[5] For example, infants are able to imitate human faces within an hour of birth and are able to recognize others'
intentions within the first year of life.[6] Earlier theorists such as Jean Piaget
thought these capacities developed much later and required a private mental
apparatus capable of abstract thought and belief. If this is not the case, then
maybe abstract inner mental capacities are less foundational for the person
than embodied interaction and a kind of bodily knowledge gained through
that interaction.

Because this is not a book on either neuroscience or experimental psychology, and because it is impossible to do justice to the immense diversity
and sheer quantity of literature on the subject of the self in these fields, in the
remainder of this chapter I limit myself to an overview of philosophical and
scientific theories of the relationship between the body and the mind, drawing
primarily on the work of philosopher Shaun Gallagher, and conclude with an
example from the work of developmental psychologist Vasudevi Reddy.

Overview: The True Size of the System That We Are

Toward the end of his remarkable book *How the Body Shapes the Mind*, Shaun
Gallagher provides a summary list of the empirical findings about body and
cognition that he has discussed. These findings come from studies done by
neuroscientists to see what neurons are activated by different events, studies
of infant development by experimental psychologists, and studies of situations
of pathology in which the usual relationship between body and cognition is
disrupted. Here is an abbreviated list:

5. Pioneers in such studies include Colwyn Trevarthen and Daniel Stern. See, e.g.,
Daniel N. Stern, *The Interpersonal World of the Infant* (New York: Basic Books, 1985); Colwyn
Trevarthen, "The Self Born in Intersubjectivity: The Psychology of an Infant Communicating,"
in *The Perceived Self: Ecological and Interpersonal Sources of Self-Knowledge,* ed. Ulric Neisser
(New York: Cambridge University Press, 1993), 121–73; Beatrice Beebe et al., "Forms of Inter-
subjectivity in Infant Research: A Comparison of Meltzoff, Trevarthen, and Stern," in *Forms of
Intersubjectivity in Infant Research and Adult Treatment* (New York: Other Press, 2005), 29–53.

6. Andrew Meltzoff is the primary investigator and spokesperson for the discovery of
infant imitation. For the earliest studies, see Andrew N. Meltzoff and M. Keith Moore, "Imitation of Facial and Manual Gestures by Human Neonates," *Science* 198.4312 (1977): 75–78.
Vasudevi Reddy has done video-taped studies of infants demonstrating their nonverbal embodied recognition of the intentions of adults. See Vasudevi Reddy, Gabriella Markova, and
Sebastian Wallot, "Anticipatory Adjustments to Being Picked Up in Infancy," *PLOS ONE* 8.6
(June 2013): e65289, doi:10.1371/journal.pone.0065289.

- Neonates are capable of imitating facial gestures from the first minutes after birth.
- With neither proprioception (bodily awareness of what the body is doing) nor vision, deafferentiated patients (rare cases where a patient has lost the sense of touch and bodily awareness from the neck down) are still able to gesture in a manner that is close to normal.
- Subjects who are congenitally blind use gestures when in conversation with other blind subjects.
- The visual observation of an object automatically evokes the most suitable motor program required for interaction with it.
- The same neuronal patterns in the premotor cortex are activated both when a subject performs a specific action and when the subject observes someone else perform the action.
- Before children attain a theory of mind (e.g., a conceptual apparatus recognizing others as thinking, feeling, intending, and acting creatures both like themselves and separate), they already have an embodied understanding of other people.[7]

This is a pretty impressive list. In what follows here I highlight and briefly discuss a few of these items and their importance for theories of the person.

First, neonate imitation: newborns imitate the facial expressions of others within an hour of birth, even though they cannot see their own faces.[8] Studies of such neonate imitation have been conducted in a variety of cultures around the world, with safeguards built into the studies to distinguish between imitation and simple reflex motor actions. Infants sometimes imitate facial expressions, but not always; also, they will imitate after a delay, and they show a marked preference for human faces.[9] Such findings imply that infants have an innate propensity for interpersonal connection long before the development of language or the capacity for abstract thought. We might say that parent and

---

7. Shaun Gallagher, *How the Body Shapes the Mind* (Oxford: Oxford University Press, 2005), 244–45.

8. Meltzoff and Moore, 'Imitation of Facial and Manual Gestures"; Andrew N. Meltzoff and Alison Gopnik, "The Role of Imitation in Understanding Persons and Developing a Theory of Mind," in *Understanding Other Minds: Perspectives from Autism,* ed. Simon Baron-Cohen et al. (New York: Oxford University Press, 1993), 335–66; Andrew N. Meltzoff and Rechele Brooks, " 'Like Me' as a Building Block for Understanding Other Minds: Bodily Acts, Attention, and Intention," in *Intentions and Intentionality: Foundations of Social Cognition,* ed. Bertram F. Malle, Louis J. Moses, and Dare A. Baldwin (Cambridge MA: MIT Press, 2001), 171–91.

9. Gallagher, *How the Body Shapes the Mind,* 71–72.

child act in concert with one another in an interpersonal dance at the very beginning of human development.

How is this possible, why do infants behave in this way, and what is the effect of such behavior on the formation of the person? What kind of movement or gesture is enacted in infant imitation of faces? Gallagher discusses the options in terms of kinds of motion, first eliminating possible modes of movement: facial imitation is not locomotive, not a way of getting from one place to another. It is not instrumental—it does not accomplish something like picking up a cup. It is not a mere reflex action, like the way our leg jerks when the doctor taps the knee with a hammer. Gallagher suggests, rather, that infant imitation is expressive movement, a kind of gesture; it is not expressive in the sense of expressing an abstract inner thought, but expressive because it "brings the infant into a direct relation with another person, and starts them on a course of social interaction." In other words, expressive gesture is not self-directed; it is other-directed. The infant's expression is a response to the presence of the parent's face, and this imitation happens through immediate bodily action. Again in Gallagher's words, "To imitate a facial gesture that it sees, however, the infant has no need to simulate the gesture internally. It is already simulating it on its own face. Its own body is already in communication with the other's body at prenoetic and perceptual levels that are sufficient for intersubjective interaction."[10]

Here at the most elemental level of infant development, the body as other-relation is the medium of communication and interaction. The resulting interaction itself motivates imitation and the further cognitive and emotional developments that follow, through a reciprocal mimetic interplay between adult and child. For some theorists, the initiative of the parent is crucial. As we shall see, Vasudevi Reddy argues that "being imitated seems to establish a powerful and immediate statement of interest, connection, and intentional relation . . . it is *being* imitated which is crucial for intimacy."[11] Here mimetic

---

10. Gallagher, *How the Body Shapes the Mind*, 128, 223. Gallagher is arguing against the "simulationist" theories of Andrew Meltzoff, which posit that imitation requires an extra internal step in which the imitator generates a neurological internal simulation of the observed action, which in turn acts as a model for action. As Gallagher observes, in such a model "second-person interaction is reduced to a first-person internal activity" (222). For Meltzoff's simulation theory, see Andrew N. Meltzoff, "Understanding Other Minds: The 'Like Me' Hypothesis," in *Perspectives on Imitation: From Neuroscience to Social Science*, ed. Susan Hurley and Nick Chater (Cambridge, MA: MIT Press, 2005), 2:56. For critique of Meltzoff's theory, see Wolfgang Prinz, "Construing Selves from Others," in the same volume, 181.

11. Vasudevi Reddy, *How Infants Know Minds* (Cambridge, MA: Harvard University Press, 2008), 64–65.

interaction is a specific mode of movement geared expressly toward interpersonal bonding and even intimacy. It is intrinsically dyadic and foundational for the development of the person.

Gallagher draws similar conclusions about the use of gesture in subjects who are congenitally blind or who lack proprioceptive awareness of their own bodily movements.[12] As in neonate imitation, what kind of movement is this? What purpose does it serve? Why do both congenitally blind and deafferentiated people gesture while telling a story? For that matter, why do any of us gesture, even when driving and talking alone in a car, ostensibly to ourselves? Gallagher suggests that this is expressive movement, and as such it is communication—expression requires interaction with another, even when our interlocutor is only imagined and not physically present. In other words, "expressive movement is expressive only on one condition: that there is already intersubjectivity." Gallagher continues his reflection on the implications of infant imitation for human nature: "Even if it were possible to have both a biological embodiment in the form of a complete human body, and a set of gestures framed for the solipsistic shaping of a mind, without other human persons the system would fall short of being a human person. . . . The body generates a gestural expression. It is, however, another person who moves, motivates, and mediates this process. To say that language moves my body is already to say that other people move me."[13]

Like Reddy's claims about the importance of being imitated for infant development, here Gallagher decodes mimetic movement in terms of its intersubjectivity; it implies and requires the motivational presence of another. He reaches similar conclusions in discussing the findings of neuroscientists regarding links between perception and action. We recall his earlier observations drawn from neuroscientific studies:

- The visual observation of an object automatically evokes the most suitable motor program required for interaction with it.
- The same neuronal patterns in the premotor cortex are activated both when a subject performs a specific action and when the subject observes someone else perform the action.

To understand Gallagher's conclusions about such findings, it is helpful to explain them in a bit more detail. He is reporting on the discovery of "mirror

12. See in particular Gallagher, *How the Body Shapes the Mind*, 111–27.
13. Gallagher, *How the Body Shapes the Mind*, 129.

neurons" by a group of neuroscientists in Parma, Italy. One of these scientists, Vittorio Gallese, has become one of the major spokespersons for the importance of neuroscience in the concept of persons and theories of mind. Gallese discusses two subcategories of "visuomotor" neurons: "canonical neurons" and "mirror neurons." Canonical neurons are activated by observation of an *object*; they supply information about what would be required to perform an action with the perceived object, in an "as if" neurological feedback loop within the body. Gallese posits that such neurons create a map for the actor in a forward model, a simulation that anticipates the outcome of an action and sends signals to the body to prepare for activity related to the perceived object. Mirror neurons, however, are a different kind of motor neuron; they fire for both the observation and the performance of an *action*, so that the same neural patterns are activated simultaneously in the actor and the observer, thereby "linking the actor and the observer" in a shared cognitive experience. Gallese suggests that these visuomotor neurons generate an implicit, automatic, and unconscious inner simulation or representation of behavior for both the performer and the observer, thereby opening up a "shared space" of embodied experience between the two. He calls this "a unified common intersubjective space," a " *'we'-centric*" space, which has a "shared implicit semantic content." This "shared informational space" acts as a "control model" for behavior and relationship, not only with objects but also with other agents.[14] Furthermore, Gallese suggests that such joint experience extends beyond the grasping actions simulated by mirror neurons, to the experience of emotions and of sensations such as pain.

What does this mean? It seems to mean that, within such a metaphoric "we-centric space," persons share cognitive experience through the parallel actions of their neural systems. Gallese posits that through the experience of an internal mapping—or simulation—of what they perceive in others, people experience a self-other identity that grounds an intersubjective "certitude" that other people are intentional agents like themselves.[15] Such a simulation theory projects a first-personal, self-referential understanding of others as being "like" oneself.

To be sure, Gallese's interpretations of the neurological data are contested. Gallagher accepts Gallese's findings in regard to mirror neurons but rejects his simulation-theory interpretation, because the theory presumes "the

---

14. Vittorio Gallese, " 'Being like Me': Self-Other Identity, Mirror Neurons, and Empathy," in Hurley and Chater, *Perspectives on Imitation*, 1:105, 111.

15. Gallese, "Being like Me," 102.

subject seemingly reads off the meaning of the other, not directly from the other's actions, but from the internal simulation of *the subject's own* 'as if' actions. . . . Here second-person interaction is reduced to a first-person internal activity." Instead, Gallagher proposes an "interaction theory" that even more strongly posits the primacy of intersubjective, immediate bodily interaction and shared cognition between human agents. Describing the personhood of very young children in terms of "primary intersubjectivity," he argues, "in most intersubjective situations we have a direct understanding of another person's intentions because their intentions are explicitly expressed in their embodied actions, and mirrored in our own capabilities for action."[16] This is a fully embodied and embedded, nonmentalist picture of the person as constituted in relationships with others.

It is beyond the scope of this book to evaluate the scientific data, or even to argue for the truth of one theory of the person over another. The point here is rather more general. Regardless of the fine points of interpretation, it has become increasingly clear that our bodies are interacting with our environments from the very beginning, all the time, and that this interaction profoundly shapes the development of the self in interpersonal ways. Gallagher talks about this development as taking place within a feedback loop that extends beyond the body into its environment, which crucially includes other people: "We are not just what happens in our brains. The 'loop' *extends through and is limited by our bodily* capacities, *into* the surrounding environment, which is social as well as physical and feeds back through our conscious experience into the decisions we make." In other words, if we think we can formulate a proper description (let alone an explanation) of what and who we are, how we think, how we decide, and how we act, by models of a brain in a vat, or even by looking at the individual body-brain system in isolation, "we fail to recognize the true size of the system that we are." We are not isolated individuals. We are "the larger system of body-environment-intersubjectivity."[17]

The System of Self-in-Relation: Second-Person Approaches to the Self

The challenge posed by the preceding theories is how to develop an account of the self that allows for both intense intersubjective engagement and the recognition of other people as similar to oneself, yet also separate and different from

16. Gallagher, *How the Body Shapes the Mind*, 222, 223–30, 224–25.
17. Gallagher, *How the Body Shapes the Mind*, 242–43.

oneself. One answer to this challenge comes from a number of experimental psychologists and philosophers who adopt what they call a "second-person perspective" on issues around the development and constitution of human selves-in-relation.[18] The work of Vasudevi Reddy provides an entrée into this perspective, both because she interacts appreciatively and critically with studies of infant imitation and mirror neurons and because her own argument is so accessible and articulate.

For Reddy, two basic misconceptions inhibit our understanding of how human personhood develops. The first is that we tend to think of babies (and adults) as "*disembedded* from other minds (and indeed from the world of objects and activities in which minds live)." Second, we tend to think of the mind itself as *disembodied*, private, and opaque.[19] Criticizing the detached stance of scientific investigation, Reddy asks, with some justification, "Who is the expert when it comes to understanding people—the detached scientist or the ordinary person in everyday life?"[20] She frankly acknowledges the motivation and insights that arise from her interactions with her own children and advocates a methodology that begins with and carefully observes relational engagement, not looking at people in isolation, but at parents and infants together.

Like Gallagher, Reddy rejects explicitly first-person, self-referential theories in which the experience of the self is the basis for understanding other minds. Here "minds" is to be taken in a generous sense, including thoughts, emotions, intentions, and actions; we could translate the term as "persons" to get at this broad meaning. In Reddy's view, such theories basically assume that other people's emotions, thoughts, and intentions are inaccessible, private, and hidden—there is a gap between one person's mind and another's, and the

18. Gallagher explicitly falls into this category. Introductions to philosophical and scientific work from this perspective appear in a special issue of the *European Journal for Philosophy of Religion* 5.4 (2013), entitled *The Second-Personal in the Philosophy of Religion*, ed. Andrew Pinsent and Eleanore Stump; Naomi Eilan et al., eds., *Joint Attention: Communication and Other Minds* (Oxford: Oxford University Press, 2005); Axel Seemann, ed., *Joint Attention: New Developments in Psychology, Philosophy of Mind, and Social Neuroscience* (Cambridge, MA: MIT Press, 2011). In philosophy, see Eleanore Stump, *Wandering in Darkness: Narrative and the Problem of Suffering* (Oxford: Oxford University Press, 2010); in theology, Andrew Pinsent, *The Second-Person Perspective in Aquinas's Ethics: Virtues and Gifts* (New York: Routledge, 2012).

19. Reddy, *How Infants Know Minds*, 4 and 5 (emphases original). Similarly, neuroscientist Marco Iacoboni criticizes the "analogy argument" that we know others' minds by reasoning from our own experience, for its "underestimation of the ability to access other minds" (*Mirroring People: The New Science of Empathy and How We Connect with Others* [New York: Farrar, Straus & Giroux, 2008], 264). See Reddy, *How Infants Know Minds*, 5; emphasis original.

20. Reddy, *How Infants Know Minds*, 5.

problem is to bridge the gap. This assumption fails to take account of three realities that may be seen in daily life: first, people commonly operate with some degree of confidence that they know what another person is thinking and feeling, because this knowledge is necessary simply to live and develop as human beings; second, because "bodies are what minds do," bodies make mind "visible"; third, the processes of the mind are not *necessarily* private.[21] To the contrary, Reddy observes that in the scheme of child development, children's emotions and thoughts and interactions are public before they are private; the capacity for and interest in private experience and communication come later. Furthermore, says Reddy, the idea of private mental experience is culturally conditioned. In some non-Western cultures, including her own Indian culture, "a problem, loss, difficulty, victory, doubt, indecision, or hardship never belongs to just one person; rather, it is always owned by those around the person as well."[22]

Thus in Reddy's view, the self-referential models proposed by simulationist theories are inadequate at best. Even though they talk at length about persons as intersubjective entities, they do so primarily from a first-person standpoint; knowledge of other people is accessible and always mediated only through knowledge of oneself and therefore through one's own experience. Ironically, this approach ends up absorbing other people into the self's own frame of reference, projecting one's own experience on others rather than genuinely engaging with them interpersonally. Therefore Gallese's proposal about a "we-centric space" is vital, but not enough: "It still does not offer an explanation of an "I-You" space in which the other is recognized as *different* from the self, a difference to which the infant is attracted and moved to *respond*."[23]

A model of the self in relationship to others that depends on self-understanding thus has several weaknesses. First, it assumes "direct and privileged access at least to our *own* mental states." Second, such understanding of other people based on our own experience is incredibly limiting, "making a huge generalization" about other people "from one case"—that is, our own experience. Third, as already noted, it starts from the conviction that other people's emotions, thoughts, and intentions are abstract, mental, conceptual and hidden; the "mind" is hidden behind and in the "body." The basic developmental task, in such a view, is to bridge the gap between ourselves and others'

---

21. Reddy, *How Infants Know Minds*, 5. Gallagher makes a similar argument, repeatedly emphasizing the immediacy of communication through bodily interaction (*How the Body Shapes the Mind*, 211–12).

22. Reddy, *How Infants Know Minds*, 16.

23. Reddy, *How Infants Know Minds*, 19–21, 57.

hidden selves. Reddy criticizes this position as an assumed mind-body dualism.[24] Fourth, such self-referential theories cannot account for the recognition of others as different from oneself. Reddy argues, to the contrary, that actual observation of infant development reveals a movement from a "we-centric" space to an "I-You" space, not the reverse. The problem is not how infants know other people are "like me" but how they know others are "not like me."

Fifth, first-person theories do not account for the reciprocal *responsiveness* between parent and child, in which parental initiative plays a major role in infant-parent interactions. The pressing question is what *motivates* the infant to imitate and otherwise initiate "conversation" with those closest to him or her. As Reddy puts it, " 'Like me' representations and mirror neurons and analogue representations of body and world could explain *how* imitation occurs, but they don't explain *why*."[25] This lack may be because methodologies based on a first-person perspective do not take into account the role of the experimenter in interactions with infants that test such behaviors as imitation, role playing, and so forth. That is, the experimenter is assumed to be a spectator, not a participant who influences the outcomes of the experiment: "Bystanders' theories about minds are likely to be a poor substitute for participants' experience of minds. Both routes [first and third person], even when they assume that interaction is the essential source of data, run the risk of positing an observer and an observed, of thinking of 'mind-reading' primarily as a 'spectatorial' process."[26]

Reddy's alternative to the first-person perspective on who we are and how we know is a second-person approach to understanding the self.[27] Her understanding of the person takes Gallese's "we-centric space" seriously as the beginning of the self, so much so that there is no assumed initial gap between the infant and other people. Such gaps develop later. It also "pluralizes the other, rejecting the assumption of singularity in the way we sometimes talk about other minds."[28] Along the way, the second-person approach recognizes that our experience of other people is very much shaped by the contexts and ways in which we engage with them. Our attitudes, goals, and style of interacting deeply influence what we see of the other person and how we know them.

24. Reddy, *How Infants Know Minds*, 19, 14–15.

25. Reddy, *How Infants Know Minds*, 59; emphasis original.

26. Reddy, *How Infants Know Minds*, 25. Gallagher similarly criticizes the limits of experiments based solely on third-personal observation, without taking into account the role and influence of the observer (*How the Body Shapes the Mind*, 218).

27. Reddy, *How Infants Know Minds*, 26–42.

28. Reddy, *How Infants Know Minds*, 26.

Reddy's observation is similar to Gallagher's notion of the way in which body schema and body image shape our perception, from the angle and posture of our vision to the categories in which we interpret what we see.[29] Reddy stresses the reciprocity of such perceptual experience when we are actively and emotionally involved; in healthy parent-child relationships, that interaction shapes and constitutes "the minds that *each* comes to have and develop, not merely providing information about each to the other."[30]

This is a picture of the self as constituted, even created, in relationship with other people—people who are similar and also, even crucially, different, distinct, and particular. Psychologists Peter and Jessica Hobson, also second-person theorists, express the delicate balance of similarity and difference as follows: "There is a sense in which one 'participates' in the other person's state, yet maintains awareness of 'otherness' in the person with whom one is sharing, while also being affectively involved from one's own standpoint."[31]

To illustrate the point, we can think again about infant imitation. When a baby boy, for example, imitates his mother's smile, he assimilates to her "state"; he shares with her the experience of the smile and, to a degree, inhabits her bodily, emotional, and mental experience. Similarly, when the mother imitates the baby's raised eyebrows, she playfully enters into the baby's world and shares his gestural language. But she is not her child's other self, nor is the child her self. Rather, the experience of *being* imitated communicates a sort of recognition of oneself as distinctive and worthy of attention. When done in loving playfulness, it causes pleasure. It invites a response, usually by carrying forward the imitative game and interaction. The interpersonal relationship itself motivates imitation and the cognitive and emotional development that follow. "Being imitated seems to establish a powerful and immediate statement of interest, connection, and intentional relation . . . it is *being* imitated which is crucial for intimacy."[32]

In short, from the standpoint of second-person theorists the starting point for the intersubjective constitution of the self is crucial. As Reddy puts it, "You have to be addressed as a subject to become one."[33] Elsewhere she says,

29. Body schema is the framework of the body and its positioning in space, which shape perception on an unconscious level; body image is the way in which people conceptualize their own bodies.

30. Reddy, *How Infants Know Minds*, 27.

31. Peter Hobson and Jessica Hobson, "Joint Attention or Joint Engagement? Insights from Autism," in Seemann, *Joint Attention*, 120–21.

32. Reddy, *How Infants Know Minds*, 64–65; emphasis original.

33. Reddy, *How Infants Know Minds*, 32.

"It is the other's attention at grips with the infant that makes attention exist for the infant."[34] A baby girl learns that she exists by being the object of her mother's and father's loving gaze. She learns what it is to see by being seen, as she sees herself reflected in the eyes of her parents. She learns what happiness or sadness or wanting is by experiencing it in and through her primary engagements with others. Her awareness of herself begins with the interaction rather than preceding or motivating it. This is the reverse of self-referential theories about the person, where self-knowledge precedes and mediates understanding of other people. Here other-relation precedes and mediates self-knowledge.

When Reddy describes stages of the interpersonal engagement between parent and child through which children begin to attend to others and to objects, each stage thus begins with the child's *response* to the parent's attending activity, followed by the child's *initiative* in directing that attention.[35] The child is not passive, but neither is he or she autonomous. From the very beginning of life, the child is a relationally constituted acting subject, not a discrete, self-aware, and self-directed agent. This is not to say that there is no individual self or that the infant begins as a blank, passive slate. With significant exceptions, infants are active participants in the interplay between parent and child, and they arrive on the scene with their own distinct genetic make-up. But they develop a sense of self, as well as recognition of other persons, *through and in* the interplay with their parents, not as a *prerequisite for* such interplay. Rather, the interaction itself is the prerequisite for the sense of self, as well as the capacity for thought.

From a first-person perspective, then, the *initiative* for mutual engagement begins with, and depends on, the infant's innate capacities and motivation to connect with others. From this perspective, it is difficult to see how an infant could develop as a person, and certainly as a knowing subject, without an innate, functioning neurobiological feedback loop and a propensity to imitate others. From a second-person standpoint, however, only through other people does the child even know that he or she exists as a feeling, thinking, wanting, related human being. This view assumes and requires the initiative of an adult partner. From this perspective, it would be difficult if not impossible to imagine the development of human capacities for personal knowledge without the presence of an attending partner who is motivated to connect with the child. The first-person perspective relies heavily on the presence of

34. Vasudevi Reddy, "A Gaze at Grips with Me," in Seemann, *Joint Attention*, 137–57.
35. Vasudevi Reddy, "Before the 'Third Element': Understanding Attention to Self," in Eilan et al., *Joint Attention*, 96.

innate capacities within the individual infant; the second-person perspective relies heavily on the presence of nurturing relational partners engaged with the infant.

Peter Hobson argues that, in fact, primary social engagement is necessary for the development of language and, furthermore, of all human capacities for thinking. In Hobson's view, "Central to mental development is a psychological system that is greater and more powerful than the sum of its parts. The parts are the caregiver and her infant; the system is what happens when they act and feel in concert. The combined operation of infant-in-relation-to-caregiver is a motive force in development, and it achieves wonderful things. When it does not exist, and the motive force is lacking, the whole of mental development is terribly compromised."[36] Note here simply the primacy of the system of self-in-relation-to-other for the development of thinking, and the role of such a system as a motive force for human development.

Both Gallagher and Reddy develop an "intersubjective" account of the self from a second-person perspective; the individual does not exist in isolation but is always in relationships that in some way are crucial to personal identity. At the same time, both Gallagher and Reddy find some degree of uniqueness in each infant born into this world. This view can be seen in second-person theorists' insistence on the distinctiveness of each partner in any intersubjective engagement. This emphasis on the delicate balance of assimilation and otherness is key. Reddy's model of the self-in-relationship does not begin with the self at all, in terms of either mental states or neural circuitry, although she certainly is interested in discoveries about both neonate imitation and mirror neurons. Her theory begins with the relational interchange between the infant and the mother, albeit with a strong focus on the mother's initiative at each developmental stage. For this reason, the quality of parent-child interaction has significant power in the development of the person.

A Brief Excursus

Two examples may serve to highlight the priority of the relational "cradle" in which human development begins. The first example is drawn from Eleanore Stump's use of a philosophical thought experiment to illustrate the difference between propositional knowledge *that* something is the case and second-

---

36. Peter Hobson, *The Cradle of Thought: Exploring the Origins of Thinking* (Oxford: Oxford University Press, 2004), 183.

person knowledge *of* something or someone. The thought experiment posits a hypothetical person, Mary, who "has been kept from anything that could count as a second-person experience, in which one can say 'you' to another person."[37] Mary has grown up in a black and white room without any color or any stimuli beyond books and computer programs through which she has learned to read. Despite this situation, she is a brilliant scientist, supplied with "the best science texts" on any subject. Mary understands propositionally—in a third-person kind of way—*that* her mother loves her. She knows the meaning of the words. But until she meets her mother, who really does love her, she does not *know* her mother's love experientially. She does not know what it is *like* to be loved. She does not have second-person knowledge *of* her mother's love.

This is a wonderful illustration of the philosophical difference between propositional (third-person) knowledge *that* something is the case, and personal (second-person) knowledge *of* another person. Nonetheless, as Stump recognizes, from a fully second-person perspective on the development of human cognition, the thought experiment lacks insight into the constitution of Mary as a human subject capable of thought in the first place.[38] In Reddy's terms, for example, even the capacity for propositional knowledge requires prior interpersonal interchange, because "mutual relation is the primary form of knowledge."[39] How can Mary learn to think without the give-and-take of human interaction? How can she learn language without such embodied give-and-take? How can she have an abstract concept of love without first experiencing what it is *like* to be loved? We know from studies of people raised with extreme social deprivation, such as children in Romanian orphanages, that severe cognitive and affective disorders accompany the prolonged absence of human contact.[40]

In my second example, the exception to my argument might seem to be high-functioning autistic persons who appear capable of propositional knowledge apart from affective engagement with others. For example, Peter Hobson

37. Stump, *Wandering in Darkness*, 52.

38. Stump, *Wandering in Darkness*, 502n38. This thought experiment might in fact be an example of Stump's claim that, "to the extent to which the absence of the distinctly Franciscan knowledge of persons would impoverish our intuitions and thus diminish our capacity to form appropriate judgments about thought experiments, to that extent Franciscan knowledge is significant for philosophy" (60).

39. Reddy, "Before the 'Third Element,'" 96.

40. There are many examples of the effects of such deprivation. See, for example, studies of children that indicate a significant decrease in brain development because of their being abandoned in Romanian orphanages (Charles A. Nelson III, Nathan A. Fox, and Charles H. Zeanah Jr., "Anguish of the Abandoned Child," *Scientific American*, April 2013, 62–67, published online March 19, 2013, doi:10.1038/scientificamerican0413–62).

quotes an interview with an intelligent young autistic man who says, "I really didn't know there were people until I was seven years old. I then suddenly realized that there were people. But not like you do. I still have to remind myself that there are people."[41] This young man knows *that* people exist, but not in the way other people know. This surely is a kind of propositional knowledge in contrast with personal knowledge; one might deduce that it arises in a purely first-person self-referential way, apart from human interaction.

Such is not the case, however. Rather, as autistics have begun to articulate their own experience through personal memoirs "from the inside," so to speak, it has become clear that embodied involvement with other people is crucial for their capacity to act as agents of their own lives. In their remarkable book *Autism and the Myth of the Person Alone*, Douglas Biklen and Richard Attfield invite autistics (including Attfield himself) to give their perspectives on their own development and growth.[42] In each case, it turns out that intensive interactions with others who attend carefully and respectfully to the autistic person are crucial for the autistic's awareness of his or her own body and capacity to act effectively. Tito Mukhopadhay, for example, describes his difficulty in learning to talk because he could not make his lips move. His mother helped him by patting him on the back, generating a little puff of breath that gave Tito access to his own sensory experience so that he could speak. His bodily self-relation was and is mediated through an intense embodied other-relation with his mother. As he puts it, his mother's presence "creates an environment" that makes it possible for him to express his thoughts through writing. Thus, although his speech is still quite limited, he communicates brilliantly through writing on a laptop. Similarly, other communicative autistics can write and sometimes talk through partnership with other people. Theirs is an explicitly intersubjective agency that allows them to be far more independent than they would be if left alone and isolated in their condition. As the authors conclude, "The central element of each person's emergence into social participation has not been behavioral training; it has been inclusion." Even here the person is interpersonally constituted, albeit in ways that are different from (and perhaps instructive for) "neuro-typicals."[43]

41. Hobson, *Cradle of Thought*, 11.

42. Douglas Biklen and Richard Attfield, *Autism and the Myth of the Person Alone* (New York: New York University Press, 2005). The book is largely a series of invited chapters written by autistics, with additional commentary by Biklen and Attfield.

43. For example, John Swinton reflects on the insights gained from talking with autistics about their experiences of love, in "Reflections on Autistic Love: What Does Love Look Like?," *Practical Theology* 5.3 (2012): 259–78.

Summary

Two observations arise from the preceding discussion, with particular salience for reframing Paul's anthropology. First, across a spectrum of views among both philosophers of science and experimental psychology, there is a broadly shared notion of the person as irreducibly embodied and socially and environmentally embedded. This model of the self-in-relationship does not begin with the individual at all, in terms of either mental states or neural circuitry. It is intersubjective all the way down. The Cartesian idea of an individual, freestanding, independent self is long gone. There are no lone rangers on this playing field; for good or for ill, there are always other players involved.

Second, theorists differ in their interpretation of the data; I have proposed a hermeneutical grid based on the distinction between first- and second-person standpoints. A first-personal standpoint, here exemplified by Vittorio Gallese, posits that the recognition of other people begins with an inner feedback loop between the body and the brain, which in turn simulates experience that we use as a basis for understanding others as like us. We might say that the self in self-relation, or more precisely, in the system of interaction between the body and the mind, is the beginning point for, and therefore the mediator of, understanding other people. From a second-person perspective, such an approach is backward; the experience of others, and indeed of oneself as the object of another's gaze, is the beginning point for all other kinds of knowledge, including the knowledge of self and of others as both like us and different from us.

These experiences of self- and other-relation are not mutually exclusive; nonetheless, a great deal may be at stake in where we start. Both the general idea of the person as embodied and socially embedded and the differences between first-person self-relation and second-person other-relation acquire distinct resonance when juxtaposed with the teaching of Epictetus.

Epictetus and Contemporary Theories

The previous chapter noted divergent approaches to Epictetus in relationship to contemporary notions of the person. Despite nuanced differences, A. A. Long and Troels Engberg-Pedersen both argue that Epictetus thinks in first-person, individualistic terms: from birth, human beings' perception of themselves is fundamental to their development as persons, and throughout life that self-perception and self-relation are central to achieving freedom and a good life. All external data of consciousness are mediated through a kind of self-talk, an evaluative filter that determines what belongs to the person and what is extraneous and therefore irrelevant. Along with the proper performance of one's given roles in society, interaction with other people is a necessary good, in large part because it provides a testing ground for practice in achieving the splendid freedom that accompanies inner detachment. The self-in-relation-to-itself is thus both the starting point and the goal of Epictetus's educational project.

In contrast, as Christopher Gill emphasizes, the person simultaneously and primarily is constituted through participation in an objective reality that exceeds the individual and is therefore not contained or determined by the individual. The turn to the inner citadel is simultaneously the recognition that one is a part of the whole, embedded in and continuous with the objective flow of divinely constituted nature. So one might say that there is no difference between self-relation and other-relation, because self and other are on a continuum. Or as Engberg-Pedersen also insists, for the Stoics objectivity requires subjectivity, and subjectivity requires objectivity. The first-person perspective relies on a third-person reality, but that third-person reality is experienced through the correct perception of oneself as connected with God.

These observations highlight a tension in Epictetus's own program for human happiness. Insofar as the person is on a continuum of being with a providentially ordered material cosmos, there is every reason for optimism about the possibility of inner freedom. But insofar as that very continuum entails vulnerability to misleading false impressions, constant vigilance is needed to guard the inner citadel against incorrect judgments. Indeed, as noted in the previous chapter, what is not to be found in Epictetus is the idea of a second-person, intersubjective constitution of the self, as argued by the theorists in this chapter. To be so vulnerable to environmental factors, including the influence of other people, would seem to be anathema to Epictetus's whole philosophical project. Empathy and understanding other minds are not goals for those who would learn *philosophia*; if they were to appear at all on Epictetus's horizon, I suspect they would simply be more *phantasia* to be managed. Ultimately, then, Epictetus is interested, not in knowing other people, but in acquiring a correct knowledge of oneself, which is also the knowledge of God. For this reason Epictetan knowledge of God cannot be construed as a genuinely second-person construction of the self; for Epictetus the rational self and God are on a continuum. Despite the devotional quality of Epictetus's language about God, ultimately there is no distinction between "I" and "Thou." Rather, the second-person grammar of his conversational style functions in a first-personal way, namely, by allowing him to put the self in conversation with itself.

There thus seems to be a wide gap between the thought of Epictetus and the contemporary theories of the self in theorists such as Gallagher, Reddy, and Hobson. It is true that the scientific model of proprioception provides an intriguing analogue to Stoic ideas of self-perception as basic to sentient beings. But for Gallagher, as for Reddy and other second-person theorists, the locus of the person is primarily in interpersonal engagement with others, not in the experience of self-awareness and the exercise of self-determination. Rather than moving from self to shared to self, we might say that, for these theorists, the person moves from shared to self to shared.

The Pauline "Body" and Contemporary Theories

The cosmic parameters of Paul's thought may seem far from the work of contemporary scientists and many philosophers, but the participatory aspects of his thought are deeply amenable to depictions of the person as a "self-in-relationship," to quote Hobson, or as "the system that we are . . . the larger system of body-environment-intersubjectivity," to quote Gallagher.[44] Insofar as the self is objectively connected to other people through the actions of the body, such that "others move me," in Gallagher's words, the self is intensely vulnerable to its relational matrix. We recall Hobson's words about the system of self in relationship: "The combined operation of infant-in-relation-to-caregiver is a motive force in development, and it achieves wonderful things. When it does not exist, and the motive force is lacking, the whole of mental development is terribly compromised."[45]

Paul also is intensely attuned to such vulnerability and to its power for good or for ill. In terms of human flourishing, he insists on the mutual dependence of the individual members of the "body of Christ" (1 Cor 12:19–20), who together are "the body of Christ" without erasing their distinctive identities. Here is assimilation to a shared state, and a concomitant recognition of difference. There is a sense in which "in Christ," human beings belong to one another and constitute one another's well-being at a foundational level, a level that also is coconstituted through the Spirit of God dwelling in the midst of the community of faith (Rom 8:9).

44. Gallagher, *How the Body Shapes the Mind*, 242–43.
45. Hobson, *Cradle of Thought*, 183.

The reverse is true as well for Paul: he depicts human dereliction in terms of a kind of enmeshment in the realm of bodily existence that he calls "the flesh," which is enslaved by sin and ends in death. The permeable and malleable human body mediates this experience of bondage and debility "under sin," just as it also may mediate participation in life-giving relational matrices constituted "in Christ."

We thus can see intriguing connections between second-person theorists in science and philosophy and participatory aspects of Paul's anthropology. The central associative motif is the notion of the body as the mode of connection and communication, and as such, a "projection of one's world." For example, one of the puzzling aspects of Paul's anthropology is the way in which *sōma* denotes both physical human bodies and corporate "bodies," which may include both cosmic powers and human beings in their mutual interaction. "Body" is qualified by belonging to Christ, on the one hand, and to "sin" and "death," on the other hand. At the same time, *sōma* denotes physical existence in the realm of "the flesh." In the next chapter we will look in depth at this Pauline picture of the body, in conversation with both Epictetus and the recent work of Gallagher and Reddy.

Conclusion

In a crucial way the theorists studied in this chapter differ from both Paul and Epictetus. As hinted at in the introduction to the last chapter, no Stoic would say that one's philosophical commitments, including one's ideas about "God," were irrelevant for their practices. For Epictetus, as for Paul, the shape of the cosmos and the shape of one's life are inextricably bound together. Most contemporary theorists of mind, however, do not link their theories to larger claims about cosmic or metaphysical realities; such matters are bracketed out of their "scientific" investigation. Such bracketing means that their methodology is functionally naturalistic, regardless of their personal views. In other words, they do not address questions of divine causality; practically speaking, their theories neither entertain nor exclude the possibility of a second-person relationship with a God who is not a part of this world but rather is qualitatively different.[46] Now it may be that their naturalistic methodology brings

46. There are notable exceptions to this pattern, for example, in the work of Malcolm A. Jeeves, ed., *From Cells to Souls—and Beyond: Changing Portraits of Human Nature* (Grand Rapids: Eerdmans, 2004); see also Warren S. Brown, Nancey C. Murphy, and H. Newton

them close to the naturalism of Epictetus, insofar as he also does not conceive of a God who is outside the natural order of things. But it is impossible to make a full equation; as Long says, Epictetus is not a secular humanist, and his natural theism is central to his philosophy. Conversely, it may also be the case that the second-person perspective on human development, in which the self is constructed in relationship to a distinctly different other who is also "like us," leaves open the door for second-person engagement with a transcendent God.[47]

The juxtaposition of Epictetan natural theology with the methodological naturalism of these contemporary theories of the person raises a further question: does a purely naturalistic material cosmos—that is, one that excludes any ontologically distinct divine action in the natural world—allow for an account of an intersubjective constitution of human persons with a relational partner who is genuinely, radically "other"? Or does such a radical intersubjectivity require an intimate and yet transcendent partnership with a God who is both Creator and incarnate in history? Rowan Williams catches the sense of this noncompetitive and transcendent Other when he describes the soul as "a whole way of speaking, of presenting and 'uttering' the self, that presupposes *relation* as the ground that gives the self room to exist, a relation developing in time, a relation with an agency which addresses or summons the self, but is in itself no part of the system of interacting and negotiating speakers in the world."[48] The last line is the key point—here is an agency that is both intensely personal and yet qualitatively other, not caught up in and constrained by other causal matrices that would impinge on a gracious, gifted relational bond with human beings.

Might such a divine-human partnership be what is disclosed in Paul's participatory account of dying and living with Christ? And might the intersubjective constitution of persons-in-relationship also inform our understanding of the constriction of the "I" in relation to sin? These are questions for part 2

Malony, eds., *Whatever Happened to the Soul? Scientific and Theological Portraits of Human Nature* (Minneapolis: Fortress, 1998).

47. It is not insignificant that Martin Buber's *I and Thou* (trans. Walter Kaufmann [New York: Touchstone, 1971]) is a lodestar for work in second-person perspective by both philosophers and experimental psychologists. See, e.g., Reddy, "Before the 'Third Element,' " 104. Theologians and philosophers who find common ground between second-person theories of the self and Christian theology include Pinsent, *The Second-Person Perspective*, and Stump, *Wandering in Darkness*.

48. Rowan Williams, *Lost Icons: Reflections on Cultural Bereavement* (London: Continuum, 2003), 196.

of this book. In any case, Paul cannot be squeezed into either a purely first-person or a purely third-person framework, and second-person theories give us reason to believe that such a framework is by no means characteristic of all "modern" thought in the twenty-first century.[49] Rather, as we shall see, Paul's cosmos is second-personal all the way down, from selves in relationship to one another, to a God who is both the supernatural Creator of all that is and intimately "like us" through the incarnation of the Son of God.

49. See the perceptive comment by Volker Rabens: "[W]e suggest that the Spirit effects ethical life primarily by means of *intimate relationships* created by the Spirit with *God [Abba], Jesus, and fellow believers*" (*The Holy Spirit and Ethics in Paul: Transformation and Empowerment for Religious-Ethical Life* [Minneapolis: Fortress, 2014], 126). This notion of "transforming relationships" moves understanding of Pauline thought beyond the false dichotomy of "relational versus substance-ontological transformation; [functional] empowerment versus [ontological] transformation; new self-understanding versus a completely new self" (143).

CHAPTER THREE

Embodied and Embedded

The Corporeal Reality of Pauline Participation

The Aristotelian insight that the human soul is an expression of the human body finds significant verification in contemporary scientific studies of human experience. Before you know it, your body makes you human, and sets you on a course in which your human nature is expressed in intentional actions and in interaction with others.

—Shaun Gallagher, *How the Body Shapes the Mind*

We are a way for the universe to know itself. Some part of our being knows this is where we came from. We long to return. And we can, because the cosmos is also within us. We're made of star stuff.

—Carl Sagan, "Cosmos: A Personal Journey"

Body language is ubiquitous in the letters of Paul. Perhaps for this reason, if for none other, studies of Paul's anthropology have tended to start with his use of the terminology of the body (*sōma*).[1] Similarly, as the first quotation that opens this chapter illustrates, contemporary theorists in philosophy and science take the body as their starting point. Interpretation of the data varies,

---

1. In addition to Rudolf Bultmann's *Theology of the New Testament*, trans. Kendrick Grobel, 2 vols. (Waco, TX: Baylor University Press, 2007), see Robert Jewett, *Paul's Anthropological Terms: A Study of Their Use in Conflict Settings* (Leiden: Brill, 1971); Robert Gundry, *Sōma in Biblical Theology, with an Emphasis on Pauline Anthropology* (Cambridge: Cambridge University Press, 1976); John A. T. Robinson, *The Body: A Study in Pauline Theology* (Philadelphia: Westminster, 1952).

but all are agreed that our cognitive and relational capacities are inextricably tied to bodily movement and interaction.

Furthermore, this bodily movement and interaction link us with the larger environment in both relational and elemental ways. Carl Sagan's famous line that we are made of stardust is also a strong empirical claim that can be traced back to earlier scientific claims. In 1929 Harlow Shapley, director of Harvard College Observatory, stated in an interview: "We are made of the same stuff as the stars, so when we study astronomy we are in a way only investigating our remote ancestry and our place in the universe of star stuff. Our very bodies consist of the same chemical elements found in the most distant nebulae, and our activities are guided by the same universal rules."[2]

As we have seen, a Stoic would agree. Twentieth-century pundits may trumpet that human beings are made of stardust, but that would have been old news to a Greco-Roman audience, who understood their bodies as existing on a continuum with the natural world. As Dale Martin observes, for people in the Hellenistic era, "Innards . . . are constituted of the same stuff as the rest of the cosmos."[3] Writing in 1995, Martin asks his readers "to try to imagine how ancient Greeks and Romans could see as 'natural' what seems to us bizarre: the nonexistence of the 'individual,' the fluidity of the elements that make up the 'self,' and the essential continuity of the human body with its surroundings."[4] But as we have seen, such ideas are no longer bizarre in the popular and scientific imagination; they are the order of the day. Indeed, many of the insights from neuroscience and experimental psychology sound eerily similar to views of the body in the Hellenistic world. *Plus ça change, plus c'est la même chose.*

In this chapter I give a brief overview of some aspects of Paul's body language and how that language might have been heard in Paul's context. Comparing such readings with the work of Bultmann and Käsemann, I then bring in contemporary views of embodiment in relationship to the person.

The Pauline "Body"

Sōma (body) does not appear as an unqualified or freestanding term in Paul's letters. Rather, it is qualified both negatively through affiliation with death,

---

2. Quoted by H. Gordon Garbedian, "The Star Stuff That Is Man," *New York Times*, August 11, 1929.

3. Dale Martin, *The Corinthian Body* (New Haven: Yale University Press, 1995), 16.

4. Martin, *Corinthian Body*, 21.

sin, and the flesh and positively through affiliation with Christ and the "body of Christ." These defining realities are so dominant in relationship to the body that in some instances it is by no means clear that Paul uses *sōma* to refer to human beings at all. Consider the following expressions:

> You have died to the law through the body of Christ [*hymeis ethanatōthēte tō nomō dia tou sōmatos tou Christou*]. (Rom 7:4)
> Who will deliver me from this body of death [*ek tou sōmatos tou thanatou toutou*]? (Rom 7:24)

How to translate the genitive phrases qualifying *sōma* in both these passages is a live exegetical issue. If *sōma* retains an anthropological referent, it denotes the human body as it "belongs to" or "originates in" either Christ or death; alternatively, "the body of Christ" may signify quite concretely Christ's physical body or the corporate "body" of all those who belong to Christ, and "the body of death" may mean some corporeal expression of "death" itself as a personified power.

Each case must of course be decided individually. In Romans 7:4 "the body of Christ" most likely refers to Christ's physical body crucified for all humanity, building on the notion of solidarity with Christ's crucified body as a means of deliverance from the "body of sin" (Rom 6:4-6).[5] In Romans 7:24 the meaning of "this body of death" is less clear; in light of the parallel with "the body of sin" (Rom 6:6), it seems more clearly a referent to the physical human body as gripped or determined by sin's reign and thereby death's power.[6]

Already it seems that "body" can express powerful connections with

5. Ernst Käsemann, *Commentary on Romans*, trans. G. W. Bromiley (Grand Rapids: Eerdmans, 1980), 189; C. K. Barrett, *The Epistle to the Romans*, Black's New Testament Commentaries 6 (Peabody, MA: Hendrickson, 2001), 128; Robert Jewett, *Romans*, Hermeneia (Minneapolis: Fortress, 2007), 433-34: "Those who accept this message become members of the church as the 'body of Christ' (1 Cor 12:27), but the vehicle of transformation that Paul describes here is not ecclesiastical. It is the power of God acting through the death and resurrection of the 'body of Christ' that brings the reign of law to an end and ushers believers into a new realm of grace dominated by Christ himself."

6. Käsemann: "Where sin reigns, the power of death qualifies our bodily existence in its total relationship to the world, as in 5:12ff." (*Romans*, 209). So also James D. G. Dunn, *Romans 1-8*, Word Biblical Commentary 38A (Waco, TX: Word, 1988), 397, who rightly emphasizes the corporeal nature of "body" here, with reference to Rom 6:6, 12. Barrett glosses *sōma* as "either the body or human nature" under the "dominion of death" (*Romans*, 141), following Bultmann in seeing "body" as designating the whole person. Jewett rather provocatively argues that Paul here has in mind his own history of persecuting Christians unto death (*Romans*, 472).

larger realities, with either life-giving or death-dealing effects. J. A. T. Robinson expressed this claim powerfully several decades ago:

> Solidarity is the divinely ordained structure in which personal life is to be lived. . . . It is from the body of sin and death that we are delivered; it is through the body of Christ on the Cross that we are saved; it is into His body the Church that we are incorporated; it is by His body in the Eucharist that this Community is sustained; it is in our body that its new life has to be manifested; it is to a resurrection of this body to the likeness of His glorious body that we are destined.[7]

Robinson's study of Paul's body language repeatedly highlights the connectivity communicated by that language; whatever else it may signify in Paul's discourse, *sōma* is a mode of participation.

In other Pauline uses of *sōma*, the anthropological designation is ambiguous at best. Consider, for example, Romans 6:6: "We know this, that our old self was cocrucified [*ho palaios hēmōn anthrōpos synestaurōthē*], in order that the body of sin [*to sōma tēs hamartias*] might be done away with, that we might no longer be enslaved to sin." On the one hand, *to sōma tēs hamartias* can be translated "sinful body," giving it an anthropological referent, as is the case in some English translations (RSV). Indeed, Paul very quickly exhorts the Roman believers, in what may be a prayer for divine deliverance, "Let not sin reign in your mortal bodies [*en tō thnētō hymōn sōmati*]" (Rom 6:12).[8] On the other hand, human "bodies" are not intrinsically "sinful"; Paul subsequently drives home his point by telling the Romans not to present their bodily members (*melē*) to sin as weapons (*hopla*) of unrighteousness, but rather to God as weapons of righteousness (Rom 6:13, 16, 19).

Furthermore, Paul does not say that human bodies as such are to be done away with; to the contrary, they are to be deployed as "weapons of righteousness" precisely because "the body of sin" has been nullified and rendered powerless. It thus is not the body per se or the "sinful body" that is rendered null by cocrucifixion with Christ, but rather "the body of Sin." In Paul's logic, "Sin" itself once held human bodies captive, but now through Christ they have been set free (6:6-7, 10-14, 16-18). Given this interplay between "body" and

---

7. Robinson, *The Body*, 9. Robinson and Käsemann are very close in their emphasis on the body as the means of communication and connection in a supra-individual way.

8. See Joel Marcus, " 'Let God Arise and End the Reign of Sin': A Contribution to the Study of Pauline Parenesis," *Biblica* 69.3 (1988): 386-95.

"Sin," perhaps the best translation for *to sōma tēs hamartias* is "the body held captive by Sin" or "the body belonging to Sin."⁹ As the subsequent imperatives make clear, it is not bodily existence that is done away with·but the body qualified in some way by sin as a distinct entity, or perhaps sin as it takes hold of embodied existence.

A parallel pattern obtains with Paul's use of the multivalent term "flesh" (*sarx*). "Flesh" is closely allied with bodily life, usually (but not always) in a negative sense. At times the term simply denotes the physical existence of human beings in general, or the embodied and socially embedded realm in which all humans live (Gal 2:20). The prepositional modifier "according to the flesh" (*kata sarka*) may refer simply to physical lineage and kinship, as in Paul's reference to his kinsfolk *kata sarka* in Romans 9:3 and his recognition that Christ was descended from David *kata sarka* (Rom 1:3). More frequently, however, actions according to the flesh (*kata sarka*) are limited to what is humanly possible, over against divine power and miracle. For example, in Galatians 4:23 Paul contrasts the birth of Ishmael *kata sarka* with the birth of Isaac through the promise of God (*di' epangelias*). Here "according to the flesh" denotes Ishmael's natural, humanly possible birth through Abraham's liaison with Hagar, in contrast with Isaac's miraculous birth from Sarah despite her barrenness. This is not intrinsically an evil or sinful notion of "flesh," but a qualification that renders "flesh" limited at best. In all these instances—physical existence, kinship, and human limitation—*sarx* participates exclusively in what Paul calls "the present evil age" (Gal 1:4). Through such participation, *sarx* denotes a realm of existence that is doomed to pass away.¹⁰

At its most heinous, *sarx* seems almost personified as a cosmic power that thinks and desires in opposition to the thinking and desiring of the Spirit. Thus in Galatians 5:16-24 the imperative "walk by the Spirit [*pneumati*

9. Käsemann glosses both the "old *anthrōpos*" and "the body of sin" simply as "existence in sin's power" (*Romans*, 169). Jewett translates the phrase as "the sinful body" but immediately interprets it in terms of "the human body that stands in the generic sense 'under the rule of sin and death' " (*Romans*, 403). Whether this wording refers to individual or to corporate existence, or both, is a matter of debate; this Pauline text illustrates the difficulty in positing an either/or between individual and corporate denotations, precisely because the self is embedded and never autonomous. As Robert C. Tannehill elegantly puts it, Rom 6:6 refers "to the old dominion as a corporate entity. When the believers were in slavery to sin, they were part of this inclusive 'old man'; their existence was bound up with his" (*Dying and Rising with Christ: A Study in Pauline Theology* [Eugene, OR: Wipf & Stock, 2006], 30).

10. John M. G. Barclay designates *sarx* as "what is merely human," locating Paul's division between "flesh" and "Spirit" within the cosmic dualism of Paul's apocalyptic worldview (*Obeying the Truth: A Study of Paul's Ethics in Galatians* [Edinburgh: T&T Clark, 1998], 206).

peripateite]" is immediately followed by its cosmic rationale: "*For* the flesh desires against the Spirit [*hē gar sarx epithymei kata tou pneumatos*], and the Spirit against the flesh; these are opposed to one another, that you may not do what you want."[11] The opposition here between "flesh" and "Spirit" is not reducible to purely human entities, and yet it takes place in human existence. To be precise, it is instantiated in the qualities of embodied social interactions among the Galatians themselves, whether those be characterized as the corrosive and destructive "works of the flesh" or the mutually upbuilding "fruit of the Spirit" (Gal 5:19–23). Insofar as the divisive effects of the "works of the flesh" parallel the community-destroying effects of the "works of the law," in Galatians *sarx* takes on a close association with the law and with doing the "works of the law." Chief among these works is circumcision, literally an inscription of the law in circumcised flesh; hence Paul can say of the circumcising missionaries in Galatians, "For even those who receive circumcision do not themselves keep the law, but they desire to have you circumcised that they may glory in your flesh" (Gal 6:13)—that is, in your circumcised flesh.[12]

Bodily existence in this realm of "flesh" is not only vulnerable to the power of sin; it is sin's handle on the person in such a way that the person is constituted inextricably in relationship to sin. Thus in Romans 7:14 the "I" that is "fleshly, sold under sin," later says, "I myself am a slave to the law of God with my mind, but with my flesh [I serve] the law of sin [*tē de sarki nomō hamartias*]" (Rom 7:25).[13] Deliverance from this impossible situation comes through the crucifixion of the Son of God in the "likeness of the flesh of sin" (Rom 8:3); that is, through entering the realm of the flesh and suffering crucifixion, the Son of God does what the law, "weakened by the flesh, was powerless to do [*to gar adynaton tou nomou en hō ēsthenei dia tēs sarkos*]" (Rom 8:3). Here the crucifixion of the Son of God uniquely constitutes a new

---

11. This sentence is a notorious crux for the interpretation of Galatians. Following the logic of Gal 4:21, I argue elsewhere that the activities that the Galatians "want to do" are "the works of the flesh," including circumcision as a way of attempting to live under the law: they "cannot be led by the Spirit and under the law at the same time" (*Recovering Paul's Mother Tongue: Language and Theology in Galatians* [Grand Rapids: Eerdmans, 2007], 164–65). For the argument that here Paul sees the flesh as a cosmic power linked to the notion of the evil inclination, see J. Louis Martyn, *Galatians*, Anchor Bible 33A (New York: Doubleday, 1997), 290–92, 493–94; Martinus C. de Boer, *Galatians*, New Testament Library (Louisville: Westminster John Knox, 2011), 335–39.

12. Martyn, *Galatians*, 290.

13. For in-depth discussion of this passage, see chapter 4 below.

human agency in which "the just requirement of the law might be fulfilled in us [*to dikaiōma tou nomou plērōthē en hymin*]" (Rom 8:4). The logic is similar to that of Romans 6:6, where the "body of sin" was done away with through cocrucifixion with Christ, so that in Christ believers might offer their bodily members to God.

Paul subsequently depicts human agency as constituted in relationship to the agency of "the flesh," on the one hand, or "the Spirit," on the other. Thus, "the mind-set of the flesh [*phronēma tēs sarkos*] is death, but the mind-set of the Spirit [*phronēma tou pneumatos*] is life and peace" (Rom 8:6). Human beings participate in these opposing mind-sets through their own "walking," "being," and "thinking," whether "according to the flesh" or "according to the Spirit" (Rom 8:4–5). In this sense, then, they are either "in the flesh" (*en sarki*) or "in the Spirit" (*en pneumati*). And walking, thinking, and being "in the flesh" signify more than simply acting in a merely human manner: here, in contrast to Paul's language in Galatians 2:20, to be "in the flesh" is to be an enemy of God (Rom 8:7–8). The opposite of such fleshly existence is not a dematerialized "spiritual" life but bodily participation in the "body of Christ" (Rom 12:4–5; 1 Cor 6:15; 12:12–27).[14] Paul apparently intends to link the behavior of singular, physical human bodies to the well-being of the communal, social "body" of believers.

Paul's "body language" thus discloses a close interplay between corporeal human existence as physical and social "bodies" and larger suprahuman realities that exercise pressure on embodied human interaction. This interplay means that Paul's uses of *sōma* and *sarx* exemplify what Ernst Käsemann termed the central tension in Paul's theology: the relationship between cosmology and anthropology.[15] I will return to Käsemann's account of Paul's understanding of the body later in this chapter; here I simply note that the push and pull between *sōma* as denoting a suprahuman power and *sōma* as denoting a physical human body or a corporate human community suggests that embodied human existence is always embedded in, and qualified by, supracorporeal forces, whether those be merely human social realities or cosmic powers.

---

14. The literature on Paul's notion of the "body of Christ" is vast. I will compare the influential and contrasting views of Bultmann and Käsemann in some depth later in this chapter. Other important works include Robinson, *The Body*; Robert Jewett, *Paul's Anthropological Terms: A Study of Their Use in Conflict Settings* (Leiden: Brill, 1971); Gundry, *Sōma in Biblical Theology*; Martin, *Corinthian Body*; and John M. G. Barclay, *Paul and the Gift* (Grand Rapids: Eerdmans, 2015).

15. Käsemann, *Romans*, 33.

The Porous Body: Ancient and Contemporary Views

One angle on the link between embodiment and embeddedness comes through study of the language of the body in Paul's Hellenistic context. Dale Martin's work *The Corinthian Body* usefully models such an approach. Martin limns the notions of the body in both elite philosophical discourse and popular culture, as much as the latter can be accessed from magical papyri and medical discourses, particularly those of Galen in the second century. This study intersects in intriguing ways with Epictetus; Martin's research displays above all the way in which embodied existence was inseparable from participation in the larger culture, and the extreme vulnerability entailed by such participation. The Stoic insistence on defending an inner space of freedom appears particularly poignant in such a world.

Here I highlight several points from Martin's overview of Greco-Roman understandings of the body. To begin with, Martin argues that the ancients knew nothing of the Cartesian ontological dualism between "natural" and "supernatural," which until very recently North Atlantic culture took for granted.[16] Like many current philosophers and cognitive scientists, Martin traces this dualism to Descartes and links it with an individualistic notion of the body as bounded and self-determining. Its hallmark is a distinction between the material "natural" world and an immaterial "supernatural" reality, traceable in accounts of the body as physical and the soul or mental processes or "spirit" as nonphysical. Such accounts find very little support in the ancient world, claims Martin. Indeed, "*all* Cartesian oppositions—matter versus nonmatter, physical versus spiritual, corporeal (or physical) versus psychological, nature versus supernature—are misleading when retrojected into ancient language."

Rather than talking about "an ontological dualism, we should think of a hierarchy of essence."[17] As Epictetus demonstrates, Stoic cosmology is a case in point, in which everything is "stuff" that exists on a spectrum of being,

---

16. Martin, *Corinthian Body*, 1–14. However, there certainly were dualisms in the ancient world, as in the dualism between "flesh" and Spirit" so evident in Paul's letters. Martin minimizes the existence of transcendent realities in Paul's thought, as well as the fundamental distinction between what is created and divine causality. Similarly, as explicated by A. A. Long, there is a kind of functional dualism operative in Epictetus's exhortations regarding the correct use of impressions. See again his "Representation and the Self in Stoicism," in *Stoic Studies* (Cambridge: Cambridge University Press, 1996), 285: "The mind's freedom from constraint, so strongly emphasized by Epictetus, gains a (transcendental?) dimension that scholars of Stoicism have tended to overlook."

17. Martin, *Corinthian Body*, 15.

including the divine Logos.[18] Martin traces out significant ways in which such a hierarchy of essence is displayed in views and practices of the body.

First, on a continuum with the larger social and cosmic realities in which it is embedded, the human body is literally a microcosm of the macrocosmic body. It both shares the same elements and mimetically corresponds to its larger matrix; Sagan's claim that "we are made of the same stuff as the stars" fits well with this view.[19] Furthermore, this cosmic connection breaks down divisions between a presumed "inner self" in any psychological or mentalist sense and an "outer self." Rather, environmental factors directly shape the "'weather' inside the body." The body is "porous" and "of a piece with the elements surrounding it and pervading it," so that "the surface of the body is not a sealed boundary."[20]

After reading the work of theorists such as Gallagher, Reddy, and Hobson, we note that such views of the body come with an odd shock of familiarity. We may recall Gallagher's conclusion, "We are not just what happens in our brains. The 'loop' *extends through and is limited by our bodily* capacities, *into* the surrounding environment, which is social as well as physical and feeds back through our conscious experience into the decisions we make." This loop is "the true size of the system that we are . . . the larger system of body-environment-intersubjectivity."[21] There are a great many ways in which such systemic breakdown of presumed boundaries between the microcosmic and macrocosmic bodies are explored in contemporary science, from neuroscience to biology. For example, current research on "the human microbiome" explores the existence of "microbial communities" of alien cells that outnumber "human" cells in the body by up to ten to one.[22] These cells colonize parts of the human body, and research increasingly shows that they affect moods and cognition, to the point that some call the "microbiome" a "second brain."[23]

18. As noted in the discussion of Epictetus, the picture is somewhat more complex. Epictetus did not oppose the naturalism of the Stoic cosmos, but in his advice regarding the way to freedom, he did hint at a functional dualism between the body and the command center of the self.

19. Carl Sagan, "Cosmos: A Personal Journey," PBS Television, 1980, online at http://www.space.com/1602-carl-sagans-cosmos-returns-television.html.

20. Martin, *Corinthian Body*, 17–18.

21. Shaun Gallagher, *How the Body Shapes the Mind* (Oxford: Oxford University Press, 2005), 242–43.

22. Essayist Michael Pollan writes that he considers himself "ten percent human" ("Some of My Best Friends Are Germs," *New York Times Magazine*, May 15, 2013).

23. Peter Andrey Smith, "Can the Bacteria in Your Gut Explain Your Mood?," *New York Times*, June 23, 2015; David Kohn, "When Gut Bacteria Changes Brain Function," *Atlantic*,

This is a topic far beyond the scope of this book, but it gives a tantalizing taste of the way in which ancient and contemporary notions of the body as an environmentally embedded system may converge. In both, there is a constant traffic between the "inner" and the "outer" through the porous surface of the body, with immediate and far-reaching implications for the psychological-*cum*-physical well-being of the person.

Second, then, because the body is of a piece with its environment, "one can read the nature of the inner body on the external surface of the body." Furthermore, "Our own divisions between the 'physical' and the 'psychological' are strikingly absent" from ancient texts about physiognomy and medical practice.[24] Martin draws the line of influence back to Aristotle's dictum that the soul is the form of the body—a principle that, not incidentally, Shaun Gallagher quotes to sum up the implications of contemporary scientific accounts of the relationship between the body and the mind. Similarly, Reddy insists that the mind is not hidden behind the body, nor is understanding other minds a process of inference from our own private experience of our own minds; thoughts and emotions are displayed and enacted in bodily events and interactions.[25] As a correlate, then, there is no need to posit an inner, essential, or continuous self that is hidden from public view.[26] Martin argues that in Greco-Roman conceptions of the body, "the individualism of modern conceptions disappears, and the body is perceived as a location in a continuum of cosmic movement. The body—or the 'self'—is an unstable point of transition, not a discrete, permanent, solid entity."[27] It appears that "the individualism of modern conceptions" is again disappearing: in at least some contemporary views, the self is visible, public, embodied, and constituted in constant interchange with its relational, material environment.

Finally, the lack of firm boundaries means that the body is malleable, to use Martin's terminology. He references the upper-class practice of massaging elite young male bodies, precisely with the goal of shaping them into beautiful "masculine" bodies that conform to the values of a hierarchical, status-conscious society.[28] The basic idea is that society molds the self: "The shape of

---

June 24, 2015. I am grateful to my student Aminah Al-Attas Bradford for alerting me to this topic and for these references.

24. Martin, *Corinthian Body*, 18, 19.

25. Vasudevi Reddy, *How Infants Know Minds* (Cambridge, MA: Harvard University Press, 2008), 4–6; Gallagher, *How the Body Shapes the Mind*, 211–12.

26. Martin, *Corinthian Body*, 19–21.

27. Martin, *Corinthian Body*, 25.

28. Martin, *Corinthian Body*, 25–29.

the body and its inner constitution are thus subject to the molding of civilization; the idea of a self left to grow all by itself appears to have been unthinkable."[29] From birth, and even before through instructions given to pregnant women, the infant's body is intimately shaped by and constituted in relationship with its environment. Once again, the overlaps with current research on the brain are striking. The effects of the relational and physical environment on infant development are well documented, as discussed in the previous chapter.

Martin's analysis of the ancient body, with its intriguing convergences with modern theory, generates further questions about the relationship between individual and corporate identity. Granted that in the ancient world bodies were permeable, unbounded, and of a piece with their environment, does this mean that there was no self in the Greco-Roman world? Or does it mean, rather, that there was no abstract concept of individuals as autonomous, self-determining, and discrete in a Cartesian sense? Or is this either/or a false dichotomy, ironically imported from the very modern conceptualities that Martin explicitly rejects as a lens for reading Paul? The reality, at least in Stoicism as demonstrated through Epictetus, seems to be more complex. Precisely because the body in all its physicality is more of a bridge than a barrier, it is immensely vulnerable to environmental factors, for good and for ill. There are different ways to navigate such vulnerability. The Stoics, as we have seen in Epictetus, narrowed down the range of the self to the "inner citadel"—the inner sanctum of correct judgments in which detachment and therefore freedom can be maintained against all the vicissitudes of bodily existence. They thus demonstrate a complex tension between the body as "other-relation" on a continuum with everything else and the body as a unique kind of self-relation. Indeed, Epictetus distances himself from affliction as well as pleasure by dismissing his "paltry body" as of no more significance than any other essentially alien part of experience: "But here is where we must begin, and it is from this side that we must seize the acropolis and cast out the tyrants; we must yield up the paltry body, its members, the faculties, property, reputation, offices, honours, children, brothers, friends—count all these things as alien to us" (*Disc.* 4.1.87). Here there does seem to be a sense of the individual, as argued by A. A. Long over against more "participatory" accounts of the structured self. Nonetheless, as a close look at Epictetus has shown, this "individual" is not self-constituting or self-determining in a modern sense; the inward turn is in fact also a turn to the objectively existing divine Logos within that also permeates all nature and is coextensive with it.

29. Martin, *Corinthian Body*, 27.

Paul's Logic of the Body

What about Paul's use of the language of the body? Is there an individual in
Paul, or is the body simply part of a continuum of being, such that body and self
are simply an "unstable point of transition"? Martin's project aims to "sketch the
logic underlying . . . ancient discourses about the body" in conversation with
"Paul's own logic of the body," which both converges with and differs from these
other discourses.[30] Along the way he exposes a priori philosophical commitments that have dominated and, in my view, hamstrung earlier interpretations
of Paul's body language. We can trace these commitments in the theological
interpretation of Paul's letters as well. Martin himself does not interact with
such interpretations, yet there are again intriguing points of convergence and
divergence between Käsemann's depiction of Paul's anthropology as "crystalized cosmology" and Martin's discussion of the body as a socially embedded
microcosm of the macrocosm. The points of convergence lie in precisely this
embedded, porous depiction of the body; the points of divergence may lie in
the question of ontological or metaphysical dualism. A closer comparison of
Bultmann and Käsemann on the body will clarify the issues.

Bultmann and Käsemann on sōma in Paul

As noted in the introduction, Bultmann begins his interpretation of Paul's
theology with the famous claim that "every assertion about God is simultaneously an assertion about man, and vice versa. For this reason and in this
sense Paul's theology is, at the same time, anthropology."[31] This assertion stems
from Bultmann's conviction that God is not knowable in Godself, but only in
God's dealings with humanity. Anthropology thus becomes for Bultmann the
entry point into Paul's thought, and he structures his investigation of Paul's
anthropology by discussing a set of "anthropological concepts," beginning with
sōma (192–203).

Rejecting any notion of sōma as the outward form of the self or merely
the physical body, Bultmann insists that for Paul, "body . . . means the whole
person" (192). This includes the physical body, but not as separable from some
nonmaterial essential soul: "man does not *have* a *soma*; he *is* a *soma*" (194).

---

30. Martin, *Corinthian Body*, xiii.
31. Bultmann, *Theology of the New Testament*, 1:191. Subsequent page references in the
text are to this volume.

What makes human beings unique is Paul's foundational conception of the embodied self: "*Man is called soma in respect to his being able to make himself the object of his own action or to experience himself as the subject to whom something happens. He can be called soma, that is, as having a relationship to himself*" (196-97, emphasis original). Indeed, "for a person his body is not a thing like the objects of the external world, but is precisely *his* body, which is given to him, and he to it. He gets his primary experience of himself by experiencing his body, and he first encounters his thralldom to outside powers in his bodily dependence upon them. So the inward aspect of the self and the outward (its sensory given-ness) remain at first undiscriminated as phenomena" (196).

As we have seen in the previous chapters, this notion of bodily experience as the primary and therefore foundational source of self-knowledge occurs in both Stoic thought and some contemporary ideas of child development. Implicit here is the idea that, as *bodies*, human beings experience self-awareness—a relationship with the self—that makes them unique and that precedes and facilitates other-awareness and other-relationship. *Sōma* is that through which we relate to ourselves. The body is what first mediates our experience *of* ourselves *to* ourselves. It is also the medium through which the self can become enthralled to "a power not one's own," which Bultmann identifies with Paul's terminology of "the flesh" (*sarx*; 196).

Note that this relationship with the self entails an inner division inherent in the capacity to stand aside from oneself and observe oneself. Such an inner division means that one's self-relation "can be either an appropriate or a perverted one; that he can be at one with himself or at odds; that he can be under his own control or lose his grip on himself" (197-98). Therefore, somewhat paradoxically after insisting on the unity of the self precisely as *sōma*, Bultmann distinguishes between the "*soma-self*" under the sway of the flesh and the "subject-self," or "real self," which separates itself from the body, insofar as the body is under the power of the flesh (197). It is only "the power of God which reconciles the cleft between self and self within a man" (199). Bultmann here sounds close to Epictetus, who does not dispute the unity of human beings with all of nature in theory, but in practice operates with a functional anthropological dualism that distinguishes between the self as *proairesis* and its insignificant body.

There is a real tension between this depiction of a divided self, or indeed "self and self," and the claim that *sōma* denotes the whole, undivided person. Bultmann argues that the experience of "outside powers," which wrest away self-control and lead to an experience of inner division, makes human beings falsely distinguish between themselves and their physical bodies, as in dualistic views of the self as imprisoned in the body (199). Such anthropological dualism is not Paul's view, but "he sees so deep a cleft within man, so great a tension between self and self, and so keenly feels the plight of the man who loses his grip upon himself and falls victim to outside powers, that he comes close to Gnostic dualism" (199). All of this depicts the body under the rule of the flesh and bound to sin, so that there is an "estrangement between the self which is the bearer of man's real will (the 'inmost self' of Rom 7:22) and the self which slips away from this will and falls under the sway of flesh" (200).

Nonetheless, Bultmann thinks the body remains intrinsically neutral, not evil or sinful. He points out that, once the "flesh" is done away with and ceases to rule over the body, the body can become "the vehicle of the resurrection-life" (201). Implicit here would seem to be a picture of the body as participating in and therefore qualified by either the realm of flesh and sin or the realm of resurrection life. But Bultmann does not narrate matters in such a participatory, other-related way. Rather, he remains committed above all to the idea of the body as *self*-relation for isolated, discrete individuals. Even in resurrection life the structure of human existence thus remains unchanged; it is still a structure of self-in-relation-*to-itself*. At the end of all things, when only faith, hope, and love remain, "in faith, hope and love, man always also *has a relationship to himself*, since in them he makes up his mind about something, adopts a definite attitude" (199, emphasis added). Note, typically, how the language of decision and intention is wedded to the concept of self-relation.

In short, in all his discussion of the body, Bultmann emphasizes one thing repeatedly—the picture of the body as a self-in-relation-to-*itself*. This is clearly "individualism about persons" in which "relationality presupposes individuality." When we put this picture of the self into conversation with contemporary theories, we thus find that it operates from a first-person perspective. That is, it begins with and constantly refers back to the perspective and experience of the "I" as a singular, self-referential entity. The bodily experience of the self precedes and mediates all other knowledge and experience.

As we have seen, this first-person perspective, in which bodily self-knowledge precedes the knowledge of others, bears interesting similarities to some contemporary theories of mind, but it clearly differs from those of others, such as Shaun Gallagher, Vasudevi Reddy, and Peter Hobson. Here I note only that, ironically, such a first-person, individualistic, and self-referential anthropology is somewhat at odds with the second-person goals and certain second-person aspects of Bultmann's interpretive project, which seeks to articulate the text's witness to the kerygma as a divine address that comes to the individual from outside, from a God who is qualitatively different and other. As noted in the introduction, Bultmann's famous claim—"Every assertion about God is simultaneously an assertion about man *and vice versa*"—is a second-person claim, insofar as God and humanity are known in their mutual relations. But as Käsemann complained, " 'and vice versa' never receives due attention."[32] Rather, Bultmann's starting point and consistent focus are on the inner experience of the individual, rather than the dynamic exchange between God and humanity in the complexities of human history.

Alternatively, Käsemann suggests, "If the dialectic of 'and vice versa' is seriously meant, neither theology nor anthropology can 'properly' be conceded priority. Yet it might be possible to develop the connection of the two in the light of Pauline Christology, thus avoiding the danger both of a Christian metaphysic and of a Christian humanism."[33] By "Christian metaphysic," Käsemann means metaphysical speculation about God; by "Christian humanism," he means an anthropological focus in which God is functionally absent. Either loses sight of the interaction between God and humanity at the heart of Paul's thought. And in Käsemann's view, Christ is the place where that interaction most decisively happens, along the way disclosing a different understanding and enactment of the person.[34]

Matters thus appear very differently in Käsemann's depiction of the body. If for Bultmann the body is inward-directed self-relation, for Käsemann it is outward-directed other-relation. The body is the means and mode of communication and connection with other people in particular environmental and historical contexts: "corporeality is the nature of man in his need to participate in creatureliness and in his capacity for communication in the widest sense."[35] Both scholars emphasize the importance of the body, and both think that Paul has a notion of the individual. But Käsemann has a very different understanding of what that embodied self is for Paul.

In the first place, Käsemann thinks that Bultmann's understanding of the body as the capacity for self-relation tends toward a division between the "human person and its corporeality." Contrary to Bultmann's own holistic understanding of the body, the physicality of the body gets lost and separated from some idealized "true self" or "subject self." This separation is linked to a division between the person as the subject of his or her actions and the body

32. Ernst Käsemann, "On Paul's Anthropology," in *Perspectives on Paul*, trans. M. Kohl (Mifflintown, PA: Sigler, 1996 [1969]), 12.

33. Käsemann, "On Paul's Anthropology," 12.

34. For discussion of Paul's Christology in Phil 2 and the construction of the person, see chapter 5 below.

35. Käsemann, "On Paul's Anthropology," 21.

as the object of the self's actions. Käsemann, to the contrary, doubts that *sōma* always denotes the whole person rather than specifically the physical body, because he insists on the centrality of physical embodiment for Paul's thought: "for Paul all God's ways with his creation begin and end in corporeality," and such embodied existence necessarily means connection with the rest of the cosmos in particular, concrete, and historical ways.[36] To be a body is to be historically entwined with one's world.

Such continuity between the human body and its world has profound consequences for the notion of the individual. On the one hand, Käsemann does develop the importance of the individual in Paul, albeit not as innate or self-directing, but rather as given through the charismata of the Spirit: "Paul only applies the category of the individual to the believer. . . . For him man under the rule of sin could never be an 'individual' but was, as representative of his world, a victim of its powers. For him, the 'individual' is not the *premise* of an anthropological theory but the *result* of the grace which takes people into its service. It differentiates in the Christian community especially."[37] Note the priority of the divine gift that comes from the Giver and creates distinctive personal identity. It is the other-relation to God through "gift" and "call" that functions to constitute each person with a unique vocation, in differentiation from others.[38] Here personhood is thoroughly relational, given as a gift that generates distinctive personal identity, not as a general idealist or humanistic construct.[39]

On the other hand, "prior to and without Christ" there is no individual, if by "individual" is meant an autonomous, self-aware, and self-directing person. There is no freestanding self under the reign of sin in the realm of flesh. Shocking as this claim is, enfolded in it are two supporting observations: first, contrary to Bultmann's view that, as bodies, human beings have a capacity for self-knowledge, Käsemann reads Paul as saying that any such capacity is lost under sin. Our self-knowledge is distorted and partial at best. Second, therefore, contrary to Bultmann's emphasis on an innate human capacity for self-control and free decision, in Käsemann's view any such capacity is also, practically speaking, an illusion. Käsemann therefore criticizes Bultmann's language of self-determination: "It is revealing to use expressions which describe

---

36. Käsemann, "On Paul's Anthropology," 19, 20–21, 18.

37. Käsemann, "On Paul's Anthropology," 31; emphasis added.

38. Käsemann is reflecting on Paul's teaching about the charismata of the Spirit in 1 Cor 12, but Paul's depiction of his own unique apostolic call "through grace" in Gal 1:15–16 would also provide a case in point.

39. See further discussion in Käsemann, "On Paul's Anthropology," 2–4.

the self as being at least potentially one with itself, under its own control, at its own disposal. For it is precisely this that is never true of the creature."[40] Käsemann's pessimism about human self-knowledge and self-determination negates any definition of the person that assumes self-consciousness or self-control as constitutive of personhood. The paradoxical correlate of such pessimism, however, is a radical inclusiveness. It amounts to a rejection of "criterialism" about persons that would exclude some people and include others.[41] No one meets Bultmann's criterion of body as "self-relation"; everyone is cognitively impaired when it comes to the knowledge of God and self; everyone stands in abject need of God's grace; ultimately everyone is included in the gift of divine mercy.

The body is thus never a neutral entity; embedded in its environment, it is always constrained and shaped by the worlds to which it belongs.[42] For this reason, the body is contested territory in the battle between cosmic powers—on the one hand, the "flesh," and on the other, the "Spirit," which for Paul is always the Spirit of God. "The flesh" is both human existence in rebellion against God and a cosmic sphere of power where the demonic holds sway. Bultmann recognizes this dual usage of the term, but his philosophical focus on the individual does not leave him with a framework to make sense of it. To the contrary, says Käsemann, for Paul "anthropological terms" don't refer to the individual at all because "existence is always fundamentally conceived from the angle of the world to which one belongs."[43]

Implicit in this way of talking is a superficial similarity to the ancient idea of self as microcosm, and yet a profound difference from Stoic naturalism. In Käsemann's view it is essential to retain Paul's "metaphysical dualism" between cosmic powers opposed to God and the Spirit of God, rather than demythologizing such dualism in terms of the individual.[44] The split is fundamentally cosmic, not private, and it enters human experience through bodily enmeshment in the larger world. This notion of cosmic dualism is in some ways the mirror opposite of the Stoic worldview, in which a functional distinction between the body and the inner citadel operates apart from any notion of cosmic dualism. In both cases, some kind of dualism seems necessary to the notion of freedom, but it is located differently.

40. Käsemann, "On Paul's Anthropology," 24, 21.

41. See Timothy Chappell, "Knowledge of Persons," *European Journal for Philosophy of Religion* 5.4 (2013): 3–28.

42. Käsemann, "On Paul's Anthropology," 20.

43. Käsemann, "On Paul's Anthropology," 26.

44. Käsemann, "On Paul's Anthropology," 24.

Along the same lines, Käsemann rejects the notion of an essential self that remains constant over time and across bodily changes. There is no such constant, abiding self; rather, any such ideas of continuous identity are completely foreign to Paul's way of thinking. To the contrary, Käsemann locates the continuity of personal existence, and indeed of all history, in God rather than in human experience.[45] Divine continuity and human discontinuity mean that death and resurrection, not development or maturation, are the watchwords of Christian existence. The result is a distinctive picture of the self over time: the embodied individual finds his or her vital existence only in and through the gifts and calling given and exercised in the body of Christ, which are "new every morning" and not innate or gradually developing.

Both Bultmann and Käsemann saw themselves as doing historical critical interpretation of Paul's letters, and both also interpreted Paul's anthropology in light of urgent questions facing their time and place in twentieth-century Germany. For Bultmann those questions were framed in an existentialist framework and the necessity of resisting National Socialism, with its "submersion of the individual into *das Volk*."[46] Käsemann shared that context and that concern, but even more urgent for him was the pressing "apocalyptic" question, who owns the earth? Decades later, he bitterly reflected on the church's abandonment of history and of responsibility in the face of the Nazi challenge: "Who owns the earth? We have again been confronted with this problem. Did not the Nazis carry on their fight against us with the slogan: 'Heaven for sparrows and Christians, earth for us'?"[47] From his perspective, any interpretation of Paul's anthropology must engage with the question of belonging and lordship in the public sphere.

Epictetus and the Pauline Body

Despite their different projects and goals, there are striking similarities as well as differences between Martin's and Käsemann's depictions of the body in Paul

---

45. Käsemann, "On Paul's Anthropology," 8-10.

46. Wayne A. Meeks, "The Problem of Christian Living," in *Beyond Bultmann: Reckoning a New Testament Theology*, ed. Bruce W. Longenecker and Mikeal C. Parsons (Waco, TX: Baylor University Press, 2014), 214. See also Angela Standhartinger, "Bultmann's *Theology of the New Testament* in Context," in *Beyond Bultmann*, 237: "With the Pauline *hōs mē* ('as though not') from 1 Cor 7:29-31, [Bultmann] emphasized, however, the distinction between God and the world order and the distance that faith must maintain from the world."

47. Ernst Käsemann, *Jesus Means Freedom* (Philadelphia: Fortress, 1968), 134.

and in the ancient world. Both emphasize the corporeal nature of *sōma* and the continuity between the human body and the larger social body, and between microcosm and macrocosm. Both reject the idea of any essential, continuous self. But whereas Martin dismisses the idea of any distinction between natural and supernatural as anachronistic in the first century, Käsemann's stress on "anthropology as crystalized cosmology" assumes the existence of metaphysical cosmic powers that are distinct from the created order. And whereas Martin says there is no individual in the ancient world, including in Paul's thought, Käsemann insists quite strongly that Paul promoted the idea of the individual, albeit in a deeply counterintuitive, non-Cartesian way. That is, Käsemann finds in Paul the existence of unique selves, while simultaneously rejecting the ideas of autonomy, continuity, or a core self. Clearly a very distinctive notion of individual is in play here.

What happens when we juxtapose Epictetus's teaching with Bultmann's and Käsemann's different interpretations of the body in Paul? The parallels between Epictetus and Bultmann are many and intriguing. To begin with, Bultmann thinks of the body as primarily the mode of relationship with oneself; "body" denotes our capacity to look at ourselves. Similarly, like other Stoics, Epictetus insists on the innate priority of self-perception in all sensate beings. Again, like the Stoics, Bultmann rejects any dualism between an immaterial soul and the material body, as well as between a rational mind and an irrational part of the self. Yet, despite his holistic and unified account of the body, in effect Bultmann's construal of Pauline anthropology tends toward a functional dualism *within* the self, in a way that is similar to Epictetus's distinction between the self as observer and as object.

Furthermore, although Bultmann emphasizes the reality of God as supernatural and ontologically "other" in Paul's thought, to the degree that anthropology becomes the only way to know anything about God, his interpretative hermeneutic for twentieth-century "modern" readers is *functionally* naturalistic. In the effects of his methodology, he thus perhaps comes superficially close to the naturalism of Epictetus. I say superficially, because the Stoic concept of God as completely immanent in nature is fundamentally at odds with Bultmann's commitment to the radical otherness of God. According to Bultmann's notion of historical criticism, any direct divine causality must thus be excluded from any historical account. For Epictetus, divine causality is everywhere.

Recalling that Käsemann sees *sōma* as the means of connection with external realities, at least initially there may seem to be similarities with the Stoic idea of the self as participating in the cosmos. Similarly, Käsemann's picture of the body as connection bears similarities to Martin's discussion of the porosity and malleability of the body in ancient practice and thought. But for Käsemann the body as other-relation is always under orders from a distinctive "other" entity, whether that be sin as a power or God. Under orders, the body is a mode of belonging; such belonging is basic to the structure of the self.

The Interconnected, Participatory Body

By seeing Paul's view of the body as primarily a mode of relationship with external realities that also operate internal to the self, Käsemann shows affinities not only with the porous, malleable, and interconnected body of ancient practices but also with some second-person notions of the self in contemporary debates. Rather than starting with an a priori notion of the person as a self-contained individual in an embodied self-relation, he says that all human beings are embedded in and impinged upon by suprahuman realities, and that the individual exists only in and through the community of faith. It is not the "will to selfhood" that is the presupposition for communion, but exactly the reverse: communion is the presupposition for a self that is capable of self-knowledge and action—and even for believers in Christ, such capacities are always limited and under threat short of the final consummation. This is "relationalism about persons" in which "individuality presupposes relationality."

The Connected Body

Several voices thread through this chapter and find some surprising common ground: Paul; Epictetus; popular practices of the body in the ancient world, as explicated by Martin; Bultmann and Käsemann; and contemporary theorists. For Paul, *sōma* is affiliated either with flesh, sin, and death, or with Christ in mutual *koinōnia* with others who "belong" to Christ. To a degree this language accords with ancient practices of the porous, malleable, visible body that exists on a vulnerable continuum with the stuff of nature, embedded in the larger hierarchical social and cosmic "body." Similarly, Käsemann interprets the Pauline body as a corporeal, other-related mode of communication and connection. Such participatory models of embodied existence intersect with contemporary second-person theories of the body as intimately shaping the mind in a loop that extends out into the environment. What all these depictions have in common is the notion of interconnectedness and participation.

These different voices all also navigate the relationship between singular and corporate or participatory identity, as well as the correlative vulnerability of environmentally shaped bodily existence, albeit in different ways. The Stoics, as represented by Epictetus, believe that the divine reason permeates and orders all things for good, linking the innermost spark of rationality in the wise person with the Logos in everything that is. Yet they also teach the correct evaluation of impressions, so as to create an inner space of freedom detached from the vicissitudes and false impressions of the world. Similarly, for Bultmann the Pauline body as self-relation maintains a certain bounded neutrality and therefore freedom of agency in and of itself. It is vulnerable to outside powers, to be sure, which create an experience of division within the self. But nonetheless, as a body in self-relation, the person maintains a capacity for self-knowledge and self-determination in relation to these outside powers.

Käsemann, in contrast, sees in Paul's body language an emphasis on corporeal other-relation without exception or remainder. There is no possibility of existence outside such other-relation. The determining factor in whether such other-relation is for good or for ill depends on the relational partner. Apart from Christ, humanity is so enslaved and deluded by sin that there is no individual at all; agency is, as it were, swallowed up by the powers of sin and death. But in Christ individuals become "partisans" in God's liberating army, each living out a unique calling under God's lordship. Such connection does not, however, entail an end to the vulnerability that goes with understanding the body as connection and communication. It may mean, rather, the capacity to endure and even flourish in the midst of affliction.

As we have seen, second-person theorists speak of the self as a system of self-in-relation-to-another; the body immediately and physically enacts such other-relation from the very beginnings of life. Such interpersonal connection is essential for human flourishing, and at the same time it may have toxic effects on the development of persons in relationship.

In this chapter I have limned a brief outline of Paul's body language. In part 2 I look in more depth at Paul's letters: his understanding of sin as a lethal "relational partner" in Romans 7 and how that intersects with current work in cognitive and experiential psychology; the redemption of relational identity through Christ's assimilation to humanity's plight, in Philippians 2; and the constitution of a new system of self-in-relationship in Galatians, embedded and bodily enacted in the new relational matrix generated by belonging to Christ.

PART TWO

Participation and the Self

CHAPTER FOUR

Relationality Gone Bad

The Evacuation of the Self in Romans 7

> The combined operation of infant-in-relation-to-caregiver is a
> motive force in development, and it achieves wonderful things.
> When it does not exist, and the motive force is lacking, the whole
> of mental development is terribly compromised.
>
> —Peter Hobson, *The Cradle of Thought*

> I do not know (or understand) what I'm doing. For I do not do
> what I want, but I do what I hate. Now if I do what I do not want,
> I agree that the law is good. So then *I no longer am doing it, but sin
> dwelling in me,* that is . . . in my flesh. . . . Now if I do what I do not
> want, *I no longer am doing it, but sin dwelling in me.*
>
> —Paul, Epistle to the Romans

Few verses in Paul's letters have caused more consternation and received more
attention than Romans 7:7-25.[1] Revisiting them in the light of both ancient
and contemporary depictions of the embodied self sharpens their meaning
and casts them in a new light. My focus is limited to the construction of the
person assumed and disclosed here; this is an "I" inhabited and overtaken

---

1. In what follows I draw on two earlier essays: "The Shadow-Side of Intersubjective
Identity: Sin in Paul's Letter to the Romans," *European Journal for Philosophy of Religion* 5.4
(2013): 125-44, and "The 'Empire of Illusion': Sin, Evil, and Good News in Romans," in *Comfortable Words: Essays in Honor of Paul F. M. Zahl,* ed. John D. Koch and Todd H. W. Brewer
(Eugene, OR: Wipf & Stock, 2013), 3-21.

by a hostile colonizing power that causes it to act against its own desires and separates the results of its actions from its own intentions. Paul calls that hostile power sin, and he attributes agency to it by making it the subject of active verbs. The actions of this agent are tied in with both the flesh and the law in complex and confusing ways.

Situating the Argument

Paul's account of sin and human beings takes on a spiral structure in Romans 1–8, in which three repetitive, overlapping narratives progressively expand the cast of characters and then intensify the personal and emotional effects of Paul's rhetoric. The first account depicts sin as what humans do (1:18–5:12). Here human beings are the subjects of the verb "to sin" (*hamartanō*; 2:12; 3:23; 5:12; 6:15). Paul expands this sense of sin as human action through other verbs as well: people accomplish (*katergazomai*; 2:9), "do" (*poieō*; 3:8), and "practice" (*prassō*; 1:32; 2:1–3) evil. Such actions reflect the human situation, in which, as a result of primal idolatry, God has "handed over" human beings into the grip of destructive powers, including an "unreasoning mind" (*adokimon noun*) that corresponds to their failure to "acknowledge God" (*edokimasan ton theon*; 1:28). Such is Paul's initial pessimistic view of human beings as cognitively impaired and out of control, full of hatred and poisonous speech, and destroying one another (3:9–18).[2]

In the second account of sin and human beings, sin appears as an agent acting in human history (5:12–7:7).[3] Sin arrives on the scene, accompanied by death: "Sin came into the world through one man and death through sin, and so death spread to all human beings, *so that [eph' hō]* all sinned" (5:12).[4] Paul

2. See Stephen Westerholm, "Paul's Anthropological 'Pessimism' in Its Jewish Context," in *Divine and Human Agency in Paul and His Cultural Environment*, ed. John M. G. Barclay and Simon J. Gathercole (Edinburgh: T&T Clark, 2006), 71–98.

3. See in particular Martinus C. de Boer, "Paul's Mythologizing Program in Romans 5–8," in *Apocalyptic Paul: Cosmos and Anthropos in Romans 5–8*, ed. Beverly R. Gaventa (Waco, TX: Baylor University Press, 2013), 13–14: "In short, Paul personifies and thereby 'mythologizes' the notions of sin and death, which is to say, he talks about them as he elsewhere does about Satan . . . Paul's cosmological language about Sin and Death as malevolent powers represents an attempt to account for anthropological realities and experiences."

4. For this translation, see Robert Jewett, *Romans*, Hermeneia (Minneapolis: Fortress, 2007), 375–76. De Boer translates *eph' hō* as "since" (all sinned) but points out that all sinned because all were under the power of sin (Rom 3:9): sin and death are twin realities ("Paul's Mythologizing Program," 14).

blames this global sinning and death on the primal transgression of Adam, the universal progenitor (5:14, 18, 19, 21), through whom all humanity now lives under the reign of death (5:14, 17) and sin (5:21). In Käsemann's striking expression, "Every person after Adam is entangled in the fate of the protoplast."[5] Henceforth sin rampages through human existence, holding humanity captive. Expanding exponentially (5:20), it reigns in death (5:21) and in mortal bodies (6:12), using human bodily members as weapons of wickedness (*hopla*; 6:13) and repaying its soldiers with death (6:23). Finally, it conscripts God's good law as a military platform (*aphormē*) for its lethal attacks on human beings, using the law to deceive and to kill (7:11).

Within this situation human actors are not simply passive victims, but rather are both captive and complicit. Paul paints himself and his auditors in a progressively damning picture: "we" were weak, sinners, and enemies of God (Rom 5:6, 8, 10). Shifting to the third person, he includes all human beings in the category of those who trespass as Adam did (5:15-20): "Through one man's disobedience the many were made sinners" (5:19). To be sure, this amplification of sin's destructive power and humanity's collusion with it serves primarily to magnify the even greater life-giving power of God's grace in Christ, the one man who undoes the lethal effects of Adam: where sin increased, grace increased even more (5:20). Paul's logic throughout this section depends on connections between all human beings over space and time, in a thoroughly participatory and interconnected web of relation. It is cosmically anthropological, in that both Adam and Christ are agents whose actions have universal consequences for all human agents. Within Cartesian notions of the self as independent, isolated, and autonomous, his logic makes no sense. But Paul's cosmos is more like the world according to the "butterfly effect," in which one seemingly small action changes the course of events on a global scale.

The passage at hand belongs to Paul's third account of sin and human beings in Romans 7:7-25. It contains a complex answer to the question, "What then shall we say? That the law is sin?" Paul's immediate answer is "By no means [*mē genoito*]!" As many commentators note, Paul goes on to distinguish carefully between the law and sin; in the process, however, he also paints a picture of sin's lethal and deceptive use of the law, so that "the very commandment which was for life was found to be death to me [*heurethē moi hē entolē hē eis zōēn hautē eis thanaton*]."

Romans 7:7-25 is marked by two significant grammatical shifts: from

---

5. Ernst Käsemann, *Commentary on Romans*, trans. G. W. Bromiley (Grand Rapids: Eerdmans, 1980), 197.

the first person plural to the first person singular at 7:7, and from the past tense to the present tense at 7:14. Both of these dramatic characteristics have occasioned endless debate over seemingly intractable problems concerning the identity of the speaker and the function of the passage. Is Paul depicting the experience of Jews who are faithful to the law, or of all humanity after Adam's fall?[6] Is this a description of life under the law apart from Christ, or a warning against going under the law, whether for Jewish or Gentile believers, or simply a powerful defense of the law's goodness? Or does the "I" describe Paul's own experience, and if so, is this a dramatization of Paul's experience under the law prior to faith, or a description of his present experience "in Christ"? In either case, does Paul use his own experience as a paradigm for his auditors? Or is the "I" purely fictive, for rhetorical effect? And so forth.

It is not the purpose of this chapter to solve all of these problems, but rather to focus on the depiction of the self as disclosed in Paul's language. I begin by noting that the first-personal "I" is not precisely singular, or at least its singularity is decidedly odd. To rephrase my earlier question: When someone says, "If I do what I do not want, it is no longer I doing it but sin dwelling in me," who is doing the action? Despite Paul's own language, the dominant answer among commentators is that the individual ego is doing the action. This answer takes many forms. One argument rings the changes on a view of the ego as isolated, discrete, and self-contained, and therefore as the source and locus of evil. This interpretation serves to exonerate the law from any charge that it operates as a source of evil. To give one example, Mark Seifrid says,

6. Käsemann wants to have it both ways, beginning with "the pious Jew" but extending to "every existence in the wake of Adam" (*Romans*, 203–5). For the view that Paul has all of Adamic humanity in mind, see Paul W. Meyer, "The Worm at the Core of the Apple: Exegetical Reflections on Romans 7," in *The Word in This World*, ed. Paul W. Meyer and John T. Carroll (Louisville: Westminster John Knox, 2004), 57–77. See also C. E. B. Cranfield, who thinks that Paul consciously has Gen 1–3 in mind and also draws on his own experience: "We may recognize Paul's use of the first person singular here as an example of the general use of the first person singular; but at the same time we shall probably be right to assume that his choice of this form of speech is, in the present case, due not merely to a desire for rhetorical vividness but also to his deep sense of personal involvement" (*Commentary on Romans*, vol. 1, International Critical Commentary [London: T&T Clark, 1975], 343–44); Cranfield thinks Paul is describing Christian experience. This is a minority view in current scholarship. The dominant view since W. G. Kümmel is that the "I" depicts the situation of humanity under the law, seen from the viewpoint of faith. Jewett, however, sees in 7:7–25 a depiction of Paul's past personal experience (*Romans*, 450–56). E. P. Sanders concludes that the "I" in 7:9–13 is "Adam, speaking on behalf of humanity," and in 7:14–25 it is "the human without Christ, who is depicted as living in total depravity" (*Paul: The Apostle's Life, Letters, and Thought* [Minneapolis: Fortress, 2015], 650, 656).

"By ascribing radical evil to the human being Paul relieves his Gospel of the charge that it betrays the goodness of *Torah.*"[7] According to this widespread view, the main purpose of Paul's rhetoric is exoneration of the law through the ascription of sin solely to the human agent. But *does* Paul ascribe radical evil to the individual human being? If this were the case, how can one make sense of Paul's depiction of sin as an agent, and his denial of a free range of activity to the "I" that laments doing actions it "hates"?

A second common solution is to read the self as divided against itself; there is a breakdown in the self as self-relation. We recall Bultmann's careful depiction of the experience of "losing one's grip on oneself," such that Paul's language sounds dualistic; according to Bultmann, Paul is depicting the human experience of an "inner cleft" that is constitutive of the person: "man is 'of the flesh' precisely because he is characterized by the split between willing and doing. . . . Just as his willing and doing are not distributed between two subjects—say, a better self and his lower impulses—but rather are both realized by the same I, so also are 'flesh' and 'mind' (or the 'inner man') not two constituent elements out of which he is put together. Man *is* the split."[8] The split, that is, is not between "flesh" and "mind," but rather between the whole self in its willing and in its doing. Or as Robert Jewett puts it, "Sin causes an objective kind of contradiction between willing and achieving the good."[9]

There is indeed an "objective kind of contradiction" between what the speaker desires and what he or she accomplishes; the question is whether this contradiction originates in the ego. Alternatively, we can take seriously the way Paul drives a wedge between the self that seeks the good and sin as an alien occupying power. Käsemann goes so far as to speak here of demonic possession: "Paul, however, really means that the I who speaks here is demonically enslaved and therefore did not will or grasp the effect of his action."[10] What is clear is that a conflicted dyadic agency that Paul names "I-yet-not-I-but-sin-dwelling-in-me" performs actions previously ascribed simply to human beings, using the same interchangeable active verbs: doing (*poieō*), practicing (*prassō*), and accomplishing (*katergazomai*) evil (7:15–21; cf. 1:32; 2:1–3, 9; 3:8). In this self-in-relation-to-sin, the agency of sin overrides the wishes of the self, so that Paul

---

7. Mark A. Seifrid, "The Subject of Romans 7:14–25," *Novum Testamentum* 34.4 (1992): 325.

8. Rudolf Bultmann, "Römer 7 und die Anthropologie des Paulus," in *Imago Dei: Festschrift für Gustav Krüger*, ed. H. Bornkamm (Giessen: Alfred Töpelmann, 1932), 53–62; Eng. "Romans 7 and the Anthropology of Paul," in *Existence and Faith: Shorter Writings of Rudolf Bultmann*, trans. Schubert Ogden (New York: Meridian Books, 1960), 151.

9. Jewett, *Romans*, 467.

10. Käsemann, *Commentary on Romans*, 204.

repeats verbatim, "It is not I bringing it to pass, but sin dwelling in me" (7:17). He describes an excruciating interaction in which one partner overpowers the other, who says, "I thought I was acting, but really it was sin acting in me."

The experience Paul describes precisely lacks what some philosophers see as essential for a sense of personal agency: "a congruence between anticipated outcome and actual outcome."[11] Rather, within Paul's account of the competing agencies of self and sin, sin confiscates the person's desire for the good for its own lethal purposes.[12] Nonetheless, there is not a complete erasure of the self, for it continues to "know" (7:18), to "want" (7:15, 16, 19, 20), to "find" (7:21), to "see another law at work in my members" (7:23), and even to "delight in the law of God in my inmost self" (7:22). The person here is described as occupied territory, his subjectivity colonized by an oppressive foreign power, his members mobilized for actions contrary to his deepest wants, but yet he remains cognizant of his loss of freedom. He may experience this combination of self-awareness and crippled capacity as inner division, but it is the internalization of sin's lethal embrace.

What, then, is Paul's purpose in dramatizing the plight of this (as yet unidentified) "I"? In my view, Leander Keck rightly identified the function of this difficult text some years ago, when he wrote that "what makes Romans tick is the inner logic of having to show how the gospel deals with the human condition on three ever deeper levels, each understood as a dimension of the Adamic condition: the self's skewed relationship to God in which the norm (law) is the accuser, the self in sin's domain where death rules before Moses arrived only to exacerbate the situation by specifying transgression, the self victimized by sin as a resident power stronger than the law."[13] That is, Paul's dramatic enactment of the plight of the self in the grip of sin and sin's use of the law is not in the first instance a defense of the law, but rather a preparation for the announcement of the good news in the depths of human despair. As Paul Meyer saw, this despair is not simply that the human being is frustrated in trying to keep the law, but that sin can twist even the doing of the commandment to lethal ends.[14]

---

11. Elisabeth Pacherie, "The Phenomenology of Joint Action: Self-Agency versus Joint Agency," in *Joint Attention: New Developments in Psychology, Philosophy of Mind, and Social Neuroscience,* ed. Axel Seemann (Cambridge, MA: MIT Press, 2011), 379.

12. Such conscription is parallel to the way in which sin conscripts the law, using it as a basis from which to deceive and kill human beings (Rom 7:11).

13. Leander E. Keck, "What Makes Romans Tick?," in *Pauline Theology,* vol. 3, *Romans,* ed. David M. Hay and E. Elizabeth Johnson (Minneapolis: Fortress, 1995), 26.

14. Meyer, "Worm at the Core of the Apple," 62–97; repr. in Meyer and Carroll, *The Word*

Paul does not speak in the past tense in Romans 7:14–25, but in the present. In doing so, he depicts a present situation or condition; I suggest that his expression of this present condition is experiential, not an ontological description mapped on a linear timeline.[15] Paul invites his audience into the experience of a shared interpersonal condition through the first person plural "we know" (7:14), progressing to the singular "I do not know" (7:15) and "I know" (7:18). Each use of the first person invites his auditors to say "I" along with the speaker.[16] As Beverly Gaventa puts it, "The 'I' has the potential to shape its hearers, so that they join with that 'I' in crying out for deliverance from the enslaving power of sin."[17] Caught up in the experience of the speaker who cries out, "Who will deliver me from this body of death?" Paul's listeners and current readers are ready to hear anew, "There is no condemnation for those who are in Christ Jesus. For the law of the Spirit of life in Christ Jesus has set you [*se*, sing.] free from the law of sin and death" (8:1–2).[18] That is, the singular "I" of Romans 7 hears the news of liberation from condemnation, death, and the power of sin, personally addressed to him or her as a singular "you." As Stanley Stowers puts it, "The character's speech ends when Paul addresses him in words of encouragement."[19]

This is a paraenetic appeal, not an ontological argument, and it builds on the preceding chapter by rephrasing and intensifying both the human dilemma and the divine deliverance. In Romans 6:1–14 Paul emphatically reassures his auditors that through baptism they have died with Christ and are no longer enslaved to sin (vv. 6–7), and that sin will not reign over them because they

in *This World*, 57–77. In Paul's own self-depiction in Phil 3:6, he was blameless with regard to righteousness through the law and simultaneously a persecutor of the church. It seems possible that in this respect his personal experience might well inform his claim that sin used the law to deceive and kill (Rom 7:11), without arguing for a full-blown autobiographical narrative.

15. See Seifrid, "Subject of Romans 7:14–25," 321–22.

16. "The whole point of Paul's account seems to lie in making his readers themselves experience the experiences of the self that he is recounting" (Troels Engberg-Pedersen, *Cosmology and Self in the Apostle Paul: The Material Spirit* [Oxford: Oxford University Press, 2010], 168).

17. Beverly R. Gaventa, "The Shape of the 'I': The Psalter, the Gospel, and the Speaker in Romans 7," in Gaventa, *Apocalyptic Paul*, 78.

18. *Se* is supported by both Alexandrian and Western witnesses—א B F G 1506* 1739* it[ar b] sy[p] Tertullian Ambrosiaster. Bruce M. Metzger comments: "It is much more difficult to choose between *me* and *se*. The latter, as the more difficult reading, is more likely to have been replaced by the former (which harmonizes better with the argument in chap. 7) than vice versa" (*A Textual Commentary on the Greek New Testament*, 2nd ed. [Stuttgart: German Bible Society, 1994], 456).

19. Stanley K. Stowers, *A Rereading of Romans: Justice, Jews, and Gentiles* (New Haven: Yale University Press, 1994), 282.

are not under law but under grace (v. 14). Why, then, the pathos-filled per-formance of the plight of the self in the grip of indwelling sin, in 7:14–25? Why does Paul keep retelling the story of sin and redemption, moving from a third-person account, to a second-person-plural address, to a first-person per-formance that culminates in a second-person-singular address? I suggest that the repetition serves to name the complexities of human experience caught between the dominion of sin and the reign of grace. Despite Paul's cosmic claims regarding the distinctions between the self-in-relation-to-sin and the self-in-relation-to-Christ, in *felt experience* and daily life the sequence from the first to the second is not so clear-cut.[20] The gap between Paul's cosmic claims and the behavior of his converts is already evident in the imperatives in the preceding chapter (6:11–13): "Let not sin therefore reign in your mortal bodies, to make you obey their passions. Do not yield your members to sin as instruments of unrighteousness, but yield yourselves to God as those who have been brought from death to life, and your members to God as instruments of righteousness." Paul would not need to give the Roman Christians this instruc-tion if in fact they were experientially and practically, as well as ontologically, free from sin. The strong implication is that their behavior and experience have not caught up with the reality of their new life in Christ.

So although Paul is sure that sin has been dealt a final blow by the death and resurrection of Christ (8:3), in Romans 7:7–25 he shifts into first-person singular, employing "speech-in-character" (*prosōpopoeia*) to enlist his listeners existentially in the experience he depicts so vividly.[21] Through profoundly af-fective language the speaker expresses what Paul earlier narrated as the cosmic and corporate reality of human bondage to sin. That is, the "I" assimilates to the affective stance of the listener who *experiences* such bondage, thereby in-viting him or her into a responsive identification with the speaker.[22] I suggest that such mutual identification has the capacity to "move" the listener moti-vationally and emotionally, as well as cognitively. The speaker identifies with the hearer, the hearer identifies with the speaker, and together they hear Paul's words of affirmation: "There is no condemnation for those who are in Christ Jesus. . . . The law of the Spirit of life in Christ Jesus has set *you* free from the law of sin and death" (8:1–2).

20. See the perceptive comments of Simeon Zahl, "The Drama of Agency: Affective Au-gustinianism and Galatians," in *Galatians and Christian Theology: Justification, the Gospel, and Ethics in Paul's Letter*, ed. Mark W. Elliott et al. (Grand Rapids: Baker Academic, 2014), 335–52.
21. Stowers, *Rereading of Romans*, 20.
22. Such a move is parallel to Christ's mimetic assimilation to the condition of human-ity in bondage and subject to death, in Phil 2:6–11; see further discussion in chapter 5 below.

This mutual engagement mirrors and enacts God's second-person involvement with humanity. Immediately after announcing liberation from sin, Paul grounds that liberation in God's act of sending "his own Son in the likeness [*en homoiōmati*] of the flesh of sin, and for sin" (8:3). God in Christ moved into the human condition, assimilated to it in bodily form, and is attuned to it. The logic of Paul's appeal to the Romans in 8:1–4 proceeds from this embodied divine participation, which in turn invites and instigates a responsive second-person assimilation to Christ.

But this divine movement and participation does not take place in a vacuum. Rather, it is a movement into a relational matrix dominated by sin and death. Insofar as human beings are embodied and embedded creatures, they are enmeshed in and constituted by that matrix. As such, they are not free agents, certainly not autonomous, and not capable of freeing themselves. They require a liberating alliance with a noncompetitive and transcendent Other, who is "no part of the system of interacting and negotiating speakers in the world."[23]

A First-Person Analysis: The View
from Epictetus and Engberg-Pedersen

Paul's depiction of the "I" in bondage to a hostile power and delivered by another external power that acts internally could not be further from the wise man of Stoic teaching. Indeed, the existence of such a hostile power is alien to the Stoic cosmos, which, despite the hardships of individuals, is seen as providentially ordered—indeed, the best of all possible worlds. Epictetus's basic optimism strikes a very different chord from the voice of the "I" in Romans 7. Epictetus might at most say that the speaker in Romans 7 is under the sway of "false impressions," but the evaluation of impressions is in the control of the wise person. Perhaps he could say that the alliance of the Stoic teacher with the pupil as a kind of coach facilitates such correct judgment, so that, in a sense, the inner citadel is not "breached." But there are fundamentally different underlying cosmologies operative in Epictetus and in Paul.[24] As Paul narrates

23. Rowan Williams, *Lost Icons: Reflections on Cultural Bereavement* (London: Continuum, 2003), 196.

24. For discussion of this issue in *Cosmology and Self*, see the review by John M. G. Barclay, "Stoic Physics and the Christ Event: A Review of Troels Engberg-Pedersen, *Cosmology and Self in the Apostle Paul: The Material Spirit*," *Journal for the Study of the New Testament* 33.4 (2011): 412: "For the Stoics, God (or 'Reason' or 'Nature') is fully immanent within the

"sin" here, it has an active, deceptive, and lethal agency of its own, exercising power over human agency and the outcomes of human actions.

Remarkably, in his analysis of Romans 7–8 Engberg-Pedersen ignores this suprahuman and cosmic aspect of Paul's depiction of sin.[25] Bypassing sin's role as the subject of active verbs, Engberg-Pedersen instead narrates the problem as merely occasional transgressions of the law, as if such periodic lapses were the issue concerning Paul. The experience of the self is, in Engberg-Pedersen's analysis, not one of bondage to an outside power but rather of an inner split between competing desires. The resulting picture of the structured self falls in line with Bultmann's picture of the body as the human capacity to be in relationship to itself: there is an "I" that acts out of control, an "I" that should have been in control, and an "I" that watches itself.[26] All of these "I"s need to be brought into a correct self-relation; indeed, that is precisely what the "watching" "I" wants to do, to "harmonize" the other selves, as it were.

Engberg-Pedersen intends his account of the experience Paul depicts in Romans 7 to be amenable to a Stoic such as Epictetus, and along the way, to us moderns as well. It describes an experience of the self in self-relation experienced as inner division, rather than the self as constituted via its participation in a larger, personalized, and death-dealing reality that holds it in bondage. In Stoic terms, what Paul enacts might be construed as the plight of one whose inner citadel has been breached. The correct response to such a breach would be through a recovery of the true self through *proairesis*, or the exercise of right judgments. As Engberg-Pedersen observes, for Epictetus such enactment of right judgment is "entirely 'up to us,' " giving Epictetus a distinctive focus "on the human freedom of mind which translates directly into the notion of individual mastery and power." *Proairesis* would be a way of "getting a grip on oneself" and thereby gaining freedom. Engberg-Pedersen applies this Stoic conception to Paul through the conduit of cognition, which

---

cosmos, guaranteeing its order and cohesion, and is distinguishable from the rest of the cosmos in quantity (the concentration of refined fire) but not quality (117–19). In contrast, Paul seems committed to the transcendence of God in a form that is not necessarily the transcendence of the 'immaterial' over the 'material', but represents a qualitative difference nonetheless, such that it is impossible to place God at one end of the spectrum of 'being.' "

25. Engberg-Pedersen, *Cosmology and Self*, 164–69. This interpretation is in line with Engberg-Pedersen's project of making Paul's thought accessible to "modern" thinkers who, in his view, cannot possibly accept the idea of supernatural cosmic powers.

26. Engberg-Pedersen, *Cosmology and Self*, 166. But where does Paul speak of two competing desires? The "I" wants only the good; it is "sin" that intrudes between that desire and its outcome.

in turn comes through the presence of the Spirit (*pneuma*). In brief, "Believers are free because they themselves understand—through the physical influx of the cognitive *pneuma*—that in the world as a whole, including the present world that is animated by evil powers, the ultimate power is God's as is shown by his acts, including the Christ event. The freedom of believers therefore is a freedom of understanding." This is a Stoic view of freedom; "the idea itself that cognition gives freedom is central to Stoicism."[27] Thus when Engberg-Pedersen interprets Romans 7, he argues that Paul's paraenesis actually transmits his *pneuma* to his auditors in order to strengthen their habitus: "It seems, therefore, that what we are witnessing in this passage is precisely a case of pneumatic transmission by Paul of *his own pneuma* through the medium of experiential language."[28]

The textual support for such a claim is thin; I note only that, when Paul cries out, "Who will deliver me from this body of death?" his answer does not come through an inward turn, nor even in the first instance through reference to the Spirit, but through God's sending of the Son into the realm of sin and death—indeed, in the likeness of "the flesh of sin." The "sending language" implies that the origin of this divine-human rescue operation lies outside of the natural order (8:3; see also Phil 2:7-11; Gal 4:4-6), from a God who is qualitatively other. Paul's cosmos is not Stoic, precisely because he is "committed to the transcendence of God."[29] Thus Paul has a very different understanding of the problem and the solution: the person is constituted in relationship to lethal, albeit ultimately transient powers and can be freed from them only by the action of a God who is both independent of the deceiving, deadly, and global power of sin, and yet intimately involved with corporeal human existence.

Second-Person Analyses: Two Models

Examples from both the ancient and contemporary worlds provide analogies for the way in which Paul talks about sin as an alien and yet invasive force that

27. Engberg-Pedersen, *Cosmology and Self*, 112-13, 138.

28. Engberg-Pedersen, *Cosmology and Self*, 168; emphasis added. Engberg-Pedersen needs to refer all the way back to Rom 1:11 to justify this interpretation. He recognizes the weakness of the argument but nonetheless says, "I have a strong sense that exactly here we are extremely close to Paul's own understanding of what is going on in this text. If he were present, he would have nodded" (168-69)! On Engberg-Pedersen's view that Paul transmits his material spirit to his auditors, see Barclay, "Stoic Physics and the Christ Event," 409.

29. Barclay, "Stoic Physics and the Christ Event," 412.

enslaves the person. The first comes from ancient medicine; the second, from contemporary theories in psychology.

Pollution and Invasion

As discussed in the previous chapter, Stoicism is not the only model on offer in the first century, and Epictetus's optimism about human resistance to environmental dangers is not the only or even the prevailing experience. Martin's discussion of the body as "of a piece with its environment" leads into the vulnerability of the body to its surroundings. Martin extensively investigates two models of disease in the ancient world: as an imbalance of the elements that make up the body, or as pollution.[30] He suggests further that the first model, that of imbalance, would be more characteristic of the upper classes, those with social capital and power, whereas anxiety about pollution would characterize those in more vulnerable and powerless positions on the social scale. For both models, disease affects not only individual physical bodies but also corporate social bodies; the two kinds of bodies cannot be separated, and their relative health or illness is intertwined. Such mingling of personal and public corporeal health goes hand in glove with the body's character as participatory and permeable. For those in relatively secure positions, perhaps such participatory existence is not threatening, but for others it is: "For both etiologies, the body is continually pervaded by cosmic forces and is even constituted by those forces; it is a vacillating moment in an energy field. For those convinced by the logic of balance, this is not necessarily bad: the body is simply a microcosm of the balanced universe and is naturally constituted of the same substances. Others perceive the penetrability of the body as threatening, however, necessitating protection against invasion, manipulation, and disintegration." In his letters to the Corinthians, Martin argues, Paul embraces the "invasion etiology" of disease, which "evinces a social position of helplessness in the face of outside powers."[31]

Martin discusses this "invasion etiology" in his interpretation of Paul's instructions about food, sex, and desire in 1 Corinthians 5–11. Romans 7:14–25 is not in view, and there is no suggestion that Paul views sin as a kind of

---

30. Dale Martin, *The Corinthian Body* (New Haven: Yale University Press, 1995), 139–62. Note how Engberg-Pedersen's Stoic depiction of the problem and solution in Rom 7:14–25 fits with Martin's depiction of the imbalance model of disease; the elements of the self are out of balance and need to be brought back into a correct mutual relation so that there is an inner harmony. Engberg-Pedersen's view leaves no room for an "invasion model" of disease—or of sin.

31. Martin, *Corinthian Body*, 153, 161, 160.

disease. Nonetheless, the discussion of *sarx* is instructive: "Human beings are flesh insofar as they partake of the fleshiness that is part of all present humanity," and at the same time, "flesh" is an "anthropomorphic or hypostatized" cosmic power.[32] Human beings unavoidably participate in the realm of flesh, which means also being caught in and subject to a power that is hostile to God. This usage is parallel to the way in which Paul talks about sin and flesh in Romans 7:14: "I am fleshly, sold under sin [*egō de sarkinos eimi pepramenos hypo tēn hamartian*]." Sin here is depicted as something that takes ownership of the ego through its fleshly existence. Or to reprise the "invasion etiology," the porous fleshly body, understood both as individual and as communal corporeal existence, is taken over by sin. Such an anthropological model is contrary to the picture of the self watching its different "selves" and attempting to reconcile them. There is no freestanding self capable of watching itself; it is already invaded by a personified power that radically compromises its agency.

Toxic Relational Systems

As noted in contemporary studies, infants mimetically interact from birth with their caregivers. That immediate interpersonal play awakens the infant's awareness, including an awareness of itself as the object of the parent's gaze.[33] The attitudes, actions, and gaze of the parent therefore have profound power in the constitution of the self of the infant. When parents basically love and attend appropriately to their infants, the infants flourish. But when, for whatever reason—and there are many—parents do not or cannot attend appropriately to their children, when their intersubjective engagement with the child is disturbed, insufficient, or destructive, the agency and cognition of the child must also be affected. For example, what happens when the parental gaze toward the infant is a blank stare that ignores the child's increasingly frantic bids for attention?[34] And how will that child in turn interact with others?

One answer is that children internalize and later replay such toxic relationships in a variety of ways. Peter Hobson discusses the internalization of patterns of relationship by citing Freud's advice concerning severely depressed patients:

32. Martin, *Corinthian Body*, 173.

33. See Vasudevi Reddy, "A Gaze at Grips with Me," in Seemann, *Joint Attention*, 138.

34. See, e.g., the studies by Ed Tronick of such parent-child interaction, in Lauren B. Adamson and Janet E. Frick, "The Still Face: A History of a Shared Experimental Paradigm," *Infancy* 4.4 (2003): 451–73.

Freud concluded that, although one seems to be listening to a single, individual patient expressing his woes, in effect one is witnessing a relationship. An *internal* relationship. And an unpleasant relationship at that. There is one part of the patient who cruelly accuses and torments another part of the patient. . . . The patient is the perpetrator as well as the victim of the horrible onslaught. Freud went further than this: he also suggested how this relationship becomes installed in the personality. It has been internalized from outside.[35]

Similarly, Paul narrates sin as both external and internal, and as both environmental and agential: human beings are "in sin" and "under sin" as a kind of relational environment, yet also indwelt by sin personified as an agent acting in and through the self. For this reason, the self-in-relation-to-sin does not fully know its own actions; it does not understand what it is doing, yet it simultaneously retains some awareness of its predicament.

The effects of such an internalized relationship might be traced out in a multitude of directions. In Paul's account, when sin increases, the capacity for effective personal action decreases. Insofar as he depicts sin as a toxic environmental matrix, the self as a system of "body-environment-intersubjectivity" is radically compromised; insofar as he personifies Sin as an agent, sin and the self are locked in a competitive embrace, and sin has the upper hand. Drawing on the language of current theorists, we might metaphorically call this embrace a distorted primary intersubjectivity. To flesh out this idea, it is helpful to draw on the wisdom and experience of psychoanalyst Dorothy Martyn. After describing the violent outbreaks of a child with whom she was working, Martyn asks:

> What is wrong with her? We can name the problem, clinically, as a "severe behavior disorder" or an "impulse neurosis," but the names do not tell us very much. . . . The etiology of the difficulty is a relational matter. For a variety of reasons the child was deprived in early infancy of what D. W. Winnicott calls "good-enough mothering," and virtually all fathering. . . . It is of course tempting to blame the mother and father, as both professionals and non-professionals, at some level, are prone to do. But if one spends a bit of time with the mother, in an attitude of listening, it becomes quickly manifest that the mother did not willfully deprive her child; the difficulty lay in the fact that she, too, was deprived.

35. Peter Hobson, *The Cradle of Thought: Exploring the Origins of Thinking* (Oxford: Oxford University Press, 2004), 162–63.

Martyn moves from this description to a reflection on Romans 5:12, "Death spread to all because all sinned": "We are caught in an infinite series of mirrors in which repetition of man's error is inevitable because internalization of one's relational matrix is axiomatic."[36] This matter of an "internalized relational matrix" links the comments of Hobson and Martyn and suggests a second-person conceptual framework for reading Paul's depiction of the self as "sold under sin" in Romans 7:14.

How, then, might such a distorted primary intersubjectivity affect other relational engagements? In a detailed and moving account of a play session between a child and a mother with borderline personality disorder, Hobson describes the gradual disintegration in their interaction. It began with competition: "The interchange began with the infant leaning across to take a carriage that was just within reach. The mother held on to the carriage so that the child could not take it, took up a figure herself, and said, 'Put the man in the train,' while performing this action herself." Things went from bad to worse; at one point the mother tugged at the carriage while the child pulled it away. The mother immediately turned her attention to another carriage rather than to her child. She attempted unsuccessfully to catch her child's attention, and the infant attempted to get the mother's attention, also unsuccessfully. Toward the end of the session, "The infant had managed to put her figure in her carriage, and for a brief instant she looked up to her mother, but they did not smile at each other."[37] In the subtleties of Hobson's detailed observation, it seems clear that both mother and child want to interact, but something intrudes between that desire and their actions. Their interaction displays the disconnect between intended and actual outcomes that characterizes Paul's depiction of sin.

I am not suggesting that this troubled mother is a personification of sin in any agential form, including intentional cruelty. Rather, Paul's depiction of sin's power, along with his distinction between what the self wants and what sin accomplishes, provides a way to name the interpersonal difficulties between this mother and her child without demonizing the mother. Their patterns of interaction display analogies with Paul's depiction of sin as a debilitating relational system in which both mother and child are caught. Their play does not take place in a vacuum. Rather, the mother herself is shaped by other internalized relationships; in addition, both she and her child are

36. Dorothy W. Martyn, "A Child and Adam: A Parable of the Two Ages," in *Apocalyptic and the New Testament: Essays in Honor of J. Louis Martyn*, ed. Joel Marcus and Marion L. Soards, JSNT Supp series 24 (Sheffield: JSOT, 1989), 321-22.

37. Hobson, *Cradle of Thought*, 130, 131.

embedded in larger complex social realities. In this case, Hobson describes the disjointed thinking and unresolved past traumas of the mother with borderline personality disorder, correlating her history with her inability to engage with her child.

Martin's account of the "invasion" model of disease in some ancient theories of medicine showcases the vulnerability of porous bodies to toxic external forces. Hobson's and Martyn's stories serve as parables of the way in which personified Sin co-opts and lays claims to the self through enmeshment in toxic relationships: sin's power increases, and the self's agency decreases. There are hints that the woman in this account may lose all differentiation between "the sin that dwells in me" and her own desires. Her own wants become opaque to her conscious awareness; she becomes subject to drives that she does not understand, and any help for her will include learning to distinguish between those drives and her own personhood.

Conclusion

In Romans 7:14–25 Paul enacts the experience of a person who unwillingly participates in a larger cosmos with hostile powers. That participation is corporeal and constitutive of the self: the "I" is "fleshly" and sold under sin, thereby shaped in its totality in relation to that dominating and indwelling power. The resulting intersubjective "I" cannot be partitioned anthropologically; rather, it participates in and is temporally constituted in relationship to cosmic powers. For Paul, there is no inner sanctum and no *proairesis* that can resist and stand outside or act upon these powers.

I have offered two conceptual analogies for framing Paul's picture of the self in relationship to sin: Martin's discussion of the "invasion etiology" model of disease as pollution, and "psychological" models drawn from contemporary therapeutic work. In fact, in contemporary science as in ancient theories of disease, these physiological and psychological models are not separable. We noted earlier that in Hellenistic conceptions, what we might call "psychological" issues are understood in "physiological" terms, and vice versa. Increasingly the same is the case today, as the body's effects on the mind and the mind's effects on the body are seen to be inseparable.[38]

---

38. For a classic exploration of this connection and divide in modern psychiatry, see T. M. Luhrmann, *Of Two Minds: An Anthropologist Looks at American Psychiatry* (New York: Vintage, 2001).

The problem remains. If the body is porous, participatory, and entangled in its social and physical matrix, then the self is vulnerable to toxic environments. How, then, to deal with this situation? The solution cannot be simply a change in self-relation or self-understanding. Insofar as the "system" that is the self is bigger than the individual, then no merely individual solutions will do. The system itself needs transformation. In the ancient world, one might try to control and limit the permeability of the social body, as Martin describes it, or to set boundaries around the inner citadel of one's capacity for correct judgment, as Epictetus taught. In the modern world, there are all kinds of attempts to protect vulnerable human beings, from face masks to hand sanitizers to walls along borders.

All such attempts are secondary to Paul's vision of the person; his diagnosis and analysis are global and radical, exempting no one from the deadly powers of sin and death. If the self is structured in other-relationship, then its liberation and health require a radically new relational matrix.[39] Paul finds that new relationship in Christ's mimetic assimilation to the situation of Adamic humanity to the point of crucifixion, and his subsequent victory over condemnation and death. Several key texts announce this divine rescue operation, beginning with Romans 8:3, as discussed above. This is what Luther called "the fortunate exchange," in which Christ takes on humanity's plight and overcomes it so that human beings may be joined with Christ through the Spirit, in a reciprocally mimetic transformation.[40] That divine-human interaction is fully displayed in the drama of Philippians 2:5–13 through the divine-human intersubjective agency of Christ himself and through Christ's mimetic assimilation to the stance of the other—that is, of all humanity in the realm of the flesh and under the power of sin and death.

---

39. Given such a radical diagnosis, however, Paul is concerned to safeguard the boundaries of that new relational matrix, the social body of Christ. See Martin, *Corinthian Body*, 163–97.

40. Martin Luther, *Luther's Works*, ed. Jaroslav Pelikan and Helmut T. Lehmann (St. Louis: Concordia, 1955–86), 26:284. For a particularly perceptive account of Luther's reading of justification and participation in Paul, see Stephen Chester, " 'It Is No Longer I Who Live': Justification by Faith and Participation in Christ in Martin Luther's Exegesis of Galatians," *New Testament Studies* 55 (2009): 315–37.

CHAPTER FIVE

Divine Participation

The New Christological Agent in Philippians 2

> Being imitated seems to establish a powerful and immediate state-
> ment of interest, connection, and intentional relation.... It is *being*
> imitated which is crucial for intimacy.
>
> —Vasudevi Reddy, *How Infants Know Minds*

A rabbinic story tells of a prince who fell into a deep delusion about his identity: he became convinced that he was not a human being but a chicken. The
prince took off all his clothes, sat under a table, ate only chicken food, and
clucked. His father and mother consulted all his physicians and counselors,
but no one could do anything to change the situation. Finally, in desperation,
the king and queen turned to a famous rabbi known for his wisdom. The rabbi
agreed to help. He took off all his clothes, joined the prince in sitting under
the table, ate chicken food, and began to cluck.

This situation went on for some time. Eventually the rabbi said to the
prince, "This chicken food is getting old; I think I'd like something else to eat.
I think I'll have some human food. How about you?" The rabbi began to eat,
and soon the prince joined him.

Time passed as they sat naked under the table, clucking and eating human food. One day the rabbi said, "It's a bit cold under this table. I'm going to
put on a robe to keep warm. How about you?" He dressed, and eventually the
prince put on a robe also.

Time passed. Finally the rabbi said, "It's so cramped under this table. I
think I'll stand up and stretch. How about you?" The prince said, "But I'm a
chicken! And now I'm eating human food, and I'm wearing human clothes and
talking. If I stand up, no one will know I'm a chicken!" The rabbi answered,

"You know you're a chicken, and I know you're a chicken, but nobody else needs to know."[1]

In this story the wise rabbi enacts the power of imitation in a counter-intuitive way. Rather than saying to the deluded prince, "Imitate me," the rabbi first joins in the prince's condition. He shares the cramped space and the cold and the pitiful chicken food. He enters into the prince's world. Only from that shared standpoint does he then invite the prince to imitate him in response: I'm hungry—how about you? I'm putting on some clothes—how about you? And so forth. The rabbi initiates a reciprocal mimetic interplay and a relational bond through which the prince is restored to his humanity.

I tell this story to frame my approach to Philippians 2:5-13, the extremely influential and controversial story of Christ's humiliation and subsequent ex-altation.[2] In discussing the relational constitution of the person and the divine action that restores humanity to its intended freedom and agency, this text is at the heart of the matter:

> Have this mind-set [*touto phroneite*] among yourselves, which is in Christ Jesus,
> Who, being in the form of God, did not consider equality with God as something to be exploited,
> but made himself as nothing,
> taking the form of a slave [*morphēn doulou*],
> being born in the likeness of human beings [*en homoiōmati anthrōpōn*]
> and being found in the trappings of a singular human being [*kai schēmati heuretheis hōs anthrōpos*],[3]
> he humbled himself [*etapeinōsen heauton*]
> becoming obedient to the point of death [*genomenos hypēkoos mechri thanatou*],

1. Attributed to Rabbi Nachman of Breslov, this story is told in many versions. See, e.g., Elie Wiesel, *Souls on Fire: Portraits and Legends of Hasidic Masters* (New York: Random House, 1972), 170-71.

2. In this chapter I build on an earlier essay, "Philippians 2:7-11: Incarnation as Mimetic Participation," *Journal for the Study of Paul and His Letters* 1.1 (2010): 1-22.

3. The KJV, RSV, and NAS move verse 7d to the beginning of verse 8. For discussion of the issues, see Peter T. O'Brien, *The Epistle to the Philippians*, New International Greek Testament Commentary (Grand Rapids: Eerdmans, 1991), 226; Markus Bockmuehl, *The Epistle to the Philippians*, Black's New Testament Commentaries 11 (Peabody, MA: Hendrickson, 1998), 137; and Gordon Fee, *Paul's Letter to the Philippians*, New International Commentary on the New Testament (Grand Rapids: Eerdmans, 1995), 214n2.

death on a cross [*thanatou de staurou*].
For this reason God highly exalted [*hyperypsōsen*] him,
    and gave him the name that is above every name,
so that at the name of Jesus every knee should bow
    in heaven and upon earth and under the earth,
and every tongue confess [*exomologēsētai*] that Jesus Christ is Lord,
    to the glory of God the Father.[4]

In the ringing finale of the passage, Paul explicitly spells out the impact of Christ's actions on human agency: "Therefore, my beloved, just as you have always obeyed, not only in my presence, but much more now in my absence, with fear and trembling work out your own salvation [*tēn heautōn sōtērian katergazesthe*]; for God is the one who is at work among you [*ho energōn en hymin*], both to will and to work [*kai to thelein kai to energein*] for his good pleasure" (Phil 2:12-13).

Here is a thoroughly intersubjective notion of human personhood, in which God works conatively, cognitively, and effectively within the person, yet the human agent remains distinct and addressable by the imperative, "Work out your salvation." Paul links the divine indicative to the human imperative, and God's action to human action, resulting in the language of "willing" and "working," with its implication of an effective union of thought and action, initiative and follow-through. This working of God "among" the Philippians repeats the union of divine initiative and follow-through in 1:6 ("the one who began a good work among you [*en hymin*] will bring it to completion [*epitelesei*] at the day of Jesus Christ") and anticipates its full effect in 3:20-21: "Our citizenship [*politeuma*] is in heaven, and from it we await a Savior, the Lord Jesus Christ, who will change [*metaschēmatisei*] our body of humiliation [*to sōma tēs tapeinōseōs hēmōn*] to be conformed [*symmorphon*] to the body of his glory [*tō sōmati tēs doxēs autou*], according to the working of the power that enables him to subject all things to himself." It is this confidence in *God's* action, christologically and soteriologically enacted, that grounds Paul's confident imperatives and mimetic appeals to the Philippians as capable agents.[5]

---

4. My translation.

5. See, e.g., Brian J. Dodd, "The Story of Christ and the Imitation of Paul in Philippians 2-3," in *Where Christology Began: Essays on Philippians 2*, ed. Ralph P. Martin and Brian J. Dodd (Louisville: Westminster John Knox, 1988), 154-61; J. Ross Wagner, "Working Out Salvation: Holiness and Community in Philippians," in *Holiness and Ecclesiology in the New Testament*, ed. Kent E. Brower and Andy Johnson (Grand Rapids: Eerdmans, 2007), 257-74; Robert C. Tannehill, *The Shape of the Gospel: New Testament Essays* (Eugene, OR: Cascade, 2007), 223-37;

Along the way, Paul reframes an understanding of mimetic interaction as a mode of participation in which agency is shared; this is quite different from models of imitation as an individual decision to follow the example of another, whether that other is Paul or Christ.[6]

In the previous chapter I discussed the constitution of persons through "fleshly" participation in the realm of sin and death, with its resulting evacuation of agency under the delusional and deadly power of sin's use of the law. Paul concludes his enactment of that situation with a cry for deliverance from the "body of death" and an affirmation of God's rescue action: sending the Son "in the likeness of the flesh of sin and for sin," and there condemning sin and annulling its power. In Philippians 2:6-11 Paul depicts in more depth this "sending of the Son" in the drama of Christ's descent into, and full participation in, that body of death and his subsequent exaltation by God. Michael Gorman rightly calls this passage "Paul's master story," which is the story of Christ's liberating action and the revelation of God's cruciform nature.[7] By including this "master story" in the frame of Philippians 2:1-13, Paul's account of intersubjective personhood is transformed and grounded in the drama of Christ, which is, after all, a drama in which Jesus Christ is both a divine and a human actor. Divine and human agencies first meet here, setting the stage for any subsequent discussion of divine and human interplay in the constitution of Paul's converts and the communities in which they live. In the next chapter I will discuss the overlay of subjects implied by Paul's language of being "in Christ" and of "Christ in me," in Galatians 2:15-21. Here that human experience is preceded by the overlay of subjects in the story of the one who existed in the form of God and took the form of a slave, acting as God and acting as a human being at the same time. This is not to say that the two—the interplay of divine and human agency displayed in Jesus Christ, and in Paul's communities respectively—are precisely equivalent, but rather to ask how they are related. The second is grounded in the first, and the first displays Christ's mimetic assimilation to Adamic humanity under the power of sin and death, an assimilation that yet retains Christ's divine identity. In other words, in Philippians 2:6-11 Paul shows his readers that they are "*being imitated*" by God in Christ, in a divine-human relationship that grounds and generates intimacy with God and each other. Recalling Hobson's argu-

---

Michael J. Gorman, *Inhabiting the Cruciform God: Kenosis, Justification, and Theosis in Paul's Narrative Soteriology* (Grand Rapids: Eerdmans, 2009), 9-39.

6. See the discussion of mimetic reciprocity in Susan Grove Eastman, *Recovering Paul's Mother Tongue: Language and Theology in Galatians* (Grand Rapids: Eerdmans, 2007), 25-61.

7. Gorman, *Inhabiting*, 12.

ment that human cognition arises out of primary relationships, we might say that Christ's mimetic assimilation to humanity establishes a new "cradle of thought" that in turn generates new willing and working by a self newly constituted in relationship to the indwelling God.

The drama of Philippians 2:6–11 displays a pattern in Pauline theology that Morna Hooker calls "interchange in Christ." She identifies this pattern in Galatians 3:13 and 4:4–7, 2 Corinthians 5:21 and 8:9, Romans 8:3, 14, and Philippians 2:5–11. In brief, "the second Adam took the form of the first Adam that human beings can be conformed to *his* likeness in a new creation." Significantly, Hooker adds that, whereas in the majority of these texts the "interchange of experience" takes place between Christ and believers, in Philippians 2:6–11 "the interchange of experience takes place within Christ himself."[8] Indeed, in the dramatic action of the passage, we see a picture of the first clause of 2 Corinthians 5:21: "For our sake he made the one who knew no sin to be sin [*ton mē gnonta hamartian hyper hēmōn hamartian epoiēsen*]." The question addressed in what follows is how such an interchange taking place in Christ's story might reshape understandings of personhood, of the relationship between divine and human actors and actions, and of the remaking of the person through a radically new system of self-in-relation instigated and sustained by God in Christ.

To explore that question, I propose a heuristic *model*: the image of Jesus Christ precisely as a divine actor playing a human role on the human stage, and of Philippians 2:6–11 as the libretto for his action. Not to put too fine a point on it, I shall argue that Christ "im-personates" Adamic humanity on the stage of human history, in a double sense:

1. Christ plays the role of Adam, taking the part of Adamic humanity and makes it fully his own, playing it to the end—death on a cross.
2. In so doing, Christ implants his person in, "im-personates," Adamic humanity precisely in its most derelict, helpless state, even when held hostage by sin and death. That "im-personation" itself is the source of paraenetic power, because in it Christ assimilates to the stance of desperate human beings, joined with them in their situation and thereby empowering and transforming them.

There are three aspects to this proposal: the model, the plot, and the implications of both for the interaction of divine and human agency in human

8. Morna Hooker, "Interchange in Christ," *Journal of Theological Studies*, n.s., 32.2 (1971): 355.

subjects. I take each in turn. At the end of the chapter, I will consider how this model of personhood intersects with contemporary notions of an inter-subjective self.

The Model

Janet Martin Soskice has demonstrated that, in both scientific and religious cases, "models and metaphorical theory terms may be reality depicting without pretending to be directly descriptive." That is, models and metaphors are ways of carrying forth investigations of that which cannot be fully described, and of denoting that which is genuinely new. They are pointers, ways of "representing reality without claiming to be representationally privileged."[9]

This is the sense in which I propose seeing Christ as an actor on the human stage: not as representationally privileged or as fully explaining the mysterious interaction of divine and human agency, but as conceptually helpful in talking about that interaction by pointing to realities that to some extent will always elude our grasp. As such, a pointer to larger realities, a theatrical model is both historically plausible in the context of the early empire and potentially helpful in decoding some of Paul's difficult terminology. In regard to plausibility, abundant evidence indicates that, in the first few centuries, the Roman Empire was permeated by a theatrical and performative mind-set, with widespread attendance at, and sometimes participation in, performances ranging from street mimes to pantomimes to theatrically staged games, gladiatorial contests, and public executions. Many witnesses evince a view of the world as a theater and human life as a drama on the world stage. Suetonius, for example, tells us that Augustus approached his death asking how fitly he had "played the comedy of life"—then answered himself:

> Since well I've played my part, all clap your hands
> And from the stage dismiss me with applause. (*Aug.* 99)[10]

"Playing a part" could be seen as hypocrisy, of course, and was frequently vilified as such. It also was a survival strategy in the capricious violence of

9. Janet M. Soskice, *Metaphor and Religious Language* (Oxford: Oxford University Press, 1987), 145, 132.

10. Suetonius, *Augustus* 99, trans. J. C. Rolfe, Loeb Classical Library (Cambridge, MA: Harvard University Press, 1997).

Roman society. But as hinted at in our discussion of Epictetus, "playing one's part" could also be seen as the proper enactment of one's providentially given character and destiny.

Furthermore, in the spectacle of both stage and arena, Roman blood-lust led to an increasing blurring of the line between "make believe" and reality as the "characters" played their roles to the death. On occasion criminals or slaves conscripted as actors bled and died onstage; in elaborately staged public executions criminals were routinely forced to play roles ending in their death, and even spectators could find themselves the victims of poisoned arrows shot by actors in a mime (Macrobius, *Sat.* 2.7.15–17) or dragged from the stands and thrown to the beasts for Caligula's entertainment (Dio 59.10.3, 4; Suetonius, *Calig.* 34, 35). As Anne Duncan puts it, "The impulse to seek more radical forms of mimesis caused a theatricalization of 'real life.' The self, under the Empire, was revealed as a theatrical role, or even roles."[11] In this world of theatrical violence, those who faked death were jeered, but those who played their role to the end were praised. There was a melding of the actor's identity with that of the character, and the ultimate proof of that fusion was the shared destiny of death. Here the body itself becomes the site of authenticity.

This blurring of the distinctions between actors and their roles, between spectators and participants, and thus between performance and reality suggests a helpful context for interpreting Paul's language of mimetic representation in Philippians 2:7–8, which describes Christ "taking the form [*morphē*] of a slave, being born in the likeness of human beings [*en homoiōmati anthrōpōn*], and being found through his outward appearance [*schēmati heuretheis*] as a human being [*hōs anthrōpos*]." Many commentators rightly argue that the terms "form" (*morphē*), "likeness" (*homoiōma*), and "appearance" (*schēma*) cumulatively "stress that Jesus humbled himself to become human, and indeed lowly, *through and through*," while yet remaining "in the form of God."[12] Yet it cannot be denied that Paul's choice of words, particularly *homoiōmati* and *schēmati*, has caused endless theological grief for subsequent interpreters. The meaning of *homoiōma* moves along a spectrum between equivalence and difference, but primarily it has the sense of a "copy" or "what is made similar." In Plato it is closely related to the idea of imitation, because "people become like" those they imitate through ac-

---

11. Anne Duncan, *Performance and Identity in the Classical World* (New York: Cambridge University Press, 2006), 24.

12. Bockmuehl, *Epistle to the Philippians*, 133–34.

tion.[13] To imitate is to become a copy (*homoiōma*) of a model and to move toward assimilation (*homoiotēs*) with that model. As we shall see later, in Paul's usage the word occurs in contexts denoting a shared state and destiny rather than complete equivalence, whether of humanity with fallen Adam, Christ with fallen humanity, or baptized persons with Christ.

Schēma conveys even more emphatically the sense of an outward appearance that renders visible the reality or essence of a thing. In association with the verb "to find" (*heuriskō*), *schēma* refers to "the quality of a person or thing *as it is discovered or recognized by others.*"[14] This is performative language. Indeed, in the theatrical lexicon, *schēma* denotes the various means, such as bearing, clothing, dance movements, or gestures, by which actors display the identity of their characters. In pantomimic dance, in games, and in triumphal processions, theatrical movements and gestures were called *schēmata*.[15] This meaning is evident in ancient Greek drama, but it persists into the first century as well; Josephus describes King Hezekiah taking off his robes of state, putting on sackcloth, and assuming a "humble appearance or costume" (*schēma tapeinon*) at the news of Sennacherib's invasion (*Ant.* 10.11; see Isa 37:1; 2 Kgs 19:1).[16] Josephus's action is a public act and an other-directed expressive gesture that assumes the presence of an audience. Similarly, I would argue, Christ's assumption of the *schēma* of a human being is a public act, an other-directed expressive gesture. Indeed, his acts of self-humbling and obedience to a reviled death by crucifixion are the *schēmata* through which his particular identity is displayed.

Such a theatrical and performative context may give us a helpful image for conceptualizing Christ's unique intersubjective agency in Philippians 2:6-11. Christ in the form of God is acting throughout, but "in character" he is

13. See, e.g., *Theaetetus* 176e, 177a. For a useful discussion, see Willis P. de Boer, *The Imitation of Paul* (Kampen: Kok, 1962), 24-28.

14. Ralph P. Martin, *Carmen Christi: Philippians ii.5-11 in Recent Interpretation and in the Setting of Early Christian Worship* (Cambridge: Cambridge University Press, 1967), 208; emphasis mine. In a parallel movement, Paul regards his own advantages as garbage so that he may be "found" (*heurethō*) in Christ (3:9).

15. For example, one of the musicians dancing in a triumphal procession recorded by Appian "caused laughter by making various gesticulations [*schēmatizetai poikilos eis gelota*]" (*Pun.* 9.66).

16. In Euripides's *Ion*, for example, Creusa's royal stature is evident from her appearance (*morphē*) and her bearing (*schēma*) (*Ion* 236-38). In Aristophanes's *Knights* (1331), Demos's transformation is enacted by a change in costume, as he appears in "grand old apparel [*archaiō schēmati lampros*]." See discussion in J. B. Lightfoot, *Philippians* (Grand Rapids: Zondervan, 1953), 127.

also the human actor in the form of a slave, subject to the plot and to his role in it.[17] Christ's role-playing is not simply play-acting, as he shares the destiny of his character to the point of death (v. 8). At the same time, God's subsequent exaltation of the divine and human Jesus in verses 9-11, echoing Isaiah 45:23, reveals that Christ has been acting throughout in the divine character. God as divine agent is thus both *in* the play and its *editor*, or producer, who by the postmortem act of exalting Jesus reveals the larger drama of salvation that exceeds the conditions governing the plot onstage.

The Plot

The plot of Philippians 2:6-11 is frequently described as a pattern of descent and ascent, humiliation and exaltation, which in turn is replicated in Paul's life (3:4-11), and put forth as an example for the Philippians.[18] This pattern is true, insofar as it describes Christ's movement to become "like" human beings and be known through the outward marks of a singular person. But this pattern means that it is *also* a plot that moves from difference to similarity and from distance to participatory union, with the line of movement extending from God to humanity. In this regard it exceeds the notion of a model or ethical example, rather functioning as a kerygmatic declaration of the drama of divine action.[19]

17. Clement of Alexandria later described Christ as "putting on the mask [*prosōpon*] of the human" in order to "act the drama of salvation" (*Protr.* 10.110.2).

18. Stephen Fowl calls it a "down-up" narrative. See "Christology and Ethics in Philippians 2:5-11," in Martin and Dodd, *Where Christology Began*, 143.

19. A purely "kerygmatic" interpretation was argued forcefully by Ernst Käsemann, "A Critical Analysis of Philippians 2:5-11," *Journal for Theology and the Church* 5 (1968): 45-88 (German, "Kritische Analyse von Phil. 2,5-11," *Zeitschrift für Theologie und Kirche* 47 [1950]: 313-60), followed by Martin, *Carmen Christi*, 294-96, 309-11. Among many who view Phil 2:6-11 as primarily exemplary, see Larry W. Hurtado, "Jesus as Lordly Example in Philippians 2:5-11," in *From Jesus to Paul: Studies in Honour of Francis Wright Beare*, ed. Peter Richardson and John C. Hurd (Waterloo, ON: Wilfrid Laurier University Press, 1984), 113-26; William S. Kurz, "Kenotic Imitation of Paul and of Christ in Philippians 2 and 3," in *Discipleship in the New Testament*, ed. F. Fernando Segovia (Philadelphia: Fortress, 1985), 103-26; Wayne A. Meeks, "The Man from Heaven in Paul's Letter to the Philippians," in *The Future of Early Christianity: Essays in Honor of Helmut Koester*, ed. Birger Pearson (Minneapolis: Fortress, 1991), 329-36; O'Brien, *Philippians*, 253-62; N. T. Wright, "Jesus Christ Is Lord: Philippians 2:9-11," in *The Climax of the Covenant* (Minneapolis: Fortress, 1993), 93; Fee, *Philippians*, 196; Stephen E. Fowl, *Philippians*, The Two Horizons New Testament Commentary (Grand Rapids: Eerdmans, 2005), 106-7; Bockmuehl, *Philippians*, 121-25. Troels Engberg-Pedersen

Before tracing this thematic movement, however, we need to pause and ask whether Christ's human role is also more precisely Christ playing the part of Adam. This is a complex and highly contested question that has instigated an immense body of secondary literature.[20] Rather than pursue a full-scale investigation of this topic, I suggest that we ask who "Adam" is for Paul. What does "Adam" represent? In the texts where Adam is named, Romans 5:12–21 and 1 Corinthians 15:21–22, 45–49, there are two dominant themes: Adam is the first human being, in contrast with Christ as the last Adam, and Adam is the one through whom death entered the world.

In 1 Corinthians 15:45–49 Paul builds on a citation from the creation story in Genesis 2:7 (LXX), which reads: "Then the LORD God formed [*eplasen*] the person [*ton anthrōpon*] from the dust of the ground, and breathed into his nostrils the breath of life; and the person became a living being [*kai egeneto ho anthrōpos eis psychēn zōsan*]." In 1 Corinthians 15:45 Paul interprets this verse as follows: "Thus it is written, 'The first person, Adam [*ho prōtos anthrōpos Adam*] became a living being'; the last Adam [*ho eschatos Adam*], [became] a life-giving spirit." Paul adds the words "first" and the name of Adam, setting up the contrast with Christ as the last Adam. He immediately expands on the meaning of this contrast by describing Adam as "the first human being, from earth [*ho prōtos anthrōpos ek gēs*]," in contrast with Christ as the second *anthrōpos*, from heaven (15:47). The citation thus serves, not to speak of Adam as the image of God, but to contrast Adam's "earthy" and "psychic" body with the pneumatic and heavenly body of Christ, the last Adam and the second *anthrōpos* (15:45–47). Insofar as humanity now bears the image (*eikōn*) of this first Adam, it bears the image of dust (15:48–49).

Thus, second, Adam is the *anthrōpos* through whom death came (1 Cor 15:21–22), the one human being (*henos anthrōpou*, Rom 5:12) through whom sin, judgment, condemnation, and death entered the world (5:12–21) and

---

claims that the primary motif of the letter is "that of *Paul modeling Christ to the Philippians*," in *Paul and the Stoics* (Louisville: Westminster John Knox, 2000), 91; emphasis original. See pp. 81–130 for a full discussion.

20. For an overview and summary of debates about the role of Adam in Phil 2:5–11, see Martin, *Carmen Christi*, 116–20, 128–33. In "Imitating Christ Imitating Us: Paul's Educational Project in Philippians," in *The Word Leaps the Gap: Essays on Scripture and Theology in Honor of Richard B. Hays*, ed. J. Ross Wagner, C. Kavin Rowe, and A. Katherine Grieb (Grand Rapids: Eerdmans, 2008), I argue, "Christ does not *begin* with likeness to Adam and then move in an opposite direction, becoming increasingly dissimilar as the plot progress. Rather, in the dramatic image of Christ as actor, there is a reverse mimetic movement from difference to similarity, and the movement is on the part of Christ himself" (442). For an overview of views on Adamic Christology in Phil 2, see Wright, "Jesus Christ is Lord," 81.

whose disobedience made many to be sinners (5:19). The effects of Adam's trespass are in explicit contrast to the "free gift of grace" of the one human being, Jesus Christ (*tou henos anthrōpou Iēsou Christou*). In point of origin as well as destiny, and above all in the effects of his actions, Adam is the mirror *opposite* of Christ. In this sense he is a type (*typos*) of the coming one—that is, Christ (5:14).

These statements suggest that, if Christ is in some way playing Adam's role in Philippians 2:5-11, that role will correspond with the situation of Adam that is so clearly portrayed elsewhere in Paul's letters. Adam is the prototypical human being, a representative figure, almost a sphere of existence. To speak of Adam is thus in the same breath to speak of all humanity within the limits of Adam's earthly origin and enslaved by the effects of Adam's primal transgression. In *this* sense one can say that Christ assumes the mantle of Adam on the human stage: Christ assumes Adam's legacy. Here indeed Paul's "shadowy" language in verses 7-8 allows him to depict both similarity and difference between the incarnate Christ and the character of Adam.

Given this construal of Christ in Adam's role, the plot goes as follows. In act 1 (2:6), Christ is offstage, existing in the form of God and possessing equality with God. At this point, Christ is distinctly different from Adam, and Paul uses language that distances him from the Genesis account of the creation.[21] Indeed, when Paul wants to speak of either Christ or humanity in terms that echo Genesis, he uses *eikōn*. Had he wanted to echo the creation of Adam in Philippians 2:6, he could have used *eikōn* here as well.[22] Adam is not yet in view; at this point, Paul is saying only that

21. Here I differ from Morna Hooker, "Philippians 2:6-11," in *From Adam to Christ* (Cambridge: Cambridge University Press, 1991); Wright, "Jesus Christ Is Lord"; Martin, *Carmen Christi*, 161-64; James D. G. Dunn, "Christ, Adam, and Preexistence," in Martin and Dodd, *Where Christology Began*, 74-83, all of whom posit similarity between Adam and Christ in Phil 2:6, reading it as an echo of Gen 1:26. As opponents of this view are quick to note, the problem is that there are no linguistic links between the verses in Philippians and in Genesis. If Paul wanted to make such a connection, he certainly could have, as he does elsewhere in his letters.

22. For example, in 2 Cor 4:4 Paul does refer to Christ as the *eikōn tou theou*, explicitly echoing Gen 1:26. In 1 Cor 11:7 he refers to the man (*anēr*) as the "image and glory of God," and later he speaks of the promise that *we shall* bear the image of Christ: Just as we have borne the image of the dusty (*tēn eikona tou choïkou*), we will also bear the image of the heavenly (*tēn eikona tou epouraniou*) (1 Cor 15:49). See Bockmuehl, *Philippians*, 132; O'Brien, *Philippians*, 264.

Christ did not exploit the equality with God that he already possessed.[23] Rather, he expressed the divine likeness precisely through his humiliation and crucifixion.

In Philippians 2:6 there is thus no parity between the preexistent Christ and Adam, because Christ the divine actor has *not yet* put on Adam's mask, become his copy, and assumed his gestures; that action begins in verse 7, when, taking the form of a slave, Christ becomes what he was not previously. He is born in the likeness (*homoiōma*) of human beings, and through his appearance (*schēma*) reveals his particular human identity. It is here, rather than in the previous verse, that possible linguistic links with Genesis come into play. Genesis 1:26 reads: "Then God said, 'Let us make humankind [*anthrōpon*] in our image [*eikōn*], according to our likeness [*kat' homoiōsin*].'"[24] In Philippians, Paul uses the cognate noun *homoiōma* to denote Christ becoming a "copy" of human beings, assimilating to Adamic humanity in a mirror reversal of Adam's creation in the likeness of God.[25]

---

23. Here I follow Roy W. Hoover's translation of *harpagmos*, in "The Harpagmos Enigma: A Philological Solution," *Harvard Theological Review* 64.1 (1971): 95–119. Hoover's analysis treats the clause as a unit and notes parallels with Rom 15:3, as well as 2 Cor 8:9. The meaning of *harpagmos* has generated its own stack of scholarly monographs. Does Paul mean that Christ did not snatch at equality with God, that he did not cling to it, or that he did not exploit it? The first option would place Christ in a position similar to that of Adam, grasping at an equality with God that he lacks. The second and third would support a reading that sees Christ as possessing equality with God at the outset. Most scholars now opt for the third; we may note, however, that the result is a distancing between Christ and Adam, unless one posits that Adam also possessed equality with God prior to the fall. For a chart laying out all the interpretive options and their variants, with a thorough discussion, see Wright, "Jesus Christ Is Lord," 81.

24. This link is not airtight, to be sure. The rare word *homoiōsis* is not in Paul's vocabulary, and indeed it occurs only once in the NT—not surprisingly, in a citation of Gen 1:26 (Jas 3:9). The words, however, are extremely close in both form and meaning. See W. Bauer et al., *Greek-English Lexicon of the New Testament*, 2nd ed. (Chicago: University of Chicago Press, 1979), 570–71.

25. The verb *genomenos* deals a fatal blow to Dunn's argument that Phil 2:6-11 refers only to Jesus's earthly life as a second Adam ("Christ, Adam, and Preexistence," 78–79). As O'Brien points out: "The *contrast* clearly expressed between 'being in the form of God' and 'becoming in the form of human beings' is very odd if it is only between two stages in the career of a human being" (*Philippians*, 267; emphasis original). The phrase also creates difficulties for linking Adam at creation with Christ as a preexistent divine being. Hooker deals with *genomenos* by interpreting verse 7 as meaning that Christ, already in his preexistent state being what Adam was meant to be ("true man"), becomes what humanity now is, in the condition of enslavement to sin and death ("Philippians 2:6-11," 98–99); see also Wright, "Jesus Christ Is Lord," 59. That argument is weakened by O'Brien's observation that the aorist

The tension between likeness and contrast is amplified by attending to Paul's four other uses of *homoiōma*. Two of these invoke Adam's original trespass: Romans 1:23 refers to the original exchange of the glory of the immortal God for the "likeness" of an image of a mortal human being and of birds and animals and reptiles. In Romans 5:14 Paul says that death spread even to those whose sins are not "like" that of Adam. The other two occurrences of the word denote patterns of interchange between Christ and humanity: in Romans 6:5 we have "grown together" with the likeness of Christ's death; in Romans 8:3 Christ was sent "in the likeness of the flesh of sin," referring to the effect of Adam's trespass (Rom 5:12–21). Paul thus uses the language of likeness or mimetic assimilation in relationship both to Adamic sin and to christological transformation.

That Christ takes on Adam's role is further suggested by the use of the singular *anthrōpos* at the end of verse 7. Genesis (LXX) repeatedly names Adam as *ho anthrōpos* (1:27; 2:7, 8, 15, 18). As we have seen in 1 Corinthians and Romans, *anthrōpos* is also Paul's preferred title for Adam as the one through whose *dis*obedience sin entered the world, bringing judgment, condemnation, and the reign of death over all people (*eis pantas anthrōpous*). I suggest that this is the one whose condition and status Christ reveals through his *schēma*— his bearing, gestures, movements, public aspect—as he steps onto the stage of human history. He does so, not by miming Adam's disobedience, but by sharing Adam's condition and destiny.

But because Adam is a stand-in for the human race, Christ also becomes *en homoiōmati anthrōpōn*, in the likeness of all human beings.[26] His assimilation to the human condition thus holds up a mirror with a double reflection. On the one hand, Christ's humiliation and crucifixion mirror back to Paul's auditors the reality of Adam's sin and the condemnation for sin. On the other hand, as a reverse echo of humankind's creation in the divine likeness, this

participle *genomenos* "stands in sharp contrast to the present participle *hyparchōn* of v. 6" and that the hymn moves from using two static verbs (*hyparchōn* and *einai*) in verse 6 to using active verbs (*ekenōsen, labōn, genomenos, etapeinōsen*) in verses 7–8 (*Philippians*, 224). It is doubtful whether a change from one "Adam" to another "Adam" captures the contrast implied by the text. Rather, the repetition of the verb brings to mind the double *genomenos* of Gal 4:4: "born of a woman, born under law." This is Paul's verb for depicting the conditions attending the advent of Christ, and it is not descriptive of a preexistent state but of a "becoming." Galatians and Philippians depict movements from Christ's prior existence into the realm of human affairs, and that prior existence bears no similarity to the abject state of Adam and his heirs. See also Lightfoot, *Philippians*, 112.

26. So Lightfoot: "The plural *anthrōpōn* is used; for Christ, as the second Adam, represents not the individual man, but the human race" (*Philippians*, 112).

"becoming" reminds the audience that, even in slavery, even bound by sin and death, Adam retains God's imprint. Throughout the drama, Christ also retains his being in the form of God and indeed expresses that being through performing Adam's role. Returning to our heuristic image of Christ as miming Adam, we can picture him as the actor who never loses his offstage identity, yet at the same time he plays the onstage role with complete and utter realism. He remains fully God; born in human likeness, he is revealed as fully human *through* the gestures with which he plays Adam's part.[27]

So we come to the third act: impersonating Adam, Christ humbles himself, becoming obedient to the point of death, even death on a cross. The object of Christ's obedience is not named, but within the plot of the drama, he is obedient to the role that is given him to perform, submitting fully to the conditions that govern the plot onstage. This is the role of the primal sinner through whom humanity's script has become a tragedy, "handed over" by God to destructive powers and ending in death (Rom 1:24–32).[28] Sent "in the likeness of the flesh of sin [*en homoiōmati sarkos hamartias*]" (Rom 8:3), the divine actor "who knew no sin" (2 Cor 5:21) plays humanity's role in this script by obediently accepting the condemnation that is its necessary ending (Rom 8:3). He never takes off his mask and walks off the stage. Yet, insofar as God is ultimately the author and producer of this drama, Christ's obedience to his role is ultimately obedience to God.

In other words, for Christ to become *en homoiōmati anthrōpōn* is for him to share fully in the desperate contingency, suffering, judgment, and death of Adam's heirs, whom I take to be the entire human race.[29] Paul is describing Christ's participatory assimilation to the likeness of humanity enslaved to the sin that came into the world through Adam (Rom 5:12; 8:3). In *this* way he repeats, replicates, and reverses Adam's story. By ultimately taking on the likeness of Adam's sin and death and playing his part, Christ opens the way for humanity to be joined to the likeness of his own death (*symphytoi gegonamen tō homoiōmati tou thanatou autou*; Rom 6:5). There is a reciprocal mimetic participation at work here. As Robert Tannehill puts it, "Participation is first

27. *Schēmati* here is read as an instrumental dative, with Martin, *Carmen Christi*, 208, and O'Brien, *Philippians*, 227.

28. For discussion of the importance of divine agency in this "handing over," see Beverly R. Gaventa, "God Handed Them Over: Reading Romans 1:18-32 Apocalyptically," *Australian Biblical Review* 53 (2005): 42-53.

29. *Pace* N. T. Wright, "Jesus Christ Is Lord," who argues that Phil 2:5-11 puts forth an Adam Christology in which "Christ as last Adam takes on the role of Israel in the purposes of God . . . to be the means of solving the problem posed by Adam's sin" (59).

of all divine participation in the human plight, which makes possible human participation in God's Son."[30]

Here is the rabbi stripping off his clothes, suffering the humiliation of clucking like a chicken, and eating chicken food, getting under the table, so to speak, with deluded and bound humanity and thereby restoring human agency and dignity. As noted above, this drama of redemption animates the exhortations that precede and follow it. Paul immediately links Christ's story with its results for the Philippians: "Therefore, my beloved [*hōste agapētoi mou*], as you have always obeyed, so now, not only as in my presence but much more in my absence, work out your salvation with fear and trembling" (2:12). "My beloved" is not insignificant as Paul's mode of address to the Philippians, because God's action in and through Christ has established Paul and his auditors in a bond of love. Through that bond God "energizes" both the willing and the working of God's will (*theos gar estin ho energōn en hymin kai to thelein kai to energein*; 2:12-13). This divine action does not supplant but rather activates the desires and effective actions of the person. Here is an intersubjective constitution of personhood that does not erase the distinct otherness of each partner, yet operates at an intimately embodied level catalyzed by Christ's incarnate assimilation to the realm of human experience. That divine-human assimilation establishes a new relational matrix of humanity bound together in love.

---

30. Robert Tannehill, "Participation in Christ: A Central Theme in Pauline Soteriology," in *The Shape of the Gospel* (Eugene, OR: Cascade Books, 2007), 229 and throughout. Gorman also discusses the centrality of participation in Phil 2:6-11, which he calls "Paul's Master Story," although his emphasis falls on the notion of participation in Christ via faith, more than on Christ's participation in the human plight. Gorman's description of faith as "cocrucifixion with Christ" gets at this idea of participation; I emphasize Christ's humiliation and death as his prior "cocrucifixion" with enslaved and condemned Adamic humanity. See Gorman, *Inhabiting the Cruciform God*, 40-104. See also Douglas Campbell, *The Deliverance of God: An Apocalyptic Rereading of Justification in Paul* (Grand Rapids: Eerdmans, 2009), 756: In the context of discussing "faith" in Rom 1-4, Campbell notes that "Christian faith" is "isomorphic with Christ's own 'faith.' . . . It ultimately makes little sense to speak of a comprehensive mimetic relationship (i.e., of a thin analogy between Christ and the Christian). More likely is a participatory relationship, the Christian being caught up into Christ's story in the deeper sense of being caught up into Christ himself." As will be clear below, I am arguing for a "thick," participatory account of a *reciprocal* mimetic relationship initiated and sustained by Christ. See also Susan Grove Eastman, "Apocalypse and Incarnation: The Participatory Logic of Paul's Gospel," in *Apocalyptic and the Future of Theology*, ed. Joshua Davis and Douglas K. Harink (Eugene, OR: Wipf & Stock, 2012), 165-82.

Implications for Intersubjectivity:
Ancient and Contemporary Perspectives

The quote from Vasudevi Reddy that began this chapter shines a sharp contemporary light on Paul's depiction of Christ. Speaking of the dynamics of human development at their outset, Reddy says, "Being imitated seems to establish a powerful and immediate statement of interest, connection, and intentional relation. . . . It is *being* imitated which is crucial for intimacy."[31] When we hear Philippians 2:5-11 in light of this claim, our attention is focused on Christ's assimilation to the human condition, initiating a reciprocal human imitation of God. Or to put it in Tannehill's terms, divine participation initiates a reciprocal human participation in Christ. This mimetic interaction occurs on a bodily, socially embedded, and fully involving level. The link between participation and imitation has underpinnings both in ancient and contemporary thought, but its christological enactment is stunning and unique, whether in the ancient world or in a modern context.

Imitation and Participation in the Ancient World

We have seen how dramatic mimesis entails bodily participation in the situation and destiny of the character one enacts on the stage or on the sand. Plato knew the transformative power of such imitation, whether for good or for ill, because "we become like" what we imitate.[32] Because this participatory mimetic power goes far deeper than a simple individual choice to mimic the actions of another, poetic representation of wicked characters is dangerous for the young and thus for the well-being of the Republic; it must be denigrated, and the poets banned (*Rep.* 393c, 602d-603e, 605a-c). But despite his well-known rejection of poetic mimesis, Plato also speaks of mimetic assimilation as a means of "participating" in God by becoming as much *like* God as possible (*Phaed.* 253a-b).

In both cases, at issue is the power of mimetic representation to transform its practitioners, either for ill or for good. Thus in *Theaetetus* 176b, Socrates advises escape from earth to heaven through "becoming as like God as possible [*homoiōsis theō kata to dynaton*]," and one becomes like God by

31. Vasudevi Reddy, *How Infants Know Minds* (Cambridge, MA: Harvard University Press, 2008), 64-65.
32. *Theaetetus* 176e, 177a.

becoming "just [*dikaion*] and pure, with understanding [*phronēseōs*]."[33] This goal of assimilation to God through virtue did not end with Plato; rather, it enjoyed a resurgence in the time of the early empire, which can be traced in part through the reception history of this particular passage from *Theaetetus*; among others, both Philo (*On Flight* 63) and Plutarch (*Sera* 550d) cite it to speak of the goal of life as assimilation to God through virtue.[34]

Such talk assumes a gap between God and humanity, a gap that needs to be bridged through a mimetic, virtuous ascent. As Epictetus has taught us, matters are different in the Stoic cosmos, in which the divine Logos is on a continuum with and immanent in everything. There need be no mimetic ascent, nor a divine mimetic descent. Rather, the person is already participating in this God-saturated world, already has the spark of divine reason implanted within. True, false impressions constantly threaten to derail such participation, but the very ontological bedrock of being is the goodness of divine providence permeating all things. In such a context, performing a role entails assent to the reality of that providence; it is a matter of enacting what is truest about oneself in the givenness of a rationally ordered world. Mimesis is not a matter of assimilation to someone or something genuinely other, but of enacting one's own identity as both embedded in one's environment and inwardly free from it.

What is unimaginable in either the Platonic or Stoic cosmos is a divine movement from a position of radical ontological difference to one of mimetic assimilation to humanity, and in particular to humanity in the stance of sin and under judgment. It is telling to note that when Engberg-Pedersen reads Philippians through a Stoic lens, he explicitly removes Paul's thought from its temporal, historical context—that is, from any story about Christ as a unique, divine-human actor in history—and re-situates it by "freezing the dynamic story into a single model devoid of its dependence on time and space." This move then allows Engberg-Pedersen to draw comparisons between Paul's identification with Christ and the Stoic's identification with divine reason,

---

33. My translation.

34. John M. Dillon, *The Middle Platonists: 80 B.C. to A.D. 220* (Ithaca, NY: Cornell University Press, 1996), 145, 193. George van Kooten provides extensive discussion and a rich collection of both pagan and Jewish primary sources on the topic of divine and human likeness, in *Paul's Anthropology in Context*, WUNT 232 (Tübingen: Mohr Siebeck, 2008), 124–80. Van Kooten argues for links between Paul and Middle Platonism, rightly noting Christ's prior *homoiōma* with humanity: "Just as man is said to become grown together with the *likeness* of Christ (Rom 6.5) and to become of *the same form* as Christ (Phil 3.10; Rom 8.29), prior to that, Christ has become *in the likeness* of man and taken on *the form* of man" (213).

setting aside the radically different cosmologies of Paul and the Stoics. And yet Engberg-Pedersen simply assumes as natural a shared anthropological starting point for Paul and the Stoics, namely, "self-identification of an individual human being, which consists in an intricate interplay between two things: (*a*) the subjective sense of being 'oneself'; (*b*) seeing that self ('oneself') as being defined by one's striving to obtain so-called natural goods for oneself."[35]

What is the source of such a first-person understanding of the self? Engberg-Pedersen does not say. He simply continues his argument that such a self-understanding is "subjective"; the move to identification with Christ or with reason is a move to an "objective" self-understanding, so that henceforth one understands oneself as part of a larger "external" reality.[36] This is Engberg-Pedersen's model of the self in both Paul and Stoicism, which moves from the individual "I" to an experience of either Christ or the Logos, and through that experience to a new self-understanding as both individual and shared—what we might call, using Gallese's term, a "we-centric" space. Notably, Christ and the Stoic Logos are interchangeable, because it is not the distinct players that matter but the overall pattern of transformation and its effects on human interaction.

Not surprisingly, what is lacking in the entire discussion is thus Christ's role as a divine-human agent from outside the Stoic continuum of being, one who becomes what he was not previously. Similarly, there is no discussion of Christ's exaltation and universal confession as Lord, to the glory of God the Father. These claims and promises do not fit within the model bridging Paul and the Stoics. Rather, Christ's actions in Philippians 2:5–11 signify above all an example that Paul replicates in his own actions toward the Philippians, correlating closely with the actions of a Stoic sage sharing his wisdom with his pupils.[37] In fact, Christ as divine agent is curiously absent, removed from a dynamic account and functioning rather as a cipher in a model of transformation that leads, ultimately, to a revised self-understanding on the part of Paul and his converts.

In short, in his analysis of Philippians Engberg-Pedersen enacts what he proposes: he removes the story of Christ in Philippians 2:6–11 from its

---

35. Engberg-Pedersen, *Paul and the Stoics*, 87, 93.

36. Engberg-Pedersen, *Paul and the Stoics*, 94. The similarities with Bultmann are explicit, including the distancing of an objectified self-understanding from bodily experience. Engberg-Pedersen thinks Paul's "self-understanding" "translates immediately into Stoicism, namely into the complex relationship that the Stoic sage will have to his body and his previous self . . . between the self as placed outside the individual bodily being and the self *as* that being."

37. See, e.g., Engberg-Pedersen, *Paul and the Stoics*, 117–18.

dependence on time and space and freezes it into a model that then guides Paul's interactions with his converts and their interactions with him and with each other. The rationale for doing so is straightforward: this is the only way, so Engberg-Pedersen believes, to move past repetition of Paul's language to a genuine interpretation for today's readers "where they actually are, in the modern present."[38]

Imitation and Participation in Contemporary Perspectives

So where are today's readers "in the modern present"? Specifically, how are imitation and participation linked in current thinking? And does every working model of the person require a purely naturalistic framework in order to be a live option for today's readers?

As we saw in chapter 2, the theories of neuroscientist Vittorio Gallese, philosopher Shaun Gallagher, and experimental psychologists Vasudevi Reddy and Peter Hobson all contain a notion of the person as intersubjectively constituted, beginning with a "we-centric" space at the foundation of the self. They do not propose a model of human development that moves from self to shared, but rather from shared to self. To be sure, there are variations among the proposals of these theorists, but they agree on the fundamental notion of the person as a system of self-in-relation-to-another. Furthermore, they agree that, from birth onward, mimetic interaction between persons is foundational for such a relational self. Rooted in neurological activity that occurs at a prevolitional level, this mimetic interaction is far deeper and more self-involving than a "free individual choice" to follow another's example. It is not simply identification, but rather assimilation in a fully participatory sense, sharing in the viewpoint and emotions of another person. Peter and Jessica Hobson quote Merleau-Ponty to express this depth of assimilation: "Mimesis is the ensnaring of me by the other, the invasion of me by the other; it is that attitude whereby I assume the gestures, the conducts, the favorite words, the ways of doing things of those whom I confront. . . . It is the power of assuming conducts or expressions as my own. . . . I live in the facial expressions of the other, as I feel him living in mine."[39]

---

38. Engberg-Pedersen, *Paul and the Stoics*, 87.

39. Maurice Merleau-Ponty, "The Child's Relations with Others," in *The Primacy of Perception* (Evanston, IL: Northwestern University Press, 1964), 145, quoted by Peter Hobson and Jessica Hobson, "Joint Attention or Joint Engagement? Insights from Autism," in *Joint*

Hobson and Hobson elaborate on Merleau-Ponty's language in terms of assimilating to the stance of another person without losing awareness of the other's difference from oneself. This is a meeting along the mimetic spectrum between absolute difference and equivalence. It matches the sense of Paul's use of *homoiōma* to signify likeness but not equivalence, union but not total absorption. Or to return to the theatrical model suggested by Paul's imagery, to "live in the facial expressions of the other" is to impersonate the other in a double sense: to assume the other's gestures as one's own, but also to put one's person into the other. I have argued that such impersonation is precisely what Christ does in Philippians 2:6–11 by being found in the *schēma* of Adamic humanity. Like the rabbi with the prince, Christ adopts the stance and situation of humanity, even in its delusions and bondage, but not in order to stay there "under the table," so to speak. Rather, Christ creates a reciprocally mimetic relational bond that strengthens the agency of human beings so that they may then become fellow-imitators (*symmimētai*) of Christ, together with Paul and each other (Phil 3:17).[40]

Merleau-Ponty's image of mimesis as "the ensnaring of myself by another" also points to the detrimental effects of a toxic environment in relational terms. As argued in the previous chapter, given the porous and connected qualities of embodied and socially embedded human existence in ancient and contemporary understandings of human existence, to be a "system of body-environment-intersubjectivity," as Gallagher puts it, is to be intensely vulnerable to distorted formation.[41] As evident from the discussion of Romans 7:7–25, Paul's analysis of this situation is global and radical, exempting no one and no part of the human being from sin's invading and ruling power. Human beings, according to Paul, are therefore not isolated individuals in need of moving from their solitary existence to a shared life with others. They inhabit a we-centric space, but that space is lethal, distorting their vision and evacuating their agency. The deliverance that Paul proclaims is not simply escape from such a relational web into a different realm of power, but rather its invasion by God's Son, who both assimilates to humanity's bondage and then subverts it through crucifixion and resurrection.

Attention: *New Developments in Psychology, Philosophy of Mind, and Social Neuroscience*, ed. Axel Seemann (Cambridge, MA: MIT Press, 2011), 130.

40. For this translation of *symmimētai*, see Wagner, "Working Out Salvation in Philippians," 267; Morna D. Hooker, "A Partner in the Gospel: Paul's Understanding of His Ministry," in *Theology and Ethics in Paul and His Interpreters: Essays in Honor of Victor Paul Furnish*, ed. Eugene H. Lovering and Jerry L. Sumney (Nashville: Abingdon, 1996), 93–94.

41. Shaun Gallagher, *How the Body Shapes the Mind* (Oxford: Oxford University Press, 2005), 242–43.

A New System of Body-Environment Intersubjectivity

We may draw several conclusions for the structure of the self as displayed in Philippians. First, the heuristic model of an actor playing a role suggests a fluidity in the identity of the human subject. As the Philippians work out their salvation, God is the one generating the motivation and the energy in and among them. This wording means that, as acting subjects, they are always corporately constituted within the *koinōnia* of the Spirit (2:1), which in this letter is emphatically the Spirit of Jesus Christ (1:19). In this model of the human agent there is no essential, stable, autonomous self; there is rather the self that is continuously reconstituted by the complex interactions between the divine actor and the characters of the Philippians. Operative here is a thoroughly second-person notion of the person as constituted and remade interpersonally at the ground level. Within that network of relationships, there occurs what Morna Hooker helpfully calls an "interchange of experience." The result is a sense of the self that is always in process and never possessed as an innate or achieved "capacity" or "moral competence." There is no room here for what Timothy Chappell calls "criterialism about persons," because the fluidity and exchange in which the person is constituted renders any criteria irrelevant. Furthermore, such an understanding of personhood implies actors who are always aware of disconnections and gaps within themselves. Rowan Williams puts this claim in provocative terms: "My 'health' is in the thinking or sensing of how I am *not* at one with myself, existing as I do in time (change) and language (exchange)."[42] That is to say, human beings are never complete in and of themselves, because they exist only in what Williams calls "a moving and expanding network of saving relationship."[43]

Second, therefore, the incompleteness of the human subject implies a continuing knowledge of one's own reliance on the divine Other. Barth comments on Paul's exemplary role in Philippians 4:9: "What is to be seen in *him*, Paul, as a Christian, is in point of fact not anything positive on which *he* could pride himself, but *Christ*—that is, however, the traces of the *dynamis tēs anastaseōs autou* (the power of his resurrection), the fellowship of his sufferings, a *gap* so to speak, a lack, a defect: he is *not* holy, *not* righteous, *not* perfect,

---

42. Rowan Williams, *Lost Icons: Reflections on Cultural Bereavement* (London: Continuum, 2003), 151.

43. According to Williams, Jesus is "the embodiment of God's act to create a moving and expanding network of saving relationship" ("Incarnation and the Renewal of Community," in *On Christian Theology* [Oxford: Blackwell, 2000], 235-36).

all for the sake of Christ. This *typos* he can really without presumptuousness commend to them for imitation."[44]

Barth's point is that Paul gestures not to his own righteousness but to that of Christ (Phil 3:9); indeed, in the economy of salvation, even Paul's defects and shortcomings may redound to the glory of God's grace.[45] There is always a gap between the human subject and Christ. The dual identity of, for example, a female actor in her role may help to conceptualize this distinction: the actor plays her role with full acceptance of its consequences yet also retains an identity that is separate from the character she plays. The distinction cuts both ways: Christ plays the role of Adamic humanity to the point of being "made to be sin," yet without knowing sin (2 Cor 5:21).[46] For Christians playing Christ's role on the human stage, that role is always a likeness, a *homoiōma* in which there are both identification and difference, because it is precisely in the midst of their sinfulness that Christ "comes near."

Third, the Christian subject's dual identity or subjectivity plays itself out in a distinction between outward appearance and ultimate reality. Paul's depiction of the person conflicts here with the visibility stressed by Reddy, Hobson, and Gallagher. For those theorists, the mind is visible in the body. But for Paul, those who are "in Christ" participate in two realms at once: the realm of embodied existence in what Paul elsewhere calls "this present evil age" (Gal 1:4), and the system of body-environment intersubjectivity in relationship to Christ and to other believers. The result of this double participation is a dialectic between weakness and power, in which weakness is most visible in believers' bodies. Just as Christ in Adam's role enacts a dialectical relationship between weakness and strength because Adamic humanity has been handed over to futility and death, so the human agency animated by Christ looks weak. This pattern is in Philippians, but even clearer in the Corinthian correspondence. In 1 Corinthians 4:9–13, for example, Paul writes: "I think that God has exhibited us apostles last of all, as those condemned to death, because we have become

---

44. Karl Barth, *The Epistle to the Philippians: Fortieth Anniversary Edition* (Louisville: Westminster John Knox, 2002), 112.

45. First Corinthians 2:2–3; 15:9–10; note also the further development of this tradition in 1 Tim 1:15–16.

46. See Tannehill, "Participation in Christ," who elucidates further: "The phrase 'likeness' or 'form of flesh of sin' may seem to express a reservation about the Son's complete identification with the human situation, particularly when we recall Paul's claim in 2 Cor 5:21 that Christ 'did not know sin,' although God made him 'sin for us.' These observations should not mislead us. The logic of God's action against sin in Rom 8:3 depends on the Son's identification with humanity in its sinful state" (227).

a spectacle to the world, to angels and to human beings." In 2 Corinthians 1:9 he speaks very personally of this experience: "We felt that we had received the sentence of death in ourselves; but that was to make us rely not on ourselves but on God who raises the dead."

This is personhood under the sign of the cross. The apparent futility and weakness in the human actor is not passivity, however, in contrast with divine activity. It is simply the way the divine activity is hidden on the human stage, within the limits set by that stage. Christ looked like a failure to those who saw only the spectacle of his death, and those who play Christ's role will look like failures too. There will be a gap between their public appearance and their inner sources of strength through solidarity with the suffering and crucified Christ, and through the eschatological promise of sharing Christ's destiny. Insofar as Paul's pattern of life corresponds with Christ's, he also demonstrates a self characterized by humble trust and solidarity at the point of weakness.

Fourth, to jump too quickly to appropriating Philippians 2:1-13 as an exhortation to the imitation of Christ is, in my view, to miss the point. The movement of the plot is not that of humanity becoming like Christ but of Christ becoming like Adamic humanity. Any talk about imitation must begin by talking about Christ's assimilation to the realm of human affairs, initiating and sustaining a relational bond that restructures the self in relationship to others. The key term is *en hymin*. Paul concludes, "*For this reason*, my beloved, . . . work out your own salvation with fear and trembling; for God is the one working *in your midst*, both to will and to work for his good pleasure" (2:12-13). "For this reason"—yes, because God who powerfully exalted Jesus is the same God who will transform you also (3:21). But also, "for this reason," because Christ's self-emptying, humiliation, and obedience to death mean that Christ *is* in the midst of *their* existence, their struggle, their "body of humiliation," no matter how futile it may appear on the human stage. In this way, Christ enacts the *phronēsis* that they are to enact "among yourselves [*en hymin*]" in 2:5. Christ's movement from difference to similarity, from distance to solidarity, is itself the source of paraenetic power.

Through mimetic assimilation to the human stance, Christ "puts himself" into humanity, animating and shaping the character of the individual and the community from the inside out. Here the *koinōnia* of the Spirit in Philippians 2:1 seems to be the way in which the animating presence of Christ is mediated throughout the community. Throughout the letter Paul has emphasized the Philippians' and his shared *koinōnia*: in the gospel (1:5), in the shared experience of grace (1:7), in conflict (*agōn*, 1:30) and affliction (4:14), and in mutual giving and receiving (4:15). Through this "interchange of experience" they have come to know the working of God among them that animates their own willing and working.

Christ's "im-personation" of Adamic humanity thus in turn instigates a shared mimetic movement and participation on the part of the Philippians, so that they may "act Christ" on the human stage. However imperfect and partial this act is, it is nonetheless real; recalling Soskice's discussion of metaphor, we may say that they act Christ "metaphorically" such that their lives become a way of "representing reality without claiming to be representationally privileged." This theatrical image suggests that the divine agent has come near to energize them in the midst of their struggles. They are not merely auditors or spectators; already they have been con-scripted into the spectacle of God's salvation, already they have been en-scripted into the saving action of God.

Conclusion

Part 1 of this book sets forth the second-person standpoint in which the starting point for the relational construction of the self is crucial. As Reddy puts it, "You have to be addressed as a subject to become one." She goes on to reflect on the dynamics of interaction between parent and children in mutual imitation games, with the provocative observation, "Being imitated seems to establish a powerful and immediate statement of interest, connection, and intentional relation. . . . It is *being* imitated which is crucial for intimacy."[47] Indeed, for all the theorists of mind that we considered, the relationship with others is crucial for the development of personal capacities for knowledge of others and of themselves; for the second-person theorists, however, it is the beginning point of such knowledge. From such a standpoint, we may see Christ's mimetic assimilation to the human condition as constitutive of human personhood on the most elemental, primal level; this assimilation does not negate the profound difference between Christ's divine origin and human dereliction, but it overcomes the distance between God and humanity through bodily solidarity. There is a sense in which God incarnate "recognizes" the human subject, who in turn recognizes himself or herself in the mirror of Christ. This is a mutual assimilation, but it is not equal; Christ never loses his divine status and origin, and human beings never lose their creaturely status.[48]

---

47. Reddy, *How Infants Know Minds*, 32, 64–65; emphasis original.

48. See particularly the insightful comments of Günter Thomas, who discusses "asymmetrical relationships of dependency" in "Human Personhood at the Edges of Life: Medical

Christ's assimilation to humanity, in incarnation and ultimately in crucifixion, breaks the power of the relational matrix that Paul calls sin and the flesh. In turn, that divine-human action instantiates and reconstitutes the human person. Paul talks intimately about such reconstitution of the self in Galatians 2, to which we now turn.

Anthropology and Theology in Dialogue," in *The Depth of the Human Person: A Multidisciplinary Approach*, ed. Michael Welker (Grand Rapids: Eerdmans, 2014), 386. Robert Spaemann develops the language of recognition in *Personnen: Versuch über den Unterschied zwischen "Etwas" und "Jemand"* (Stuttgart: Klett-Cotta, 1998).

CHAPTER SIX

The Saving Relation

Union with Christ in Galatians 2

We ourselves, who are Jews by nature and not Gentile sinners, knowing that a person is not rectified on the basis of works of the law but *dia pisteōs Iēsou Christou*, we also have put our trust in Christ, in order to be rectified *ek pisteōs Christou* and not on the basis of works of law, because no flesh will be accounted righteous on the basis of works of law.

Now if seeking to be rectified in Christ, we ourselves were found to be sinners, then is Christ a servant of sin? Certainly not! For if I build up again what I tore down, I establish myself as a transgressor. For through the law I died to the law so that I might live to God. *I have been crucified with Christ. I no longer live, but Christ lives in me. And the life I live in the flesh, I live in trust—that is, in the trustworthiness of the Son of God who loved me and gave himself over for me.* I do not nullify the grace of God; for if righteousness were through the law, Christ died for nothing.

—Paul, Epistle to the Galatians

The verses cited here in the epigraph, Galatians 2:15–21, are a prime example of the need to interpret Paul's letters in experiential terms, and also of the difficulty of doing so![1] Engagement with the grammar and vocabulary of the

---

1. My translation of these verses reflects a number of interpretative decisions regarding two key terms: *dikaiosynē/dikaiousthai* and *pistis Christou*. With regard to the first, Paul's terminology does indeed carry the legal sense of "accounted righteous"; however, he clearly envisages an existential transformation of the person. As Martinus de Boer points out, Paul keeps the forensic sense of "justification" but radicalizes it precisely because it is sinners, not doers of

text is necessary but hardly adequate for grasping the sense of Paul's words, which leave us scratching our heads. In biomedical terms his self-description in Galatians 2:19–20 sounds simply impossible and delusional; in psychotherapeutic terms it sounds like a kind of splitting of the self, antithetical to the integration that is deemed central to psychological health. In fact, it is not unusual to read these verses as referring to a division within the self, based on an unexamined model of the person as a bounded, freestanding entity. As we shall see, however, an intersubjective account of the person points the way to a different interpretation.

First, it is necessary to see what is at stake in Paul's letter to the churches he founded in Galatia. His urgent concern is the unity of these fledgling communities and their continued faith in Christ. In Paul's view, this unity derives solely and sufficiently from God's redeeming action in Christ Jesus and the ongoing, interpersonal indwelling of the Holy Spirit within the community of believers. But now his converts are listening to the divisive teaching of other missionaries who insist on circumcision for Gentile believers. Paul is not opposed to circumcision per se, but he is opposed to imposing practices of law observance—"works of the law" of Moses—on Gentile believers, because such practices divide the community by setting up an erroneous litmus test for belonging to Christ.[2] In Paul's view, to set up such a test would be to put the

---

the law, who are "justified." For this reason, and in order to convey not simply forgiveness for human misdeeds but liberation from sin as a power, *dikaiosynē* takes on a larger cosmic sense as well: "Paul adopts the language of justification, but the context in which he places it forces it to take on a different meaning, that of God's rectifying power" (*Galatians: A Commentary*, New Testament Library [Louisville: Westminster John Knox, 2011], 165). For fuller discussion of the combined forensic and liberationist meanings of *dikaiosynē/dikaiousthai*, see de Boer, *Galatians*, 151–57. Given the history of interpretation of "justification" in a purely legal and nontransformative sense, here I have chosen to use the term "rectification" in order to get at both the legal and the existential senses of Paul's language. John M. G. Barclay, *Paul and the Gift* (Grand Rapids: Eerdmans, 2015), 375–78, also argues strongly for the forensic sense of *dikaiousthai*, while also noting that Paul radicalizes its meaning by making "faith in Christ," not law-observance, the basis of being accounted "worthy" of salvation. Barclay and de Boer agree on the translation of *dikaiosynē/dikaiousthai* but disagree on the translation of *pistis* in relation to Christ. On that issue, see further below.

2. James D. G. Dunn (*Jesus, Paul, and the Law: Studies in Mark and Galatians* [London: SPCK, 1990], 191–96, 220–24) has argued that, for Paul, "works of the law" refers to portions of the law of Moses that set Jews apart from Gentiles and thereby serve as "identity markers" that divide the community. Although it certainly is the case that law observance is proving divisive among the Galatian believers, insofar as Paul warns against the obligation to "do the whole law" (Gal 5:3), this verse reiterates Paul's quotation of Deut 27:26 in Gal 3:10, amplified in 3:11–12, where the emphasis is on *doing* "all that is written in the book of the law." Hence I

cart before the horse, as if doing the law was the way to union with Christ. To the contrary, says Paul, life in union with Christ is the way to truly fulfilling the loving intent of the law (Gal 5:14).

This is the context for our passage. Paul, as is typical for him, immediately goes for the heart of the matter: God's action in Christ is the only sure foundation for the life of faith, which is lived out in the common life of believers. That divine action takes place in and through the crucifixion and resurrection life of Jesus the Messiah, the Son of God. It gains traction in human lives through a mutually participatory union between Christ and those "in Christ," of whom Paul is Exhibit A.[3] For my purposes, the important point is that such union discloses a relational notion of the person, which in turn provides crucial insight into the way in which people change. This chapter aims to explicate that claim as it plays out in Galatians.

Literary Analysis

Paul's astounding self-description is all about death and life. On the one hand, "I died to the law"; "I have been crucified with Christ"; "I no longer live." On the other hand, "that I might live to God"; "Christ lives in me"; "I live in the flesh"; "I live in the faith of the Son of God." This language of death and life comes to a climax in reference to Christ's death, depicted as a kind of gift: "who loved me and gave himself (or delivered himself over) for me." Here Paul amplifies his central claim in Galatians 1:4, in which Christ's self-donation "for our sins" delivers us from the power of "the present evil age." This self-giving death is also the source of divine grace, or gift.[4] Paul puts this link between Christ's death and God's grace negatively: "I do not nullify the grace of God; for if righteousness were through the law, then Christ died for nothing" (2:21).

This distilled affirmation of both death and life in union with Christ is surely experiential language, vibrating like a bell in the midst of a dense and complex treatment of the law, righteousness, and faith—both Christ's faithfulness and human faith in Christ. As Beverly Gaventa emphasizes, "The canvas on which Paul depicts the gospel has been enlarged from legal language

---

follow de Boer in interpreting "works of the law" as "the actions or deeds demanded by the law without distinction and without regard to the manner in which these deeds are performed" (*Galatians*, 148). See de Boer's excellent analysis, *Galatians*, 145–48, followed by Barclay, *Paul and the Gift*, 373–75.

3. J. Louis Martyn, *Galatians*, Anchor Bible 33A (New York: Doubleday, 1997), 258.

4. See now the discussion by Barclay, *Paul and the Gift*, 351–87.

to existential language."[5] Furthermore, the speaker has not simply died or peacefully "expired" but has been "crucified with Christ." The speaker has been executed as a criminal, violently and involuntarily nailed to a cross along with the Son of God. The speaker has suffered the punishment meted out to slaves and traitors, suffering this punishment together with the Son of God. The "I" had no choice in the matter.[6]

Here is no partial account of the person in the sense of deadening one part of the self or exercising mastery over undesirable passions or simply cutting oneself off from a law-observant past. Rather "It is the whole of the *ego* that is gone."[7] How can we make sense of such language? Commentators refer to the "real and total demolition of the self, as previously constituted," or the "execution of [Paul's] own identity."[8] Accurate as these restatements of Paul's language are, they leave us wondering what this crucifixion of the self looks like in practice (and what keeps it from being a masochistic rejection of one's personhood or a case of schizophrenic personality disorder).

If Paul's paradoxical and visceral imagery of death is shocking, the imagery of life is equally paradoxical. First, the "I" has been put to death and no longer lives, but rather Christ lives "in me" (*en emoi*). This language leads commentators to say such things as, "Paul is provocatively denying his own role as the acting 'subject' of his own life and claiming that he has been supplanted in this capacity by Christ" and "Christ becomes the acting subject of Paul's life, apparently replacing Paul himself as the agent of his own life."[9] As these comments illustrate, on the face of it, Galatians 2:20 looks like a competitive account of the relationship between God's action and human action: either Paul acts or God acts, but they do not act at the same time.[10] Such an account

5. Beverly R. Gaventa, "The Singularity of the Gospel Revisited," in *Galatians and Christian Theology: Justification, the Gospel, and Ethics in Paul's Letter*, ed. Mark W. Elliott et al. (Grand Rapids: Baker Academic, 2014), 194. As noted above, this interplay between legal and existential language complicates the translation of *dikaiosynē* and its cognates.

6. Gaventa, "Singularity," 191–93. We may recall here the agency disclosed in Phil 2:6–11, in which Christ in the place of Adam is the recipient of God's action.

7. Gaventa, "Singularity," 193.

8. The first quotation comes from John M. G. Barclay, "Paul's Story: Theology as Testimony," in *Narrative Dynamics in Paul: A Critical Assessment*, ed. Bruce W. Longenecker (Louisville: Westminster John Knox, 2002), 143; the second is from Douglas Campbell, *The Deliverance of God: An Apocalyptic Rereading of Justification in Paul* (Grand Rapids: Eerdmans, 2009), 848.

9. Richard B. Hays, *The Faith of Jesus Christ: The Narrative Substructure of Galatians 3:1–4:11* (Grand Rapids: Eerdmans, 2002), 154; Martyn, *Galatians*, 258.

10. In his introduction to *Divine and Human Agency in Paul and His Cultural Environ-*

might follow from the passive voice of "I have been crucified" (*synestaurōmai*); Paul certainly was not the agent of his cocrucifixion with Christ.

Yet immediately preceding this self-depiction, Paul claims that his death to the law was precisely so that *he* might "live to God." And in the next breath, Paul again employs the verb "to live," with himself as the acting subject. "I live in the flesh" and simultaneously, "I live in the faith." Is this the same "I" that was put to death? Paul's extreme language forestalls such an interpretation, leaving open the question of how to understand Paul's disjunctive language over the course of a human life.[11] Three factors guide the following attempt to wrestle with these questions: the reconstitution of the "I" in relationship with Christ, the repeated use of "in" to depict spatial realms of existence, and the this-worldly location of Christ's redemptive gift of himself.

Who's Talking? The Intersubjective "I"

First, at the center of the action is an "I" that has been dramatically reconstituted in union with Christ. It thus is not precisely correct to say that the ego is gone, because it reappears immediately as the subject of active verbs. Rather, the claim of 2:19–20a—"I have been crucified with Christ. I no longer live, but Christ lives in me"—affects the agency and identity of the acting subject of the verb "to live" in the following verse. Christ as an acting subject indwells the self that continues to live "in the flesh"; similarly, Christ as an acting subject also indwells the self that lives "in the faith." Furthermore, this christological reconstitution of the subject retrospectively restructures the agency and identity of the "we" who "have trusted in Christ Jesus" in verse 16. If Christ lives in me or in us, then who is doing the trusting? One answer is simply to say that the indwelling Spirit inspires and animates faith, and on one level that response may be sufficient. But in fact Paul does not invoke the Spirit at this point in the letter. He speaks instead about the indwelling of the Christ "who loved me and gave himself for me," and in whom somehow Paul also lives while simultaneously living "in the flesh." Such language suggests that Paul's

---

ment, ed. John M. G. Barclay and Simon J. Gathercole (London: Continuum, 2006), Barclay offers an insightful analysis of different models for the relationship between divine and human agency in Paul's letters.

11. For discussion of this problem of continuity and discontinuity in Paul's account of life in Christ, see Susan Grove Eastman, *Recovering Paul's Mother Tongue* (Grand Rapids: Eerdmans, 2007), 33–43, 184–89.

threefold use of the preposition "in" (*en*) in verses 19–20 provides further clues regarding the identity of the speaker.

Life "in the Flesh" and Life "in the Faith"

Christ lives in me; I live in the flesh; I live in the faith. This is spatial language in the midst of a temporal account of transformed identity, suggesting two contrasting yet concurrent realms of existence in which "I live."[12] The first is characterized as "the flesh" and the second is characterized as "the faith."

I return later to the debated question of how "in the faith" relates to "the Son of God" in verse 20. Here I note only that to live "in faith" is parallel to living "in Christ"; it is to be rectified "in Christ" (2:17); to be crucified "with Christ" (2:19); to be baptized "into Christ," and thereby to belong to a new family in which, "in Christ," all are "sons of God" and old social divisions are abrogated (3:26–28). As Volker Rabens puts it, to be in Christ is to be transformed in a new realm of existence in which the Spirit has established "new relational realities."[13] This is a realm and mode of interpersonal existence "in the sphere of Christ," which is "the territory where Christ is Lord (1:3). That territory is the community of people, both Jew and Gentile, who have 'come to believe in Jesus Christ.' "[14]

Conversely, to live "in the flesh" plays off the multiple connotations of "flesh" in Paul's letter. As we have seen in discussion of the body and the flesh, most of these connotations are negative. In Galatians "the flesh" is opposed to the Spirit (3:3) and linked with works of the law (3:2–5), which are identified specifically with circumcision (6:13) but which also include other bodily actions such as observance of the liturgical calendar and kosher eating practices. The desires of the Spirit are opposed to those of the flesh (5:16–17), and Paul contrasts the "works of the flesh" with the "fruit of the Spirit" (5:19–23). All these activities involve interpersonal interaction insofar as they construct and

---

12. Rightly noted by Gaventa, "Singularity," 194; John M. G. Barclay, *Obeying the Truth: A Study of Paul's Ethics in Galatians* (Edinburgh: T&T Clark, 1998), 181; de Boer, *Galatians*, 162–63: "The present situation of every believer is that the believer both lives 'in the flesh' and 'in the faith of God's Son.' Living 'in the flesh' is the universal human condition; living 'in the faith of God's Son' is the privilege of believers."

13. Volker Rabens, " 'Indicative and Imperative' as the Substructure of Paul's Theology-and-Ethics in Galatians? A Discussion of Divine and Human Agency in Paul," in Elliott et al., *Galatians and Christian Theology*, 303.

14. De Boer, *Galatians*, 157.

shape both the physical body, quite literally in the case of circumcision and food laws, and the social body; the two cannot be separated. Similarly, the "works of the flesh" also take place through embodied social interactions with others, insofar as at its most basic meaning, "flesh" signifies "the material substratum of all human existence at the present time."[15] Because the mental and the physical cannot be divorced from one another, the works of the flesh are not simply mental states but the acting out of passions that lodge in the body. Hence, when Paul claims confidently, "Those who belong to Christ Jesus have crucified the flesh with its passions and desires" (5:24), his claim concerns the demolition of bodily practices that harm the interpersonal constitution of the community.[16] Finally, to "sow to the flesh" is to reap corruption, in contrast with the eternal life promised to those who "sow to the Spirit" (6:8). At the great assize, the community-destroying "works of the flesh" end in decay and death, not life. In short, "the flesh" is both a reference to actions of the body and a relational term, implying enmeshment in, and determination by, a set of damaging constructs and divisive social practices. "The flesh" thereby appears to denote both a realm and a mode of embodied interpersonal existence that at the very least are limited to the "present evil age" under the sentence of death, and that at their worst tend to oppose and destroy God's new creation—that is, God's new community. It is the outworking of the body's connectivity with what Paul dubs "the present evil age" in Galatians 1:4.

The contrast between the realm of the flesh and the realm of faith therefore raises a further question: How can Paul *simultaneously* live "in the flesh" while mutually inhabiting and being inhabited by Christ? One answer is to interpret "flesh" in this instance, as in 2:16, as simply physical life in a neutral sense, denoting, in de Boer's words, "the substance that covers a human being's bones." But as the previous discussion of Paul's body language demonstrated, bodies mean connection, and hence vulnerability to one's relational matrix. That understanding implies, as de Boer puts it, that "the flesh" entails "vulnerability to malevolent cosmic powers such as Sin" (Gal 2:17; 3:22).[17] To be embodied is to be embedded in social structures, for good or for ill. To be en-fleshed is to be en-meshed in the world in which one lives. The life that Paul lives "in the flesh" would seem to take place in the midst of this realm of existence that resists God's new creation. "In the flesh" and "in faith" thus

---

15. De Boer, *Galatians*, 162.

16. Insofar as both "works of the law" and "works of the flesh" divide and thereby destroy the community, they are closely identified as socially embodied practices with parallel effects. At the very least, the "works of the law" are inadequate to combat the "works of the flesh."

17. De Boer, *Galatians*, 162.

appear to be incompatible arenas of existence, just as Paul opposes being "in the flesh" and "in the Spirit" in Romans 8:9.

The Embodied and Socially Embedded Self-Giving of the Son of God

The key to the paradox is the short clause that fills out the basis for Paul's new life "in the faith": "the Son of God, who loved me and gave himself over for me."[18] The phrase echoes Galatians 1:4: Christ "gave himself for our sins, to deliver us from the present evil age." It anticipates Galatians 4:4-5: "God sent forth his Son, born of a woman, born under the law, to redeem those under the law, so that we might receive adoption as sons." In other words, the realm of faith and trust *within* which Paul now lives was established by Christ's self-giving love and solidarity in death with all humanity, from the universal inclusion of all who are born of women to the Jewish particularity of those who are under the law. The love and self-giving of the Son of God took place through his full immersion in fleshly existence. As we have seen in Romans 8:3 and Philippians 2:7, in later writings Paul works this claim out through the language of "likeness" (*homoiōma*). Here in Galatians we see enacted the reconstituting power of this divine participation in the life of the apostle, who uses himself as a paradigm for the Galatians themselves.

The mode of life "in faith" is therefore precisely as a gift that brings the presence of the Giver into solidarity with the receiver in the messiness of daily, corporeal, social existence in the midst of the present evil age. Paul makes this relationship clear through the third use of "in" in 2:20: "Christ lives in me." This divine presence is the source of the gift's transforming power, mediated through a mutual indwelling that remakes the receiver in a new relational system characterized by undeserved and thus noncompetitive grace.[19] This gift

18. See Hays, *Faith of Jesus Christ*, 153-55, and Martyn, *Galatians*, 259. Both note the parallel with Rom 5:15, where Paul speaks of "the gift of God in the grace [which is] of the one man Jesus Christ." In fact, Rom 5:15-17 is all about the contrast between the free gift of God in Jesus Christ and the judgment following Adam's sin, which brings condemnation. That this free gift is tied directly to Christ's death is clear from Rom 5:6-10, which emphasizes above all the incongruence of Christ's self-giving death on behalf of undeserving recipients: the weak, the sinners, God's enemies. See also Barclay, *Paul and the Gift*, 387: "There emerges here a perfect homology between the narrative shape of the Christ-event and its character as incongruous gift."

19. See in particular the comments of Barclay on the incongruity of the Christ gift, in *Paul and the Gift*, 387: "The good news stands or falls with the realization, in thought and practice, of the incongruous Gift."

took place on a Roman cross and is mediated through the presence of Christ in the Spirit in the midst of the community.[20] It is the gift of divine solidarity in extremis, with the disobedient, the criminals, the traitorous slaves, and the accursed (Gal 3:13–14; cf. Phil 2:5–11). To be joined in company with Christ on such a cross is to share fellowship with his companions there, which is surely to suffer the loss of all other sources of identity.[21]

In other words, "Christ lives in me" in the midst of "the life I live in the flesh"; the location of life in the sphere of trust generated and sustained by the Son of God is not somewhere else, in some heavenly or other-worldly realm, but precisely here in the midst of daily life under the shadow of death.[22] Such life is emphatically not a private mystical experience, because life "in the flesh" is life embedded in the complex social networks that constitute the present evil age. Paul resists any account of spiritual experience as some kind of "conscious mental going-on."[23] Yet at the same time, life "in the realm of faith and trust generated by the self-gift of the Son of God" is instantiated and sustained only through the surpassing bond with Christ "in faith."[24]

---

20. Gal 3:2–5; 5:22–26.

21. Martyn describes the loss in terms of Paul's separation from the law as the guide to his former "cosmos" (*Galatians*, 280). But as Gaventa rightly argues, this loss entails all other possible sources of identity, not simply the law ("Singularity," 190–95). See also Barclay, *Paul and the Gift*, for amplification of this loss of cosmos in terms of ancient systems of honor and shame, and thereby of all "pre-constituted systems of worth" (388–400 and throughout).

22. For a sustained argument in favor of this view, see Susan Grove Eastman, "Apocalypse and Incarnation: The Participatory Logic of Paul's Gospel," in *Apocalyptic and the Future of Theology*, ed. Joshua Davis and Douglas K. Harink (Eugene, OR: Wipf & Stock, 2012), 177–81; Martyn, *Galatians*, 258–59. My this-worldly interpretation is the opposite of Troels Engberg-Pedersen's reading of Gal 6:14, where he interprets Paul's crucifixion "to the cosmos" in other-worldly terms: "Just as Christ has been literally crucified to the whole world, and then of course *lives elsewhere*, so Paul too, through being aligned with Christ, has died (been crucified) to the world and (now) lives in a way that means new creation. . . . He already lives as he will come to live in heaven" (*Cosmology and Self in the Apostle Paul: The Material Spirit* [Oxford: Oxford University Press, 2010], 162; emphasis original). For discussion of Engberg-Pedersen's interpretation of Gal 2:19–21, see further below.

23. This is Richard Swinburne's definition of experience in *The Existence of God* (Oxford: Clarendon Press, 1979), 244. See, by way of critique, the perceptive essay by Nicholas Lash, "Human Experience and the Knowledge of God," in *Theology on the Way to Emmaus* (Eugene, OR: Wipf & Stock, 2005), 144.

24. This distinction and relationship between human experience and cosmic realities is parsed out by Tannehill: "This new reality is not first of all a matter of the individual's subjective experience, but a new form of existence under a new power" (*Dying and Rising with Christ: A Study in Pauline Theology* [Eugene, OR: Wipf & Stock, 2006], 59). At the same time, Paul surely also has in mind an experiential transformation; for a subtle discussion of the role of

I have argued that these two realms of existence may be conceptualized as relational matrices or networks within which the person is constituted. In Galatians 2:15, when Paul appeals to Peter with the phrase "we ourselves, who are Jews by nature," he identifies himself with a source of identity via kinship "in the flesh."[25] Insofar as those "fleshly" familial ties continue to play a role in Paul's personhood and social identity, he lives "in the flesh." And yet he does so *only* as one who also and primarily lives "in the faith," and thus as one who has "died to the law through the law" and been "crucified with Christ." At the least, such wording must mean that Paul's ties "in the flesh" are mediated by his new life "in faith." He has an independent stance toward those old sources of identity; they no longer tell him who he is, but he is free to interact with them.[26] In other words, his perception and actions are mediated through a new other-relation with Christ, which in turn finds experiential expression through interpersonal ties in the new community. In this new community there is neither circumcision nor uncircumcision, because all old systems of worth are "recalibrated."[27]

Insofar as the self is always a self-in-relationship, when it is embedded in a new relational matrix it becomes a new self. Insofar as this new self still lives "in the flesh," it repeatedly must confront the old relationally constructed existence that was "crucified with Christ." Because these two spheres of existence are mutually opposed, to live in both simultaneously is to live in the midst of conflict, where one's allegiance is tested daily.[28] Implicit in Paul's larger argument is the constitution of the self-in-relation, not only to Christ, but also to different human interpersonal systems. These systems are never *merely* human, but they *are* mediated in human interaction and structures.

---

experience in Gal 5, see Simeon Zahl, "The Drama of Agency: Affective Augustinianism and Galatians," in Elliott et al., *Galatians and Christian Theology*, 335–52.

25. For Paul's deployment of "flesh" to denote his ties to Israel, see Rom 9:3. In Gal 4:23, 29, "flesh" is contrasted with "promise" as a mode of reproduction and used as shorthand for circumcision (6:12–13). See further below.

26. For example, in 1 Cor 9:19–22 Paul claims, "Though I am free from all people, I have made myself a slave to all, that I might win some [to the gospel]." He goes on to depict himself as voluntarily "under the law" in order to preach to those "under the law," and so forth. He is not defined by being either under or outside the law, but he can enter into relationship with those under or outside the law.

27. The recalibration of worth is argued extensively by Barclay, *Paul and the Gift*. To speak of a new self-perception sounds close to Bultmann's argument that faith results in a new or revised self-understanding. The difference is my emphasis on the way in which such self-relation is never unmediated, but rather mediated through relationship with Christ (or, alternatively, with sin).

28. As argued extensively by Martyn, *Galatians*, 524–36.

Pistis Christou: Christ, Faith, and Second-Person Agency

Taken together, the reconstitution of the self in union with Christ, the contrasting realms of life "in the flesh" and life "in faith," and the location of Christ's self-giving love in the midst of embodied, socially embedded existence illuminate the relationship between faith and "the Son of God, who loved me and gave himself for me." I suggest that the "overlay of subjects" between the self and Christ renders both the believer and Christ as the subject who "has faith" or "trusts."[29] In other words, the believer as indwelt by Christ is structured by trust that is extrinsically sourced, as well as directed to Christ as divine "other." Recalling our earlier discussion of second-person notions of the person as never existing on his or her own, and as involving a loop that involves the whole person in relationship with another, we can see here a picture of the believer exercising faith and at the same time indwelt by Christ who engenders such faith.

Indeed, the spatial language suggests that such faith is exercised in a relational interchange instigated and sustained by Christ's trustworthiness. Christ demonstrated and enacted that trustworthiness through his self-giving and sacrificial love on the cross, and that act of love and self-giving in turn awakens believers' trust in Christ. This suggestion is admittedly circular: the object of the trust animated and exercised by Christ's energizing work in and through believers is Christ himself. The paradox, however, is not insurmountable. The meaning is captured in part by the poet Gerard Manley Hopkins: "Faith is God in man knowing his own truth."[30] I say "in part," because Paul does not

---

29. I will not rehearse here the extensive literature on this topic. But I will note the way in which discussion of faith as either "in" or "of" Christ frequently presumes a notion of the believer as an individual, deciding agent. This view is ironically implicit in the supposition of "an antinomy between human activity and God's action in Christ" (de Boer, *Galatians*, 150; see also Martyn, *Galatians*, 271), which draws heavily on Paul's insistence that his call and his gospel are not from human beings but from God (Gal 1:1, 11–12). Paul's point concerns the origin and source of his calling and proclamation, not the locus or means by which they occur. Paul received his gospel from God, and at the same time he is the active agent who proclaimed it to the Galatians. There is no competition here between divine and human agency, but rather an undergirding of human agency sourced by divine action. For a recent concise review of the arguments on both sides, see de Boer, *Galatians*, 148–50.

30. Gerard Manley Hopkins, *Sermons and Devotional Writings*, ed. Christopher Devlin, SJ (London: Oxford University Press, 1959), 157. Hopkins's definition of faith is more cognitive than I would wish, but it is structurally akin to my argument. My argument has some similarities with that of N. T. Wright, who sees "Christ" as an incorporative term. But I part company with Wright's identification of Christ with Israel and his redefinition of "Is-

depict himself simply as a passive channel for divine action. Rather, Paul's whole self has been crucified with Christ, and his whole newly constituted self-in-relation-to-Christ now acts as a believing agent. Christ indwelling and thereby re-creating the self is the source of faith in Christ; Christ crucified in human history is the basis and goal of such trust, because the self-giving of the Son of God generates and sustains trust in himself.

It is crucial not to slide into a competitive account of divine and human agency at this point. For Paul, "Christ lives in me" in no way supplants Paul's own agency; rather, it establishes it in a new way, for he immediately says, "I live."[31] Paul does not refer to himself as a channel for the divine life; rather, he himself is the subject of active verbs: he lives, he believes, he exhorts the Galatians, he wishes and wonders and is perplexed; he pleads with his converts, "Become like me, my brothers and sisters, I beg of you, because I have become like you" (4:12). This apostle is not lacking in a strong awareness of himself, and he certainly is not passive! But neither is he autonomous. His paradoxical self-depiction can be grasped only when we realize that his notion of the person is thoroughly participatory and relational. In a description of human "believing" that could be shared by many on different sides of the *pistis Christou* debates, J. Louis Martyn says,

> We can reiterate that Paul is serious when he allows human beings to be the subject of the verb "to place one's trust." Those who believe in Christ are not puppets, moved about and made to speak by others. . . . But just as these persons are not puppet believers, so they are not believers as a result of an act of their own autonomous wills, as though the gospel were an event in which two alternatives were placed before an autonomous decider, and faith were one of two decisions the human being could make autonomously. . . . Thus, when Paul speaks about placing one's trust in Christ, he is pointing to a deed that reflects not the freedom of the will, but rather God's freeing of the will.[32]

Such an interpretation makes sense in light of Paul's cryptic self-depiction in 2:19–20. As noted, the larger context is Paul's concern for the unity of the Galatian congregations, a unity that is under threat from other

---

rael" as the church. See Wright, "Messiahship in Galatians?", in Elliott et al., *Galatians and Christian Theology*, 3–23.

31. See Rabens, "Indicative and Imperative," 303–4.

32. Martyn, *Galatians*, 276.

missionaries' insistence on Gentile circumcision and other distinctive marks of obedience to the law of Moses. Immediately preceding our passage, Paul recalls his rebuke of Peter for withdrawing from table fellowship with Gentile believers in Antioch (2:11–14). He bolsters his argument against requiring the "works of the law" for Gentile converts by contrasting a status of righteousness based on law observance with a status of righteousness based on faith—faith that comes from and is returned to Christ (v. 16). This contrast frames verses 19–20 (2:15–18 and 21).[33]

Given this narrative frame, we must ask what Paul's language of death and life in union with Christ contributes to his urgent concern for the unity of the Galatian congregations. The answer seems to be twofold, operating on two levels. On one level, Paul single-mindedly presses for the primacy and sufficiency of the gift of grace through Christ. This indeed is the climax of the passage: "I do not negate the grace of God; for if righteousness is through the law, then Christ died for nothing" (2:21). On another level, this divine grace establishes and requires a new social matrix in which "life in the faith" mediates all human relationships—that is, all life "in the flesh." Because human beings are always selves in relationship to another, the character of the community of faith is central to the reality of faithful life "in the flesh." In the last two chapters of the letter, Paul develops the contrast between the "fleshly" social system and one gifted by the Spirit.[34]

Reading "I Yet Not I" from a First-Person Perspective

Galatians 2:19–20 depicts a gracious divine-human mutual indwelling that transforms the self in the midst of daily life. Such mutual indwelling, however, does not square well with an anthropology premised on the notion that human beings are essentially autonomous, discrete, and self-directing individuals. Rather, it discloses and requires an intersubjective picture of the person all the way down. Otherwise there is no possible way to make sense of Paul's conviction that the death and resurrection of Jesus accomplish redemption and transform the lives of his Gentile converts throughout the Roman world, let alone to claim any such conviction twenty-one centuries later.

---

33. On the relationship between the "justification" language in 2:15–18 and 21 and the "participation" language in 2:19–20, see particularly Gaventa, "Singularity," 187–99.

34. Barclay, *Paul and the Gift*, develops the countercultural reckoning of worth in this new social matrix (423–46). See also Eastman, *Recovering Paul's Mother Tongue*, 161–79.

Bultmann makes this impossibility ruthlessly clear in his provocative essay on the necessity of demythologizing the New Testament. He confidently traces the outlines of "our self-understanding as modern persons": "We ascribe to ourselves an inner unity of states and actions"; "we look upon [dependence] as our true being, over which we are able to take dominion by understanding, so that we can rationally organize our life"; we distinguish our "true selves" from our physical bodies. "We know ourselves to be responsible for our own existence and do not understand how through water baptism a mysterious something or other could be communicated to us that would then become the subject of our intentions and actions." According to our modern worldview, says Bultmann, "we each understand our self to be a closed inner unity that is not open to the interference of supernatural powers." Knowing guilt only as "a responsible act" by individuals, "we cannot understand the doctrine of substitutionary atonement through the death of Christ," nor can we "understand Jesus' resurrection as an event whereby a power to live is released that we can now appropriate through the sacraments."[35] All of this is to say, at the very least, that in our private silos we cannot understand another's actions as reaching across time and space to transform us, even if that other is God. If we are essentially isolated, lonely individuals whose greatest capacity for connection is through a revised self-understanding within ourselves, how can we be touched by others and reconstituted in new relationships?

Troels Engberg-Pedersen's analysis of Galatians 2:19–20 interprets Paul's functional view of the person from the angle of such a "modern" notion of the self.[36] Engberg-Pederson sees several "I"s in Paul's cryptic self-depiction: there is the "I" that has died and the "I" that now lives for God, but third, there is a dual "underlying" and "self-identical I" that transcends the radical death and new life that Paul describes. This "I" was present before Paul's conversion, it has been and is crucified with Christ, and it "is still there for Christ to live in it" (159). Engberg-Pedersen calls this continuous entity both a "superior I" that has "a kind of reflective self-awareness" and "an empty, abstract, underlying 'I' . . . which may in one instantiation be 'filled in' to become the fleshly [I] and in another instantiation become the Christ-believing [I]." In other words Paul has in mind two "different kinds of self: a concrete, 'filled' one . . . and an abstract, empty one . . . which underlies the change" from the "I" that dies with

35. Rudolf Bultmann, "New Testament and Mythology: The Problem of Demythologizing the New Testament Proclamation," in *New Testament and Mythology and Other Basic Writings*, ed. and trans. Schubert M. Ogden (Philadelphia: Fortress, 1984), 5–7.

36. Engberg-Pedersen, *Cosmology and Self*, 157–62. Page numbers in the text refer to this volume.

Christ to the "I" in which Christ now lives. This abstract self is also the self that watches itself, "an 'I' of a more powerful kind of second-order reflection" (160).

Like Bultmann, Engberg-Pedersen is committed to the notion of an essential, continuous ego, characterized above all by the capacity for self-awareness and self-reflection. We recall Bultmann's commitment to the idea of the body as the human being in his or her capability for self-knowledge, and the resulting inner split between the watching self and the physical self. Similarly, in Engberg-Pedersen's account of Galatians 2:19–20, the continuous self is theoretically embodied, yet at the same time curiously abstract, floating above its different concrete embodiments and watching them from an unchangeable, unthreatened, safe distance. It is neutral, freestanding, and essential. Furthermore, according to Engberg-Pedersen, precisely this element of "reflective distance from the change" is necessary for Paul's "notion of the self" (161). In other words, there has to be a continuous self for there to be a self at all, and that continuity is sustained by locating the core of the person in an abstract, neutral, somewhat removed realm of existence.[37] This understanding accords with Engberg-Pedersen's cognitivist bent; it is no surprise that he refers to the conflict in Galatia as "a setting of *intellectual* conflict."[38]

To his credit, Engberg-Pedersen is wrestling with the experiential meaning of the paradox of an "I" that dies and yet lives. He is offering one possible answer to the question I posed earlier: When Paul says, "I no longer live but Christ lives in me," who is talking? For Engberg-Pedersen the speaker is a neutral, reflective, continuous, and (practically speaking) disembodied self that has been present from the beginning, watching itself change and now describing the change.[39]

But is this understanding credible in light of Paul's own words? Does it do justice to the extremity of his language of crucifixion and new life? Paul

37. This position is in explicit contrast with Dale Martin's depiction of the ancient body in *The Corinthian Body* (New Haven: Yale University Press, 1995). Engberg-Pedersen is well aware of this debate and discusses it in "A Stoic Concept of the Person in Paul? From Galatians 5:17 to Romans 7:14–25," in *Christian Body, Christian Self: Concepts of Early Christian Personhood*, ed. Clare K. Rothschild and Trevor W. Thompson (Tübingen: Mohr Siebeck, 2011), 85–86.

38. Engberg-Pedersen, *Cosmology and Self*, 160; emphasis added.

39. Engberg-Pedersen reads the indwelling of Christ as a reference to the indwelling Spirit, in line with Phil 3:7–11, understood as a bodily *pneuma*. He then emphasizes the change as a bodily event enacted by the indwelling *pneuma*, but he does not make clear how that bodily *pneuma* interacts with the essential "underlying I" that transcends the change (see *Cosmology and Self*, 159–62). For further comment, see John M. G. Barclay, "Stoic Physics and the Christ Event: A Review of Troels Engberg-Pedersen, *Cosmology and Self in the Apostle Paul: The Material Spirit*," *Journal for the Study of the New Testament* 33.4 (2011): 411–12.

PARTICIPATION AND THE SELF

repeats the language of crucifixion in personal terms at key points later in the letter. He tells the Galatians themselves: "Those who belong to Christ Jesus have crucified the flesh with its passions and desires" (5:24), and later he again describes himself as one who has been crucified: "but far be it from me to glory except in the cross of our Lord Jesus Christ, through which (or whom) the world has been crucified to me and I to the world" (6:14). There is no indication of an independent, somewhat abstract, empty self in Paul's language. Such a self seems to be, rather, a basically alien construct, whether Stoic or modern, pasted onto Paul's language to render it more comprehensible to "us" (whoever "we" are) in ways that are "accessible to human reasoning" and therefore "constitute an 'option for us.'"[40]

Engberg-Pedersen calls his project an exercise in "philosophical exegesis," by which he means that he builds "on philosophical accounts of the world, in the sense of modern theories of what the world is actually like."[41] Clearly a great deal depends on which "modern theories" guide the exegesis and "what the world is actually like"; Engberg-Pedersen appears to operate from a Cartesian perspective. But the contemporary horizon is changing, as Käsemann so presciently predicted when he spoke of the "interdependence" of all humanity.[42] As has become clear, the understanding of the person as an autonomous, self-aware, self-contained, and continuous unity is on the wane, to put it mildly.[43] Consequently, given the revolutions in contemporary notions of the person, the options for a current understanding and appropriation of Paul's language have changed dramatically.

Reading Galatians from a Second-Person Perspective

Alternatively, Paul's language gains new traction when approached from a second-person perspective in which the self is always and irreducibly consti-

---

40. Engberg-Pedersen, *Cosmology and Self*, 2, 6.

41. Engberg-Pedersen, *Cosmology and Self*, 2.

42. To be sure, Engberg-Pedersen recognizes this shift, but he holds to his Cartesian and indeed Kantian worldview, as he makes clear in his essay "Stoic Philosophy and the Concept of the Person," in *The Person and the Human Mind: Issues in Ancient and Modern Philosophy*, ed. Christopher Gill (Oxford: Oxford University Press, 1990), 109–35.

43. Similarly, quantum physics shows that "what the world is actually like" turns out to be far less determined and more open to divine action than Engberg-Pedersen allows. See, e.g., John Polkinghorne, *Quantum Physics and Theology: An Unexpected Kinship* (New Haven: Yale University Press, 2008).

tuted interpersonally. As we have seen, such a model of the person parts company with both existentialist and some ancient notions of the person, albeit in different ways. The person is not self-contained and purely self-directing, but neither is the person simply a part of the whole without distinction. Rather, insofar as embodied existence connects one with the larger world, when that system or world is done away with, that relationally constituted self also ceases to have any traction in the structure of the person. If there is no a priori individual prior to or apart from the intersubjective engagement within which the person exists, there is no need to posit some abstract, essential, self-reflective, and continuous "I." Rather, bonded with its relational environment, the whole self lives or dies with that matrix. For this reason Paul's crucifixion with Christ is also his crucifixion to the cosmos and the world's crucifixion to him (6:14).

As we have seen, "the flesh" (*sarx*) denotes aspects of the relational system constituting the self that has died with Christ, including "flesh" as kinship relations and "flesh" as the physical and social locus of the "works of the law." These two denotations cohere, insofar as the "works of the law" are enacted by physical bodies acting in a community guided, sustained, and governed by such shared praxis. "Flesh" also signifies bodily passions that overtake the self, so that the person acts contrary to his or her desire for the good. All these aspects of "the flesh" have bodily components, but they are not reducible to the body as a thing in itself. Rather, they concern the body-in-relation to others. Paul has no hesitation in calling such an embodied relational system "the cosmos."[44] It is a world that shapes the individuals who belong to it.

In parallel fashion, the progressive references to crucifixion also reveal the contours of the system of self-in-relation that has been abolished by Christ's crucifixion in solidarity with human dereliction. Paul has died to the law because he has been crucified with Christ.[45] He has publically portrayed Christ crucified to the Gentile Galatians (3:1), who by belonging to Christ have

44. As Martyn has argued persuasively in his comments on Gal 6:14 (*Galatians*, 564), in Paul's world prior to Christ, his "cosmos" was constructed by the antinomy of Law/Not Law.

45. In crucifixion Christ came under the curse of the law (Gal 3:13); in union with Christ's law-cursed death, then, Paul "died to the law through the law." For discussion of the relationship between crucifixion and the law, see Martyn, *Galatians*, 257. De Boer, *Galatians*, 160, says rather that "Paul's zealous devotion to the law and its 'works' led him to persecute the very church of God" and therefore led to a "collision between the law and Christ." The choice of interpretations depends to some degree on whether one reads 2:19 primarily in light of 1:13–14 or in light of 3:10–13. I am more persuaded by the latter move, particularly given the sense of *Ioudaismos* in 1:13 as a "political cause" rather than simply "devotion to the works of the law." See now Matthew Novenson, "Paul's Former Occupation in *Ioudaismos*," in Elliott et al., *Galatians and Christian Theology*, 24–39.

crucified the flesh with its passions and desires (5:24). Finally, Paul has been crucified to the cosmos and the cosmos to him; the evidence for this radical change is in the explanatory *gar* clause that follows: neither circumcision nor uncircumcision but a new creation (6:14–15).

In a word, for both Paul and his listeners every element of personhood shaped by their social milieu has been nullified by the obscene execution of the Son of God. Specifically, insofar as Paul once depended on and drew his identity from law observance, thereby differentiating himself from nonobservant Gentiles, his "nomistic self" has "died."[46] Furthermore, insofar as Paul and his communities live in a culture pervasively shaped and dominated by systems of honor, union with Christ in the shame of crucifixion puts all such values to death, nullifying identities constructed on the basis of honor.[47] Insofar as the self cannot be imagined apart from its ties of kinship and community, the abrogation of such ties destroys the primal foundations of identity; Paul now looks upon his own infant circumcision and membership in the tribe of Benjamin as excrement (Phil 3:5, 8). Indeed, because the gospel produces a single new humanity, "every source of human identity is taken up by and into the gospel."[48]

To use Peter Hobson's terminology, we might say that the death of these socially constructed selves is the death of a "system of self-in-relation." The movement of God in Christ into embodied, socially enmeshed existence inaugurates a newly constructed self-in-relation "in Christ." This radical remaking of the person is therefore not a splitting off of one part of the self, designated as "flesh." It is the reintegration of the whole person within a new intersubjectively constituted identity. This new intersubjectively shaped identity in relationship to Christ also plays out in human interactions. Paul uses social and family metaphors to get the point across. Believers are "adopted" into a new household whose members jointly attend to God as Father through the Spirit sent into the "hearts" (4:5–6). Paul appeals to them to embrace a reciprocally mimetic relationship instigated by Paul's own mimetic movement into their world, in and through Christ's participation in the human condition (4:12). In light of this reciprocity, Paul's mimetic language does not impose an infantile relationship between Paul and his converts. Rather, like infant imitation, it implies a reconstitution of Paul's converts, like Paul himself, at the primal level

---

46. Martyn, *Galatians*, 280.

47. John M. G. Barclay, "Grace and the Countercultural Reckoning of Worth: Community Construction in Galatians 5–6," in Elliott et al., *Galatians and Christian Theology*, 306–17.

48. Gaventa, "Singularity," 196.

of identity formation.[49] They are free heirs, not slaves, living together in a new relational matrix in which the old division between circumcision and uncircumcision, slave and free, male and female, has been abrogated and replaced by a new creation (3:28; 5:6; 6:15). In contrast to the divisive "works of the law" that operate in tandem with the "works of the flesh," this new life together is characterized by "faith working through love [*pistis di' agapēs energoumenē*]." The evidence and outworking of life "in faith" is mutual loving service, in contrast with the "desires of the flesh" that correlate with rapacious mutual destruction (5:13–16). Just as the "works of the flesh" take place in interpersonal relationships (5:19–21), so also are the "fruits of the Spirit" evidenced in the way in which people treat one another (5:22–23). Such relationships constitute the socially embedded instantiation of life in the realm of faith generated by Christ's gift (2:20).

Furthermore, just as participation in "the flesh" happens through the body, so also the body mediates and signifies what it means to belong to Christ. Paul explicitly contrasts the bodily mark of circumcision in the flesh (6:12–13) with the bodily brand marks (*stigmata*) of Jesus (6:17).[50] In a nutshell, Paul anticipates in 6:17 what he will later say in 2 Corinthians 4:10–11: in the persecutions he and his colleagues suffer, they are "always carrying in the body the death of Jesus so that the life of Jesus also may be manifested in our bodies. For while we live we are always being given up to death for Jesus' sake, so that the life of Jesus may be manifested in our mortal flesh." Paul's self-depiction assumes a thoroughly second-person understanding of the body as connecting believers to Christ and as communicating this assimilated yet distinct Other to all those with whom Paul and his colleagues interact.

Paul's Relational Self in Contemporary Terms

In chapter 4 I suggested that in Romans 7:7–25 Paul personifies sin as both a destructive relational system and a hostile agent that enslaves the human subject and evacuates his or her agency. An example of this deforming system and relationship came from the contagious effects on children of parents with borderline personality disorder. Conversely, in Galatians 2:15–21 Paul depicts

---

49. I have argued for this interpretation exegetically in *Recovering Paul's Mother Tongue*, 44–61.

50. For the argument that the stigmata are Paul's scars from being stoned and whipped, see Martyn, *Galatians*, 568; de Boer, *Galatians*, 409.

a newly constituted self that lives in union with Christ in a network of relationships characterized by trusting faith, which originates in and returns to Christ. Taking its bearings from the new creation, not the old cosmos, this new relational matrix belongs to the future and pulls its members away from the past.

A Gifted Interpersonal Network

The reconstitution of the self has both corporate and individual dimensions. In Galatians 2:18-21 Paul speaks in first-person singular, dramatically depicting the transformation wrought by union of the self with Christ; in 5:13-6:10, however, he speaks primarily in the second-person plural, as he limns the effects of this transformation in the interpersonal life of the Christian communities in Galatia.[51] In both the individual and the communal instances, relationships grounded in gift are central to the transformed intersubjective life that Paul proclaims. Rabens puts this well when he claims, "Paul does not present the believer as needing, in the sense of a fusion, to 'tune in' to the ethical conduct of the Spirit at the core of the person's being. Rather, the Spirit enables ethical living by drawing believers into the loving and empowering presence of the divine and of the community of faith. The moral character and the ethical actions are that of the believer, but they are lived within these loving relationships and can to a large extent be regarded as an outflow of the continual experience of love."[52] The point here is that the change that takes place as persons are reconstituted in Christ is not discovered through an inward look for the Spirit within some core self, but rather in the interactions that take place between believers. We might even say that the quality of social interaction that Paul enjoins in Galatians 5:13-6:10 enacts corporately the newly constituted intersubjective bond between Christ and the individual, which itself is generated by Christ's loving self-gift.

51. The temporary shift to third-person plural in 5:24 appears to be a general theological claim undergirding the paraenesis of the preceding verses. The subsequent first-person plural in 5:25-26 sums up the preceding exhortations in an inclusive appeal. As Volker Rabens notes, the summary statement "if (since) we live by the Spirit, let us also walk by the Spirit" grounds that appeal in a relational bond between God and the Galatians; the Spirit is the living presence of Christ in their midst ("Indicative and Imperative," 285-305).

52. Rabens, "Indicative and Imperative," 304. See also Volker Rabens, *The Holy Spirit and Ethics in Paul: Transformation and Empowerment for Religious-Ethical Life* (Minneapolis: Fortress, 2014), 130-31, for the effects of intimate relationships on personal development.

How might such an intersubjective model of the person work in contemporary terms? I have suggested that the gift of God's gracious and self-giving presence in the midst of daily life forms personal identity around the reception of a gift rather than around competition or achievement.[53] In his reflection on Augustine and Descartes, Timothy Chappell puts the idea of personhood as relational gift succinctly: "Each of us becomes a mind, and a person, only by being 'always already' in relation with other persons, both human and divine, as a precondition of her own mindedness. Personhood, in short, is not something I achieve on my own; it is a gift, the gift to me of others."[54] In a passage worth quoting at length, Chappell traces out the implications of understanding personhood as interpersonal gift:

> If persons depend for their very being upon a pre-existing relationship, then there is something deeply wrong with the usual approach to persons in applied ethics. This begins from the claim that personhood is a status which we attain by satisfying criteria of various sorts: rationality, the ability to speak, emotionality, and so on. Such an approach to personhood makes sense if *individualism about persons* is true: on an individualist approach, there can't be anything wrong with just subjecting individuals to a tick-list of properties they might have, and seeing whether in fact they do have them. But if *relationalism about persons* is true, how can it make sense? If persons—and so *a fortiori* personal qualities like rationality and emotionality—are only constituted in the first place by the antecedent relationships in which persons are to be found, then to approach the question whether someone "counts as a person" by seeing whether they pass this or that test is to step away from the relationship that we already have with them.[55]

In his letter to the Galatians, Paul is combating a kind of *criterialism* about what counts as justification, and therefore what counts for membership in the community of persons constituted in Christ, by reminding his converts of the relationship they already share. The criteria are the works of the law,

---

53. John M. G. Barclay has extensively developed this effect of the gift on noncompetitive communal life, in *Paul and the Gift*, 493–519. See also his "Under Grace: The Christ-Gift and the Construction of a Christian *Habitus*," in *Apocalyptic Paul: Cosmos and Anthropos in Romans 5–8*, ed. Beverly R. Gaventa (Waco, TX: Baylor University Press, 2013), 59–76.

54. Timothy Chappell, "Knowledge of Persons," *European Journal for Philosophy of Religion* 5.4 (2013): 18.

55. Chappell, "Knowledge of Persons," 26; emphasis added.

with circumcision as a necessary mark of belonging. Paul, however, sets such criteria in explicit opposition to the singular and completely sufficient gift of "the Son of God, who loved me and gave himself [*paradontos*] for me." Therefore, says Paul, "I do not nullify the grace of God; for if justification were through the law, then Christ died for nothing ['gratuitously'—*dōrean*]" (2:21).[56] This gift is the only criterion by which the Galatians' identity and belonging are established, thereby linking their personal worth directly to the worth of Christ. Henceforth they are to live together in the intersubjective bond of trust established by Christ's love.

Furthermore, the fellowship the Galatians already share with Paul and each other is the medium through which they are to know this truth about their life. Paul uses every relational gambit he can muster to drive home to the Galatians this unique, interpersonal gift: he reminds them of their former welcome of him (4:12–16) and of the bond and history they share, and he draws on family metaphors to depict the formation of an identity at the primal level of birth and infancy. God has sent the Spirit of his Son into the Galatians' hearts, so that in their common worship they cry out to God as "Abba" (4:6), thereby expressing their new interpersonally expressed identity as "sons of God" in Christ Jesus (3:26). Finally, Paul appeals to the Galatians as "my children, with whom I am again in labor until Christ be formed in you" (4:19). This maternal imagery surely has apocalyptic overtones, and as such it tells the Galatians that they are being remade at the very roots of their identity.[57] The metaphor is notoriously mixed: Paul is in labor with the Galatians, but the desired result is that Christ take form among them, like an embryo taking form in the womb.[58] Despite the shift in denotation, however, the meaning is clear: precisely because the Galatians never exist on their own, Paul wants Christ's self-giving life to shape their common life, recognizing that their character is formed and transformed in this mutual exchange. Paul does not speak of Christ taking form in the Galatians individually, but "among you [*en hymin*]."

56. Noted by Barclay, *Paul and the Gift*, 332n2, in his summary of gift language in Galatians (331–33).

57. For the apocalyptic context of Paul's use of *ōdinō* in Gal 4:19, see Beverly R. Gaventa, "The Maternity of Paul: An Exegetical Study of Galatians 4:19," in *The Conversation Continues: Studies in Paul and John in Honor of J. Louis Martyn*, ed. Beverly R. Gaventa and Robert T. Fortna (Nashville: Abingdon, 1990), 189–201; Martyn, *Galatians*, 426–31. In *Recovering Paul's Mother Tongue*, 89–126, I argue that the echoes of Isa 45:10; 42:13–16 and Jer 8:21 suggest that Paul's "labor" mirrors and enacts God's "labor" in solidarity with the suffering of Israel.

58. De Boer notes Galen's use of *morphoō* to denote the formation of an embryo (*Galatians*, 284n415).

At issue here are the quality and character of the interactive bonds in which personhood is gifted and sustained.[59] In turning from a singular depiction of Christ "in me" in 2:19–21 to the corporate experience of the life of the Spirit, Paul shifts the expectation of changed behavior from individual selves to corporately constituted agents. This wording does not mean the erasure of individual agents, however, as quickly becomes clear through Paul's return to a third-person-singular address in 6:3–5. But it does mean that the Spirit is known through working in and among the believers, and that the transformation Paul expects is not a matter of individual ontological change but, rather, of participation in a relational interchange that is larger than the self. And that interchange in turn creates both a network of reciprocal exchange and truth telling and the room to name the vicissitudes and failures of actual human experience. Through the intersubjective constitution of the self with other believers, which takes place in the presence of Christ in the Spirit, the newly constituted person "in Christ" is intersubjective all the way down, in relationship to Christ and in relationship to others. Such an intersubjective transformation is mediated by the presence of the Spirit, who operates among and between believers, generating a new interpersonal "cradle of thought."

Pulled into the Future

Finally, I earlier suggested that the image of an actor playing his or her role suggests a fluidity in the identity of human subjects and argues against any essentialist notions of the person as a continuous, self-contained agent. Something similar happens in Galatians through Paul's deployment of temporal markers, but to somewhat different ends. One of the most notable features of this letter is the frequent contrast between "then" and "now" in Paul's depiction of himself, the Galatians, and the scope of human history. The entire thrust of the gospel is Christ's self-donation on the cross "to deliver us from the present evil age" (1:4). In Paul's life that deliverance means a dramatic break with his "former life in Judaism" (1:13–14) and his cocrucifixion with Christ (2:19–20). Indeed, his break with the cosmos is complete, because he has been crucified to the cosmos, and the cosmos to him (6:14). In the lives of his converts, he

59. See now the perceptive and suggestive comments of Rabens, who cites work on attachment theory in psychology in support of his claim that "it nonetheless is possible to draw out a number of significant components of relational transformation and empowering" ("Indicative and Imperative," 304n48).

also limns a contrast between their former "bondage to those who by nature are not gods" and the present, in which they "have come to know God, or rather, to be known by God" (4:8–9). Speaking of Israel's history, he contrasts the former bondage under the pedagogy of the law with the new reality, "now that faith has come" through the coming of Christ (3:23–25). The structure of the letter as a whole contrasts "the present evil age" (1:4) with the new creation through the crucifixion and resurrection of Christ (6:15).

This thematic contrast between then and now certainly depicts a radical rupture in the constitution of the self. It means, for example, that the past does not determine the present or the future, whether on a macrohistorical level or on a micropersonal level. Insofar as the past is coextensive with fleshly existence, it is nailed to the cross with Christ. There is, to be sure, a certain paradoxical continuity of the person: Paul's own calling came from God while he was in his mother's womb (1:15); although his "former life in Judaism" might be construed as interrupting that call, the apocalypse of Christ in him connected him to his original and perhaps originating call.[60] Similarly, Israel's story is one of deep discontinuity and divine continuity. On the one hand, the coming of Christ is the fulfillment of God's primal promise to Abraham; on the other, the coming of the Mosaic law temporarily interrupted the pattern of promise and fulfillment, such that "in Paul's retelling of both his own history and Israel's history, life under the law is bracketed by divine call and divine apocalypse."[61] Thus in Paul's own life and in the history of Israel, there are both a radical break with the past and a connection with the point of origin.

A great deal could be said about this pattern of continuity and discontinuity; here I am concerned with the effects of such language on the concept of the person. When the "I" is crucified with Christ, the ego is unmoored from any prior sources of identity, worth, and direction, or conversely, all sources of shame, dishonor, and despair; it is severed from the relational matrix shaped by family of origin, social context, economic status, and so forth. Henceforth all access to such sources of identity passes through union with Christ on the cross. To put this in contemporary terms drawn from philosophy of mind, a new relational system remaps the old. Or put more simply, only through the grace and judgment of the cross can there be a true knowledge of oneself and others.

60. Eastman, *Recovering Paul's Mother Tongue*, 33–43. See also Barclay, "Paul's Story," for a similar argument regarding the lines of continuity and discontinuity in Paul's self-narration.

61. Eastman, *Recovering Paul's Mother Tongue*, 36; see also Barclay, "Paul's Story," 140.

The reverse side of this claim is that human personhood, as intersubjectively constituted in relationship with Christ, belongs to the future, not to the past. There is no hint of nostalgia in Paul's letters; they are completely forward-looking. There is no longing for the good old days or for any youthful innocence.[62] He repeatedly calls his converts to set their sights on the "hope of righteousness" that comes through Christ alone (5:5), and on the promise that "the one who sows to the Spirit will reap eternal life" (6:8). Such eschatological identity has profound implications for the ways in which believers may navigate loss and hope, not only in the face of death, but also in the face of destructive patterns of social connections in this life.

62. It is true that Paul reminds the Galatians of the former welcome of him (4:13–15), but this reminder is in service of the larger warning not to return to their old bondage by taking up law observance. Rather, they are to wait hopefully for the hope of righteousness (5:5); both the warning and the hope look to the future, not the past.

Conclusion

Pushing the Reset Button on Paul's Anthropology

> Traditional—specifically Christian—doctrine and exhortation are meaningless in our present context so long as we have no idea of what *sense of self* such teaching is addressed to; to hear what is said in religious discourse, we must build a selfhood radically unlike what we take for granted as the modern norm of subjectivity.
>
> —Rowan Williams, *Lost Icons*

The necessary *sense of self*, envisioned in the above epigraph, includes "the possibility of understanding what it might mean to say that I am because I am *seen* at a certain depth, or that I require a faithful presence to hear my narrative, or that I have no reality as a subject that is not also a reality for and in another subject."[1] Williams wrote these words more than a decade ago. In the preceding pages I have tried to show that at least some modern norms of subjectivity have changed, making them more amenable to the sense of self he describes and thereby opening up new opportunities for interpreting and articulating Christian thought. In the introduction, I described the purpose of this book as an attempt to seize those opportunities, to push the reset button on our approach to Paul's answer to the ancient question in the Psalms: "What is man, that Thou art mindful of him?" This is not a question that Paul addresses directly; nonetheless, his answer is implicit in his understanding of sin, of Christ, of the work of redemption, and of the redeemed community in the body of Christ. Persons are those creatures whose bodily form Christ

---

1. Rowan Williams, *Lost Icons: Reflections on Cultural Bereavement* (London: Continuum, 2003), 203.

assumed and thereby dignified in its most socially liminal state, that of a slave and a crucified criminal. Every human being is thereby a person in the divine image. Paul's answer, like the psalmist's question, is grounded in a second-person perspective: the question of human identity cannot finally be answered from the standpoint of the individual or of merely human relations, let alone other environmental factors in the natural order, but only in relation to a transcendent God who is "mindful" of human beings. And Paul's answer takes its bearings from Christ, who enacts God's concern for humanity by taking on human flesh and blood for the redemption of all humanity.

I have argued that this second-person standpoint pervades Paul's thought and points a way out of dead ends in Pauline interpretation arising from a purely individualistic notion of the self. As bodies, persons are relationally constituted beings from the very beginning of life and are never "free" agents, if "freedom" is understood in terms of individual autonomy; they are from the beginning selves-in-relation-to-another. From the perspective of understanding the body as primarily the mode of other-relation, and only secondarily as self-relation, self-knowledge is always mediated through interpersonal interaction, both for good and for ill.

Sin is thus not a decision made by self-determining individuals, but rather a socially mediated power greater than human beings yet operative through human thoughts, words, and deeds. Yes, persons make decisions and are responsible on one level for those choices; but on another level the very perception of what choices are available is already constrained and deceived by sin. Redemption is therefore not a matter of moving from isolated turning in on oneself to participation in Christ, but rather of liberation from one realm of power to another, from the rule of sin and death to life in Christ. In both cases, the person is constituted by participation in realities larger than the self or than merely human relations.

Paul's thought is thus thoroughly participatory, and understanding the participatory nature of his perspective is crucial to grasping not only his anthropology but also his Christology. But there are many ways to talk about participation. Juxtaposing Paul's thought with the naturalistic theology of Epictetus sharpens and clarifies Paul's distinctive views; Epictetus may in one way be seen as participatory, because like all Stoics he sees human existence on a continuum with the spectrum of the natural order in which God is completely immanent. Paul's cosmology is radically different, insofar as God is the transcendent Creator, whose actions in the world originate outside the natural order. The radicalism of Paul's participatory worldview is grounded in his depiction of Christ's participation in and assimilation to human existence to the point of death, thereby enacting a transforming union with humanity operative in, but not limited to, bodily existence here and now. Both qualitatively other and fully immanent, God in Christ affords a structure of the self that is intersubjective all the way down.

This structured self intersects in intriguing ways with current work in psychology, neuroscience, and philosophy of mind, which sees persons as constructed in relationship with their environment through the actions of the body. My hope in juxtaposing Paul's voice with the work of current theorists is twofold: to generate new interpretive possibilities for articulating Paul's gospel in contemporary terms, and to bring his voice to bear in current conversations about personhood and human flourishing. In writing this book, my hope has been to invite its readers into a fruitful, provocative conversation between Paul and contemporary theorists of the person, across the spectrum of philosophy, neuroscience, and psychology. The connections I have explored between Paul's anthropology and both his first-century context and contemporary thought thus represent an introductory rather than a comprehensive survey. I have not covered every topic: I have not discussed current work in social-scientific interpretations of Paul, for example, nor the issue of Paul's relationship to the Roman Empire. I have not explored comparisons between Paul's anthropology and that of his first-century Jewish contemporaries, valuable as such comparisons would be. Rather, I have sought to model a new interdisciplinary approach to the topic of Paul and the person. By reframing Paul's voice in conversation with current work in the cognitive sciences and philosophy, I hope to set the groundwork for bringing his anthropology to bear on current issues around human dignity, suffering, and flourishing. A great deal remains to be done. Here I name some findings from this book and suggest topics that invite further exploration.

The Category of "Personhood"

How does the notion of gifted identity transform ideas of what is necessary for the status of personhood? I have suggested that Paul's anthropology counters any criterialism about qualifications for being a person, precisely because it is grounded in the story of Christ's mimetic assimilation to the human condition. Paul's "master story" about what is most deeply true about human beings is not, in the first instance, the creation narrative but the story of Jesus Christ: his being sent into the world in the likeness of the flesh of sin, his identification with sinful humanity to the point of death, and his victorious resurrection from the dead. This socially embodied divine action grants dignity and worth to every human being—that is, to every creature whose "form" Christ assumed. In this regard, it is not insignificant that Christ assumed the form of a slave, one whose legal standing as a person was liminal at best in the Roman Empire. Christ's assimilation to the most vulnerable form of human existence suggests that the status of personhood is not attained by any achievement, including participation in Christ; it is granted globally by Christ's participation in the depths of human life. For this reason, the incarnation affords a radical argument for the validity of every human body, irrespective of any criteria of rationality, mobility, race, gender, relationality, or any other characteristic. Furthermore, what distinguishes human beings from other animals is not, according to this argument, any innate quality or even the assertion that we possess souls and other animals do not, but rather the theological claim that *Homo sapiens* is the form in which God took flesh.

It is of course entirely possible to speak of personhood as relationally constituted and in this sense "gifted" without invoking any theological claims, as we have seen in the work of Gallagher, Reddy, and Hobson, for example. But here's the rub: if we take this idea of gifted identity to its logical end apart from any certainty of divine benevolence, we end with horror, because what is given by other human beings can also be withheld by others. I have suggested examples of this negative consequence on the personal level, in accounts of children of parents with borderline personality disorder. But the denial of humanity to other human beings operates globally as well. History is full of examples of such dehumanization on a massive scale, from slavery around the globe, to the genocidal demonization of people groups, from Armenians, to Jews, to Tutsis, to the sense of negation that people of color describe in contemporary American society, and on and on. Who determines the standing and worth of another human being and by what criteria? If that determination is limited to human judgments, then human flourishing is deeply at risk.

Herein are the intense fragility and danger of relational constructions of the person. One attempt to counter that danger is through the language of individual rights, which inevitably come into conflict with others' rights. Paul's theology points in a different direction, through an enduring and christologically grounded affirmation of every human body based on the human incarnation of the divine. That Christ took the form of the very lowest human being on the social ladder of the Roman Empire and then died the most ignoble death possible drives home the radical inclusivity of Paul's anthropology. But the consequent affirmation of all humanity needs repeated social enactment in every situation, requiring a nimble and embodied theological interpretation—not simply repetition—of his letters.

Rethinking Dualism

Following Käsemann, I have argued that Paul's anthropology does not support a dualistic picture of the self as divided between material and immaterial parts, but rather a holistic understanding of persons, together with a metaphysical dualism between creation and the Creator. But insofar as "anthropology is crystalized cosmology," metaphysical dualism also shapes the person; like his contemporaries, Paul thinks the structure of human beings cannot be disassociated from the structure of the cosmos.[2] For this reason, as Käsemann also said, "The tension between cosmology and anthropology characterizes the whole of Paul's theology."[3] Reading Paul through a second-person hermeneutical lens provides a way to think about this correspondence and tension in relational terms, as a distinction between (1) personhood constituted through "the flesh" in a fully embodied and socially embedded way and (2) personhood constituted through the Spirit of the incarnate, crucified, and resurrected Christ, also in a fully embodied and socially embedded way. When Paul writes, "God sent his Son, born of a woman, born under the law" and "God sent the Spirit of his Son into our hearts," the parallel clauses convey a new dualistic construction of human beings as indwelt by the Spirit of the Son, who is qualitatively distinct from the natural order yet participates fully in it. This is the insight implicit in Käsemann's suggestion, "It might be possible to develop the connection [of theology and anthropology] in the light of Pauline Christology, thus avoiding the danger both of a Christian metaphysic and of a Christian humanism."[4]

This tension between anthropology and cosmology is temporal as well as spatial in its orientation and function. The constitution of human beings in relationship to the realm of flesh, sin, and death has existential traction in the

2. For an interesting contemporary attempt to analyze this relationship from a nontheistic standpoint, see Thomas Nagel, *Mind and Cosmos: Why the Materialist Neo-Darwinian Conception of Nature Is Almost Certainly False* (Oxford: Oxford University Press, 2012): "We should seek a form of understanding that enables us and other conscious organisms as specific expressions simultaneously of the physical and mental character of the universe" (69–70). As this quote illustrates, Nagel argues for anthropological as well as cosmological dualism between "physical" and "mental" realities, contrary to the majority of scientific assumptions currently on offer.

3. Ernst Käsemann, *An die Römer*, Handbuch zum Neuen Testament 8A (Tübingen: Mohr Siebeck, 1980), 30; Eng. trans., *Commentary on Romans*, trans. G. W. Bromiley (Grand Rapids: Eerdmans, 1980), 33.

4. Ernst Käsemann, "On Paul's Anthropology," in *Perspectives on Paul*, trans. M. Kohl (Mifflintown, PA: Sigler, 1996 [1969]), 12.

present time, yet it has no final, lasting reality; it belongs to what is passing away. The constitution of persons in relationship to the lordship of Christ and the indwelling Spirit, however, has existential traction in the present time and persists into the future, because such an interpersonal identity is held and constituted by the Lord who holds the future.

Furthermore, since at the present time believers participate in both worlds simultaneously, this understanding complicates Paul's evident expectation of transformation in the lives of his converts, leading to the puzzling juxtaposition of affirmations such as "Those who belong to Christ Jesus have crucified the flesh, with its passions and desires" (Gal 5:24), with warnings such as "Let us not become conceited, competing against one another, envying one another" (v. 26). We are certainly right to ask why such warnings are still necessary if the flesh, with its passions and desires, has been put to death. Recognizing the complex relational networks in which all human life is entangled and constituted may provide a way to speak about this interpretive issue with more existential precision than simply evoking the tension between "already" and "not yet" in Paul's eschatology.

Anthropological Realism and the Promise of Change

The social, intersubjective constitution of the self supports ways of talking about personal transformation that honor Paul's language of radical change and yet also honor the reality that such transformation seems elusive and fragile at best. I have argued that Romans 7 articulates the slippage between what seems to be an *ontological* conversion from the flesh to the new creation, absolutely enacted through baptism into Christ's death (Rom 6:3–4), and the *experience* of ongoing struggle against sin as a hostile, deceptive. and lethal power. Rather than describe this struggle as an inner conflict, I suggest it displays and enacts the believer's simultaneous participation in the realm of sin and death and in the life of Christ. Sin ultimately is a fleeting falsehood, whereas Christ's rule endures forever; nonetheless, as history abundantly demonstrates, a lie may have tremendous power to do harm, precisely because it operates and spreads through interpersonal systems.

If human beings, then, live and move and have their being in complex, often conflicting networks, transformation also happens through those networks. This truth means that, rather than talking about change in individuals in a substantial or linear sense, perhaps it is more accurate and closer to Paul's thought to describe change rendered effective and visible through the quality of relationships.[5] Change happens "between ourselves" more than within discrete individuals. There are many examples of how such a shift to a second-person perspective on human transformation might afford more nuanced and ultimately hopeful accounts of change. For example, consider the case of a woman who suffers dementia toward the end of a long, faithful, and loving life; she becomes someone her family does not recognize. Through chemical changes in the brain, to all appearances her transformation into the image of Christ seems undone. Or alternatively, one might consider a person who struggles through a lifetime of addiction, never able to overcome it fully, or someone whose childhood traumas erupt in destructive behaviors after many years of apparently Christ-like service. Change is elusive, evanescent, and impossible to judge fully in this life.

But insofar as change happens, it happens through the characteristics of communal interaction that mediate Christ. It may be impossible to discern the transforming presence of the Spirit in a dementia victim (although many times the opposite is also the case); but it is possible to see that divine presence in the love extended to her by others. It certainly is impossible for a person to discern accurately the change within himself or herself, as Paul well understood when he said, "I do not even judge myself" (1 Cor 4:3). Rather, when Paul tells the Romans to think of themselves "with sober judgment, each according to the measure of faith that God has assigned," he immediately turns their attention to the interplay of God-given gifts between them; whatever faith-informed self-assessment they do exercise will be discovered and tested in the giving and receiving of divinely gifted ministry (Rom 12:3-8). That web of relationships in the body of Christ, not isolated or inward-turned individuals, is the arena in which change happens.

5. Kyle B. Wells articulates the interactive mode of transformation in Paul as well as its implications for contemporary notions of the self: "For Paul, it is this reciprocal relationship of giving and receiving, a relationship set in motion by the divine initiative, on which human competency is founded. Paul's perspective, it would thus appear, sits uncomfortably with many substantialist notions regarding the Self: a Self which exists complete, apart from the acts and relations which make up this new existence. Rather, Pauline imperatives are predicated upon the fact that, clinging to God through Christ, his communities have been *freed* to obey, and are *continually freed* to obey by the Holy Spirit." *Grace and Agency in Paul and Second Temple Judaism: Interpreting the Transformation of the Heart* (Leiden/Boston: Brill, 2015), 296.

Hope and Eschatological Identity

In terms of relationally constituted personhood, the tension between cosmology and anthropology means that there is never resolution of personal or social issues in this life. If a woman, for example, is incomplete, never whole in herself, and if her own well-being is tied in with that of others, then in the present she must live with a lack of closure, including a lack of full healing of whatever wrongs she has suffered or committed. The good of the part and the good of the whole are so intertwined that individuals can be fully transformed only when everyone is transformed. To say that I have achieved wholeness or full integration of myself is nonsensical from a Pauline perspective. Rather, as Rowan Williams puts it, "My 'health' is in the thinking or sensing of how I am not at one with myself, existing as I do in time (change) and language (exchange)."[6]

Similarly, the complex overlapping of relational systems means that social institutions must live with imperfection rather than demanding closure and a resolution of differences that will inevitably benefit some and harm others. One aspect of Christian witness is thus to name the lack of closure and the continued ruptures and suffering in all humanity, including the body of Christ.[7] To fail to do so betrays the bodily interconnectedness that underlies Paul's thought; when a community claims to have achieved perfect unity, one wonders who has been left out; when an individual claims to have achieved wholeness, one wonders at what expense that "integration" has happened. Rather than pushing for some kind of personal or social perfection, perhaps speaking truthfully about the lack of wholeness most perfectly manifests Paul's realism about Christian existence this side of the eschaton.

Yet, Paul is supremely confident in the final victory of Christ's death and resurrection and of its present effects in the lives of believers: "Sin will not rule over you, because you are not under the law, but under grace" (Rom 6:14). If there is thus a kind of persistent patience and realism engendered by eschatological reservation, there is also a profound hope engendered by eschatological identity. Again, the relational constitution of the person reshapes the picture of human hope: the person whose identity is ultimately grounded in relationship with Christ is pulled into the future, not finally determined by past or even present sufferings or achievements.

---

6. Williams, *Lost Icons*, 186.

7. Ernst Käsemann argued for such a witness by interpreting Rom 8:26–27 as Spirit-inspired groaning in solidarity with all humanity ("The Cry for Liberty in the Worship of the Church," in Kohl, *Perspectives on Paul*, 122–37).

Second-Person Hermeneutics

Perhaps all methodologies have a polemical edge; certainly the approach of this book does. Employing what I have called second-person hermeneutics, I have attempted to put distinctive voices into shared conversation across disciplinary boundaries, in the service of a theological interpretation of Paul's anthropology. Implicit in this approach is a commitment to an embodied, contextual interpretation of Paul's theology. If we cannot understand human cognition via the model of a brain in a vat, we also cannot understand Paul's thought through a model of cognition or a mode of interpretation that operates from the neck up. Rather, bodily practices, which necessarily express and engage with environmental contexts, are necessary sources of knowledge when it comes to interpreting Paul's letters. We can grasp this insight particularly because Paul depicts the body as the way in which human beings are enmeshed in larger social and cosmic realities. The theological grounding and affirmation of such bodily participation is the sending of the Son in the likeness of the flesh of sin (Rom 8:3). The second-person hermeneutics employed in this book is thus an attempt to take seriously what such incarnational cognition might mean for understanding Paul's functional anthropology—which is a way of getting at how the grace of God in Christ impacts and changes existential reality for human beings now.

The Care of the Person

I close with some questions for further exploration. In this book I have sought to reframe Paul's anthropology in light of relational accounts of the person, in conversation with both Epictetus and contemporary work in science and philosophy. My goal, however, is not simply to gain a new understanding of Paul's christologically shaped understanding of human suffering and human flourishing. Rather, in line with both Bultmann and Käsemann, I seek to catalyze a fresh hearing of Paul's "word of address" to contemporary readers in our varied contexts. There are many possibilities for such a word in relation to current issues. For example, how might Paul's embodied and socially embedded account of sin, Christ's incarnation, and new life in the body of Christ be deployed in regard to issues of racial identity and social injustice? How does the notion of divinely gifted interpersonal identity speak to the status and identity of human beings in light of rapid developments in science, such as genetic engineering or the development of nearly human artificial intelligence and robotics? How do we define health in light of both fundamental human relatedness and inevitable death, and how might Paul's anthropology bring fresh perspectives on the goals and methods of health care? Does Paul's complex understanding of the body as connection provide opportunities for rethinking the ways children and adolescents learn to view their bodies?[8] These are just a few of the potential research questions generated by reframing Paul's anthropology.

My own interests focus on the care of persons in extremis. I suggest that a conversation between Paul and current work on the person affords new opportunities for resourcing Paul's thought in pastoral and clinical settings. Paul was a missionary and pastor addressing specific social contexts in his churches; the participatory logic of his gospel needs interpretation and articulation to address particular contexts of care in churches and other institutions today. Those contexts include situations in which the worth and identity of the person seem to be at risk, such as the understanding and care of those who suffer from dementia and those who care for them; the articulation of personhood and relationship among and with autistic persons; support for people suffering the aftereffects of trauma; and articulating real hope in the face of death. All of these situations often result in social isolation; all of them are unavoidably embodied; all of them require care in interpersonal networks. How might Paul's understanding of the body as a mode of connection and communication be deployed in such care? How might his depiction of sin as a hostile, enslaving agent be deployed diagnostically in some traumatic situations? Does his view of persons as relationally constituted overlap with debates in psychology and psychiatry about the relationship between biomedical care and talk therapy? Does the understanding of personhood as a criteria-free divine gift speak to debates about the human status of limit-cases, such as fetuses, those in comas, extreme dementia, and so forth?

These questions are far beyond the scope of the present book; I offer them as an invitation to further exploration and conversation across disciplinary boundaries. No less than the person, this book exists only "in time (change) and language (exchange)"; as such, it witnesses to its own incompleteness. I make no apologies for that incompleteness. Rather, in eschatological reservation and hope, let it be a contribution to further, indeed unceasing, engagement with Paul's gospel as a word of hope and transformation in our complex world. The apostle would expect no less in the service of the liberating good news of Jesus Christ.

8. See, e.g., Emily Peck-McClain, "Agency in Paul and Implications for Adolescent Girls," *Religious Education* 110.1 (2015): 95–109.

Works Cited

Adamson, Lauren B., and Janet E. Frick. "The Still Face: A History of a Shared Experimental Paradigm." *Infancy* 4.4 (2003): 451–73.

Barclay, John M. G. " 'By the Grace of God I Am What I Am': Grace and Agency in Philo and Paul." In *Divine and Human Agency in Paul and His Cultural Environment*, edited by John M. G. Barclay and Simon J. Gathercole, 140–57. London: T&T Clark, 2008.

————. "Grace and the Countercultural Reckoning of Worth: Community Construction in Galatians 5–6." In *Galatians and Christian Theology: Justification, the Gospel, and Ethics in Paul's Letter*, edited by Mark W. Elliott et al., 306–17. Grand Rapids: Baker Academic, 2014.

————. "Humanity under Faith." In *Beyond Bultmann: Reckoning a New Testament Theology*, edited by Bruce W. Longenecker and Mikeal C. Parsons, 79–99. Waco, TX: Baylor University Press, 2014.

————. "Interpretation, Not Repetition: Reflections on Bultmann as a Theological Reader of Paul." *Journal of Theological Interpretation* 9.2 (2015): 201–9.

————. *Obeying the Truth: A Study of Paul's Ethics in Galatians*. Edinburgh: T&T Clark, 1998.

————. *Paul and the Gift*. Grand Rapids: Eerdmans, 2015.

————. "Paul's Story: Theology as Testimony." In *Narrative Dynamics in Paul: A Critical Assessment*, edited by Bruce W. Longenecker, 133–56. Louisville: Westminster John Knox, 2002.

————. "Security and Self-Sufficiency: A Comparison of Paul and Epictetus." *Ex Auditu* 24 (2008): 60–72.

————. "Stoic Physics and the Christ Event: A Review of Troels Engberg-Pedersen, *Cosmology and Self in the Apostle Paul: The Material Spirit*." *Journal for the Study of the New Testament* 33.4 (2011): 406–14.

————. "Under Grace: The Christ-Gift and the Construction of a Christian Habitus." In *Apocalyptic Paul: Cosmos and Anthropos in Romans 5–8*, edited by Beverly R. Gaventa, 59–76. Waco, TX: Baylor University Press, 2013.

Barclay, John M. G., and Simon J. Gathercole, eds. *Divine and Human Agency in Paul and His Cultural Environment*. London: T&T Clark, 2008.

Barrett, C. K. *The Epistle to the Romans*. Black's New Testament Commentaries 6. Peabody, MA: Hendrickson, 2001.

Barth, Karl. *The Epistle to the Philippians: Fortieth Anniversary Edition*. Louisville: Westminster John Knox, 2002.

———. *The Epistle to the Romans*. Translated by E. C. Hoskyns. Oxford: Oxford University Press, 1977 (1933).

Beebe, Beatrice, et al. "Forms of Intersubjectivity in Infant Research: A Comparison of Meltzoff, Trevarthen, and Stern." In *Forms of Intersubjectivity in Infant Research and Adult Treatment*, 29–53. New York: Other Press, 2005.

Biklen, Douglas, and Richard Attfield. *Autism and the Myth of the Person Alone*. New York: New York University Press, 2005.

Bockmuehl, Markus. *The Epistle to the Philippians*. Black's New Testament Commentaries 11. Peabody, MA: Hendrickson, 1998.

Boter, Gerard. *The Enchiridion of Epictetus and Its Three Christian Adaptations: Transmission and Critical Editions*. Leiden: Brill, 1999.

Brooks, Arthur C. "Lent: It's Not Just for Catholics." *New York Times*, March 12, 2015, http://www.nytimes.com/2015/03/12/opinion/arthur-c-brooks-lent-its-not-just-for-catholics.html?emc=eta1.

Brown, Warren S., Nancey C. Murphy, and H. Newton Malony, eds. *Whatever Happened to the Soul? Scientific and Theological Portraits of Human Nature*. Minneapolis: Fortress, 1998.

Brunschwig, Jacques. "The Cradle Argument in Epicureanism and Stoicism." In *The Norms of Nature: Studies in Hellenistic Ethics*, edited by Malcolm Schofield and Gisela Striker, 113–44. Cambridge: Cambridge University Press, 1986.

Buber, Martin. *I and Thou*. Translated by Walter Kaufmann. New York: Touchstone, 1971.

Bultmann, Rudolf. "Antwort an Karl Jaspers [1953]." In *Kerygma und Mythos*, vol. 3, *Das Gespräch mit der Philosophie*, edited by Hans-Werner Bartsch, 49–59. Hamburg-Volksdorf: Reich, 1954.

———. "New Testament and Mythology: The Problem of Demythologizing the New Testament Proclamation." In *New Testament and Mythology and Other Basic Writings*, edited and translated by Schubert M. Ogden. Philadelphia: Fortress, 1984.

———. "Romans 7 and the Anthropology of Paul." In *Existence and Faith: Shorter Writings of Rudolf Bultmann*, translated by Schubert Ogden, 147–57. New York: Meridian Books, 1960.

———. "Römer 7 und die Anthropologie des Paulus." In *Imago Dei: Festschrift*

für Gustav Krüger, edited by H. Bornkamm, 53–62. Giessen: Alfred Töpelmann, 1932.

―――. *Theology of the New Testament*. Translated by Kendrick Grobel. 2 vols.
Waco, TX: Baylor University Press, 2007.

Burton, Robert A. *A Skeptic's Guide to the Mind: What Neuroscience Can and
Cannot Tell Us about Ourselves*. New York: St. Martin's Press, 2013.

Campbell, Douglas. *The Deliverance of God: An Apocalyptic Rereading of Justification in Paul*. Grand Rapids: Eerdmans, 2009.

Chappell, Timothy. "Knowledge of Persons." *European Journal for Philosophy of
Religion* 5.4 (2013): 3–28.

Chester, Stephen. " 'It Is No Longer I Who Live': Justification by Faith and Participation in Christ in Martin Luther's Exegesis of Galatians." *New Testament
Studies* 55 (2009): 315–37.

Congdon, David. *The Mission of Demythologizing: Rudolf Bultmann's Dialectical
Theology*. Minneapolis: Fortress, 2015.

―――. "The Word as Event: Barth and Bultmann on Scripture." In *The Sacred
Text: Excavating the Texts, Exploring the Interpretations, and Engaging the
Theologies of the Christian Scriptures*, edited by Michael Bird and Michael
Pahl. Piscataway, NJ: Gorgias Press, 2010.

Cranfield, C. E. B. *Commentary on Romans*. Vol. 1. International Critical Commentary. London: T&T Clark, 1975.

Croasmun, Matthew. *The Emergence of Sin: The Cosmic Tyrant in Romans*. Oxford: Oxford University Press, 2017.

―――. " 'Real Participation': The Body of Christ and the Body of Sin in Evolutionary Perspective." In *"In Christ" in Paul: Explorations in Paul's Theology
of Union and Participation*, edited by Kevin J. Vanhoozer, Constantine R.
Campbell, and Michael J. Thate, 127–56. WUNT 2.384. Tübingen: Mohr
Siebeck, 2014.

Darwall, Stephen. *The Second-Person Standpoint: Morality, Respect, and Accountability*. Cambridge, MA: Harvard University Press, 2006.

Davis, Joshua B., and Douglas Harink, eds. *Apocalyptic and the Future of Theology: With and Beyond J. Louis Martyn*. Eugene, OR: Cascade, 2012.

De Boer, Martinus C. *Galatians*. New Testament Library. Louisville: Westminster
John Knox, 2011.

―――. "Paul's Mythologizing Program in Romans 5–8." In *Apocalyptic Paul:
Cosmos and Anthropos in Romans 5–8*, edited by Beverly R. Gaventa, 1–20.
Waco, TX: Baylor University Press, 2013.

De Boer, Willis P. *The Imitation of Paul*. Kampen: Kok, 1962.

Dillon, John M. *The Middle Platonists: 80 B.C. to A.D. 220*. Ithaca, NY: Cornell
University Press, 1996.

Dodd, Brian J. "The Story of Christ and the Imitation of Paul in Philippians 2–3."
In *Where Christology Began: Essays on Philippians 2*, edited by Ralph P.

Martin and Brian J. Dodd, 154–61. Louisville: Westminster John Knox, 1988.

Duncan, Anne. *Performance and Identity in the Classical World*. New York: Cambridge University Press, 2006.

Dunn, James D. G. "Christ, Adam, and Preexistence." In *Where Christology Began: Essays on Philippians 2*, edited by Ralph P. Martin and Brian J. Dodd, 74–83. Louisville: Westminster John Knox, 1998.

———. *Jesus, Paul and the Law: Studies in Mark and Galatians*. London: SPCK, 1990.

———. *Romans 1–8*. Word Biblical Commentary 38A. Waco, TX: Word, 1988.

———. *Romans 9–16*. Word Biblical Commentary 38B. Dallas: Word, 1988.

Eastman, Susan Grove. "Apocalypse and Incarnation: The Participatory Logic of Paul's Gospel." In *Apocalyptic and the Future of Theology*, edited by Joshua Davis and Douglas K. Harink, 165–82. Eugene, OR: Wipf & Stock, 2012.

———. "The 'Empire of Illusion': Sin, Evil, and Good News in Romans." In *Comfortable Words: Essays in Honor of Paul F. M. Zahl*, edited by John D. Koch and Todd H. W. Brewer, 3–21. Eugene, OR: Wipf & Stock, 2013.

———. "Imitating Christ Imitating Us: Paul's Educational Project in Philippians." In *The Word Leaps the Gap: Essays on Scripture and Theology in Honor of Richard B. Hays*, edited by J. Ross Wagner, C. Kavin Rowe, and A. Katherine Grieb, 427–51. Grand Rapids: Eerdmans, 2008.

———. "Philippians 2:7–11: Incarnation as Mimetic Participation." *Journal for the Study of Paul and His Letters* 1.1 (2010): 1–22.

———. *Recovering Paul's Mother Tongue: Language and Theology in Galatians*. Grand Rapids: Eerdmans, 2007.

———. "The Shadow-Side of Intersubjective Identity: Sin in Paul's Letter to the Romans." *European Journal for Philosophy of Religion* 5.4 (2013): 125–44.

Eilan, Naomi, et al., eds. *Joint Attention: Communication and Other Minds*. Oxford: Oxford University Press, 2005.

Engberg-Pedersen, Troels. *Cosmology and Self in the Apostle Paul: The Material Spirit*. Oxford: Oxford University Press, 2010.

———. *Paul and the Stoics*. Louisville: Westminster John Knox, 2000.

———. "Philosophy of the Self in the Apostle Paul." In *Ancient Philosophy of the Self*, edited by Pauliina Remes and Juha Sihvola, 179–94. New York: Springer, 2008.

———. "A Stoic Concept of the Person in Paul? From Galatians 5:17 to Romans 7:14–25." In *Christian Body, Christian Self: Concepts of Early Christian Personhood*, edited by Clare K. Rothschild and Trevor W. Thompson, 85–112. Tübingen: Mohr Siebeck, 2011.

———. "Stoic Philosophy and the Concept of the Person." In *The Person and the Human Mind: Issues in Ancient and Modern Philosophy*, edited by Christopher Gill, 109–35. Oxford: Oxford University Press, 1990.

Engberg-Pedersen, Troels, and Niels Henrik Gregersen. "Introduction." The Centre for Naturalism and Christian Semantics (CNCS) at the University of Copenhagen website, http://teol.ku.dk/english/dept/cncs/dokumenter /cncs_project_description.pdf.

Everson, Stephen, ed. *Psychology*. Companions to Ancient Thought 2. Cambridge: Cambridge University Press, 1991.

Fee, Gordon. *Paul's Letter to the Philippians*. New International Commentary on the New Testament. Grand Rapids: Eerdmans, 1995.

Fowl, Stephen E. "Christology and Ethics in Philippians 2:5–11." In *Where Christology Began: Essays on Philippians 2*, edited by Ralph P. Martin and Brian J. Dodd, 140–53. Louisville: Westminster John Knox, 1998.

———. *Philippians*. The Two Horizons New Testament Commentary. Grand Rapids: Eerdmans, 2005.

Gallagher, Shaun. *How the Body Shapes the Mind*. Oxford: Oxford University Press, 2005.

———. *Phenomenology*. New York: Palgrave Macmillan, 2012.

Gallese, Vittorio. " 'Being like Me': Self-Other Identity, Mirror Neurons, and Empathy." In *Perspectives on Imitation: From Neuroscience to Social Science*, edited by Susan Hurley and Nick Chater, 1:101–18. Cambridge, MA: MIT Press, 2005.

Garbedian, H. Gordon. "The Star Stuff That Is Man." *New York Times*, August 11, 1929.

Gaventa, Beverly R. "God Handed Them Over: Reading Romans 1:18–32 Apocalyptically." *Australian Biblical Review* 53 (2005): 42–53.

———. "The Maternity of Paul: An Exegetical Study of Galatians 4:19." In *The Conversation Continues: Studies in Paul and John in Honor of J. Louis Martyn*, edited by Beverly R. Gaventa and Robert T. Fortna, 189–201. Nashville: Abingdon, 1990.

———. "The Shape of the 'I': The Psalter, the Gospel, and the Speaker in Romans 7." In *Apocalyptic Paul: Cosmos and Anthropos in Romans 5–8*, edited by Beverly R. Gaventa, 77–79. Waco, TX: Baylor University Press, 2013.

———. "The Singularity of the Gospel Revisited." In *Galatians and Christian Theology: Justification, the Gospel, and Ethics in Paul's Letter*, edited by Mark W. Elliott et al., 187–99. Grand Rapids: Baker Academic, 2014.

Gill, Christopher. "The Ancient Self: Issues and Approaches." In *Ancient Philosophy of the Self*, edited by Pauliina Remes and Juha Sihvola, 35–56. New York: Springer, 2008.

———. *The Structured Self in Hellenistic and Roman Thought*. Oxford: Oxford University Press, 2006.

Goodman, Lenn E., and D. Gregory Caramenico. *Coming to Mind: The Soul and Its Body*. Chicago: University of Chicago Press, 2014.

Gopnik, Alison, Andrew N. Meltzoff, and Patricia K. Kuhl. *The Scientist in the*

Crib: What Early Learning Tells Us about the Mind. New York: Harper, 2001.

Gorman, Michael J. *Inhabiting the Cruciform God: Kenosis, Justification, and Theosis in Paul's Narrative Soteriology.* Grand Rapids: Eerdmans, 2009.

Green, Joel B. *Body, Soul, and Human Life: The Nature of Humanity in the Bible.* Grand Rapids: Baker Academic, 2008.

———, ed. *What about the Soul? Neuroscience and Christian Anthropology.* Louisville: Abingdon, 2004.

Green, Joel B., et al., eds. *In Search of the Soul: Perspectives on the Mind-Body Problem.* 2nd ed. Eugene, OR: Wipf & Stock, 2010.

Gundry, Robert. *Sōma in Biblical Theology, with an Emphasis on Pauline Anthropology.* Cambridge: Cambridge University Press, 1976.

Haugeland, John. "Mind Embodied and Embedded." In *Having Thought: Essays in the Metaphysics of Mind*, edited by John Haugeland, 207–40. Cambridge, MA: Harvard University Press.

Hays, Richard B. *The Faith of Jesus Christ: The Narrative Substructure of Galatians 3:1–4:11.* Grand Rapids: Eerdmans, 2002.

Hickok, Gregory. *The Myth of Mirror Neurons: The Real Neuroscience of Communication and Cognition.* New York: Norton, 2014.

Hobson, Peter. *The Cradle of Thought: Exploring the Origins of Thinking.* Oxford: Oxford University Press, 2004.

Hobson, Peter, and Jessica Hobson. "Joint Attention or Joint Engagement? Insights from Autism." In *Joint Attention: New Developments in Psychology, Philosophy of Mind, and Social Neuroscience*, edited by Axel Seemann, 115–36. Cambridge, MA: MIT Press, 2011.

Hooker, Morna. "Interchange in Christ." *Journal of Theological Studies*, n.s., 32.2 (1971): 349–61.

———. "A Partner in the Gospel: Paul's Understanding of His Ministry." In *Theology and Ethics in Paul and His Interpreters: Essays in Honor of Victor Paul Furnish*, edited by Eugene H. Lovering and Jerry L. Sumney. Nashville: Abingdon, 1996.

———. "Philippians 2:6–11." In *From Adam to Christ.* Cambridge: Cambridge University Press, 1991.

Hoover, Roy W. "The Harpagmos Enigma: A Philological Solution." *Harvard Theological Review* 64.1 (1971): 95–119.

Hopkins, Gerard Manley. *Sermons and Devotional Writings.* Edited by Christopher Devlin, SJ. London: Oxford University Press, 1959.

Hurtado, Larry W. "Jesus as Lordly Example in Philippians 2:5–11." In *From Jesus to Paul: Studies in Honour of Francis Wright Beare*, edited by Peter Richardson and John C. Hurd, 113–26. Waterloo, ON: Wilfrid Laurier University Press, 1984.

Hutchinson, Ian. *Monopolizing Knowledge.* Belmont, MA: Fias, 2011.

Iacoboni, Marco. *Mirroring People: The New Science of Empathy and How We Connect with Others.* New York: Farrar, Straus & Giroux, 2008.

Jeeves, Malcolm A., ed. *From Cells to Souls—and Beyond: Changing Portraits of Human Nature.* Grand Rapids: Eerdmans, 2004.

Jewett, Robert. *Paul's Anthropological Terms: A Study of Their Use in Conflict Settings.* Leiden: Brill, 1971.

———. *Romans.* Hermeneia. Minneapolis: Fortress, 2007.

Johnson, Luke T. *Among the Gentiles: Greco-Roman Religion and Christianity.* New Haven: Yale University Press, 2009.

Kahn, Charles. "Discovering the Will: From Aristotle to Augustine." In *The Question of "Eclecticism": Studies in Later Greek Philosophy*, edited by John Dillon and Anthony Long, 234–59. Berkeley: University of California Press, 1988.

Käsemann, Ernst. *An die Römer.* Handbuch zum Neuen Testament 8A. Tübingen: Mohr Siebeck, 1980.

———. *Commentary on Romans.* Translated by G. W. Bromiley. Grand Rapids: Eerdmans, 1980.

———. "A Critical Analysis of Philippians 2:5–11." *Journal for Theology and the Church* 5 (1968): 45–88.

———. "The Cry for Liberty in the Worship of the Church." In *Perspectives on Paul*, translated by M. Kohl, 122–37. Mifflintown, PA: Sigler, 1996 (1969).

———. *Jesus Means Freedom.* Philadelphia: Fortress, 1968.

———. "Kritische Analyse von Phil. 2,5–11." *Zeitschrift für Theologie und Kirche* 47 (1950): 313–60.

———. "On Paul's Anthropology." In *Perspectives on Paul*, translated by M. Kohl, 1–31. Mifflintown, PA: Sigler, 1996 (1969).

Keck, Leander E. "What Makes Romans Tick?" In *Pauline Theology*, vol. 3, *Romans*, edited by David M. Hay and E. Elizabeth Johnson, 3–19. Minneapolis: Fortress, 1995.

Keener, Craig S. *The Mind of the Spirit: Paul's Approach to Transformed Thinking.* Grand Rapids: Baker Academic, 2016.

Kohn, David. "When Gut Bacteria Changes Brain Function." *Atlantic*, June 24, 2015.

Kurz, William S. "Kenotic Imitation of Paul and of Christ in Philippians 2 and 3." In *Discipleship in the New Testament*, edited by F. Fernando Segovia, 103–26. Philadelphia: Fortress, 1985.

Lange, Armin, and Eric M. Meyers, eds. *Light against Darkness: Dualism in Ancient Mediterranean Religion and the Contemporary World.* Göttingen: Vandenhoeck & Ruprecht, 2011.

Lapsley, Jacqueline E. *Can These Bones Live? The Problem of the Moral Self in the Book of Ezekiel.* Berlin: de Gruyter, 2000.

Lash, Nicholas. "Human Experience and the Knowledge of God." In *Theology on the Way to Emmaus*, 141–57. Eugene, OR: Wipf & Stock, 2005.

Lee, Michelle V. *Paul, the Stoics, and the Body of Christ*. Cambridge: Cambridge University Press, 2006.

Levinas, Emmanuel. *Totality and Infinity: An Essay on Exteriority*. Translated by Alphonso Lingus. Dordrecht: Kluwer Academic, 1991.

Lightfoot, J. B. *Philippians*. Grand Rapids: Zondervan, 1953.

Long, A. A. *Epictetus: A Stoic and Socratic Guide to Life*. Oxford: Oxford University Press, 2002.

———. *Stoic Studies*. Cambridge: Cambridge University Press, 1996.

Long, A. A., and D. N. Sedley. *The Hellenistic Philosophers*. 2 vols. Cambridge: Cambridge University Press, 1988.

Luhrmann, T. M. *Of Two Minds: An Anthropologist Looks at American Psychiatry*. New York: Vintage, 2001.

Luther, Martin. *Luther's Works*. Edited by Jaroslav Pelikan and Helmut T. Lehmann. St. Louis: Concordia, 1955–86.

MacIntyre, Alasdair. *Whose Justice? Which Rationality?* South Bend, IN: University of Notre Dame Press, 1989.

Marcus, Joel. " 'Let God Arise and End the Reign of Sin': A Contribution to the Study of Pauline Parenesis." *Biblica* 69.3 (1988): 386–95.

Martin, Dale. *The Corinthian Body*. New Haven: Yale University Press, 1995.

Martin, Ralph P. *Carmen Christi: Philippians ii.5–11 in Recent Interpretation and in the Setting of Early Christian Worship*. Cambridge: Cambridge University Press, 1967.

Martyn, Dorothy W. "A Child and Adam: A Parable of the Two Ages." In *Apocalyptic and the New Testament: Essays in Honor of J. Louis Martyn*, edited by Joel Marcus and Marion L. Soards, 317–33. Journal for the Study of the New Testament, Supplemental Series 24. Sheffield: JSOT, 1989.

Martyn, J. Louis. "Afterward: The Human Moral Drama." In *Apocalyptic Paul: Cosmos and Anthropos in Romans 5–8*, edited by Beverly R. Gaventa, 157–66. Waco, TX: Baylor University Press, 2013.

———. "De-apocalypticizing Paul: An Essay Focused on *Paul and the Stoics* by Troels Engberg-Pederson." *Journal for the Study of the New Testament* 24.4 (2002): 61–102.

———. *Galatians*. Anchor Bible 33A. New York: Doubleday, 1997.

Meeks, Wayne A. "The Man from Heaven in Paul's Letter to the Philippians." In *The Future of Early Christianity: Essays in Honor of Helmut Koester*, edited by Birger Pearson, 329–36. Minneapolis: Fortress, 1991.

———. "The Problem of Christian Living." In *Beyond Bultmann: Reckoning a New Testament Theology*, edited by Bruce W. Longenecker and Mikeal C. Parsons, 211–29. Waco, TX: Baylor University Press, 2014.

Meltzoff, Andrew N. "Understanding Other Minds: The 'Like Me' Hypothesis."

In *Perspectives on Imitation: From Neuroscience to Social Science*, edited by Susan Hurley and Nick Chater, 2:55–77. Cambridge, MA: MIT Press, 2005.

Meltzoff, Andrew N., and Rechele Brooks. " 'Like Me' as a Building Block for Understanding Other Minds: Bodily Acts, Attention, and Intention." In *Intentions and Intentionality: Foundations of Social Cognition*, edited by Bertram F. Malle, Louis J. Moses, and Dare A. Baldwin, 171–91. Cambridge MA: MIT Press, 2001.

Meltzoff, Andrew N., and Alison Gopnik. "The Role of Imitation in Understanding Persons and Developing a Theory of Mind." In *Understanding Other Minds: Perspectives from Autism*, edited by Simon Baron-Cohen et al., 335–66. New York: Oxford University Press, 1993.

Meltzoff, Andrew N., and M. Keith Moore. "Imitation of Facial and Manual Gestures by Human Neonates." *Science* 198.4312 (1977): 75–78.

Merleau-Ponty, Maurice. "The Child's Relations with Others." In *The Primacy of Perception*, 96–155. Evanston, IL: Northwestern University Press, 1964.

Metzger, Bruce M., ed. *A Textual Commentary on the Greek New Testament*. 2nd ed. Stuttgart: German Bible Society, 1994.

Meyer, Paul W. "Worm at the Core of the Apple." In *The Word in This World*, edited by Paul W. Meyer and John T. Carroll, 57–77. Louisville: Westminster John Knox, 2004.

———. "The Worm at the Core of the Apple: Exegetical Reflections on Romans 7." In *The Conversation Continues: Studies in Paul and John in Honor of J. Louis Martyn*, ed. Beverly R. Gaventa and Robert T. Fortna, 62–84. Nashville: Abingdon, 1990.

Nagel, Thomas. *Mind and Cosmos: Why the Materialist Neo-Darwinian Conception of Nature Is Almost Certainly False*. Oxford: Oxford University Press, 2012.

Nelson, Charles A., III, Nathan A. Fox, and Charles H. Zeanah Jr. "Anguish of the Abandoned Child." *Scientific American*, April 2013, 62–67. Published online March 19, 2013, doi:10.1038/scientificamerican0413–62.

Newsom, Carol A. *The Self as Symbolic Space: Constructing Identity and Community at Qumran*. Leiden: Brill, 2004.

Novenson, Matthew. "Paul's Former Occupation in *Ioudaismos*." In *Galatians and Christian Theology: Justification, the Gospel, and Ethics in Paul's Letter*, edited by Mark W. Elliott et al., 24–39. Grand Rapids: Baker Academic, 2014.

O'Brien, Peter T. *The Epistle to the Philippians*. New International Greek Testament Commentary. Grand Rapids: Eerdmans, 1991.

Ogden, Schubert, ed. "Introduction." In *Existence and Faith: Shorter Writings of Rudolf Bultmann*, 9–21. New York: Meridian, 1960.

Pacherie, Elisabeth. "The Phenomenology of Joint Action: Self-Agency versus Joint Agency." In *Joint Attention: New Developments in Psychology, Philos-*

ophy of Mind, and Social Neuroscience, edited by Axel Seemann, 343–90. Cambridge, MA: MIT Press, 2011.

Pascal, Blaise. "Discussion with Monsieur de Sacy." In *Pensées and Other Writings*, translated by H. Levi. Oxford: Oxford University Press, 1995.

Peck-McClain, Emily. "Agency in Paul and Implications for Adolescent Girls." *Religious Education* 110.1 (2015): 95–109.

Pinsent, Andrew. *The Second-Person Perspective in Aquinas's Ethics: Virtues and Gifts*. New York: Routledge, 2012.

Plantinga, Alvin. *Where the Conflict Really Lies: Science, Religion, and Naturalism*. Oxford: Oxford University Press, 2011.

Polkinghorne, John. *Quantum Physics and Theology: An Unexpected Kinship*. New Haven: Yale University Press, 2008.

———. *Science and Religion in Quest of Truth*. New Haven: Yale University Press, 2012.

Pollan, Michael. "Some of My Best Friends Are Germs." *New York Times Magazine*, May 15, 2013.

Prinz, Wolfgang. "Construing Selves from Others." In *Perspectives on Imitation: From Neuroscience to Social Science*, edited by Susan Hurley and Nick Chater, 2:180–82. Cambridge, MA: MIT Press, 2005.

Rabens, Volker. *The Holy Spirit and Ethics in Paul: Transformation and Empowerment for Religious-Ethical Life*. Revised 2nd edition. Minneapolis: Fortress, 2014.

———. " 'Indicative and Imperative' as the Substructure of Paul's Theology-and-Ethics in Galatians? A Discussion of Divine and Human Agency in Paul." In *Galatians and Christian Theology: Justification, the Gospel, and Ethics in Paul's Letter*, edited by Mark W. Elliott et al., 285–305. Grand Rapids: Baker Academic, 2014.

Reddy, Vasudevi. "Before the 'Third Element': Understanding Attention to Self." In *Joint Attention: Communication and Other Minds*, edited by Naomi Eilan et al., 85–109. Oxford: Oxford University Press, 2005.

———. "A Gaze at Grips with Me." In *Joint Attention: New Developments in Psychology, Philosophy of Mind, and Social Neuroscience*, edited by Axel Seemann, 137–57. Cambridge, MA: MIT Press, 2011.

———. *How Infants Know Minds*. Cambridge, MA: Harvard University Press, 2008.

Reddy, Vasudevi, Gabriella Markova, and Sebastian Wallot. "Anticipatory Adjustments to Being Picked Up in Infancy." PLOS ONE 8.6 (June 2013): e65289, doi:10.1371/journal.pone.0065289.

Remes, Pauliina, and Juha Sihvola, eds. *Ancient Philosophy of the Self*. New York: Springer, 2008.

Rizzolatti, Giacomo, and Carrado Sinigaglia. *Mirrors in the Brain: How Our Minds Share Actions and Emotions*. Oxford: Oxford University Press, 2006.

Robinson, John A. T. *The Body: A Study in Pauline Theology*. Bristol, IN: Wyndham Hall Press, 1988.

Rose, Nikolas S., and Joelle M. Abi-Rached. *Neuro: The New Brain Sciences and the Management of the Mind*. Princeton: Princeton University Press, 2013.

Rowe, Kavin. *One True Life: The Stoics and Early Christians as Rival Traditions*. New Haven: Yale University Press, 2016.

Sacks, Oliver. *The Man Who Mistook His Wife for a Hat*. New York: Perennial Library, 1987.

Sagan, Carl. "Cosmos: A Personal Journey." PBS Television, 1980, http://www .space.com/1602–carl-sagans-cosmos-returns-television.html.

Sanders, E. P. *Paul: The Apostle's Life, Letters, and Thought*. Minneapolis: Fortress, 2015.

Seemann, Axel, ed. *Joint Attention: New Developments in Psychology, Philosophy of Mind, and Social Neuroscience*. Cambridge, MA: MIT Press, 2011.

Seifrid, Mark A. "The Subject of Romans 7:14–25." *Novum Testamentum* 34.4 (1992): 313–33.

Shantz, Colleen. *Paul in Ecstasy: The Neurobiology of the Apostle's Life and Thought*. Cambridge: Cambridge University Press, 2009.

Smith, Peter Andrey. "Can the Bacteria in Your Gut Explain Your Mood?" *New York Times*, June 23, 2015.

Soskice, Janet M. *Metaphor and Religious Language*. Oxford: Oxford University Press, 1987.

Spaemann, Robert. *Personnen: Versuch über den Unterschied zwischen "Etwas" und "Jemand."* Stuttgart: Klett-Cotta, 1998.

Standhartinger, Angela. "Bultmann's *Theology of the New Testament* in Context." In *Beyond Bultmann: Reckoning a New Testament Theology*, edited by Bruce W. Longenecker and Mikeal C. Parsons, 233–55. Waco, TX: Baylor University Press, 2014.

Stern, Daniel N. *The Interpersonal World of the Infant*. New York: Basic Books, 1985.

Stowers, Stanley K. *A Rereading of Romans: Justice, Jews, and Gentiles*. New Haven: Yale University Press, 1994.

Stump, Eleonore. *Wandering in Darkness: Narrative and the Problem of Suffering*. Oxford: Oxford University Press, 2010.

Swinburne, Richard. *The Existence of God*. Oxford: Clarendon Press, 1979.

Swinton, John. "Reflections on Autistic Love: What Does Love Look Like?" *Practical Theology* 5.3 (2012): 259–78.

Tallis, Raymond. *Aping Mankind: Neuromania, Darwinitis, and the Misrepresentation of Humanity*. London: Routledge, 2014.

Tannehill, Robert C. *Dying and Rising with Christ: A Study in Pauline Theology*. Eugene, OR: Wipf & Stock, 2006.

————. *The Shape of the Gospel: New Testament Essays*. Eugene, OR: Cascade, 2007.

Tappenden, Frederick S. *Resurrection in Paul: Cognition, Metaphor, and Transformation*. Atlanta: SBL Press, 2016.

Taylor, Charles. *The Ethics of Authenticity*. Cambridge, MA: Harvard University Press, 1991.

————. "The Person." In *The Category of the Person: Anthropology, Philosophy, History*, edited by Michael Carrithers, Steven Collins, and Steven Lukes, 258–81. Cambridge: Cambridge University Press, 1985.

Thomas, Günter. "Human Personhood at the Edges of Life: Medical Anthropology and Theology in Dialogue." In *The Depth of the Human Person: A Multidisciplinary Approach*, edited by Michael Welker, 370–94. Grand Rapids: Eerdmans, 2014.

Trevarthen, Colwyn. "The Self Born in Intersubjectivity: The Psychology of an Infant Communicating." In *The Perceived Self: Ecological and Interpersonal Sources of Self-Knowledge*, edited by Ulric Neisser, 121–73. New York: Cambridge University Press, 1993.

Vanhoozer, Kevin J., Constantine R. Campbell, and Michael J. Thate, eds. *"In Christ" in Paul: Explorations in Paul's Theology of Union and Participation*. WUNT 2.384. Tübingen: Mohr Siebeck, 2014.

Van Kooten, George. *Paul's Anthropology in Context*. WUNT 232. Tübingen: Mohr Siebeck, 2008.

Wagner, J. Ross. "Working Out Salvation: Holiness and Community in Philippians." In *Holiness and Ecclesiology in the New Testament*, edited by Kent E. Brower and Andy Johnson, 257–74. Grand Rapids: Eerdmans, 2007.

Welker, Michael, ed. *The Depth of the Human Person: A Multidisciplinary Approach*. Grand Rapids: Eerdmans, 2014.

Wells, Kyle B. *Grace and Agency in Paul and Second Temple Judaism: Interpreting the Transformation of the Heart*. Leiden: Brill, 2014.

Westerholm, Stephen. "Paul's Anthropological 'Pessimism' in Its Jewish Context." In *Divine and Human Agency in Paul and His Cultural Environment*, edited by John M. G. Barclay and Simon J. Gathercole, 71–98. Edinburgh: T&T Clark, 2006.

Wiesel, Elie. *Souls on Fire: Portraits and Legends of Hasidic Masters*. New York: Random House, 1972.

Williams, Rowan. "Incarnation and the Renewal of Community." In *On Christian Theology*, 225–38. Oxford: Blackwell, 2000.

————. *Lost Icons: Reflections on Cultural Bereavement*. London: Continuum, 2003.

Wright, N. T. "Jesus Christ Is Lord: Philippians 2:9–11." In *The Climax of the Covenant*, 56–98. Minneapolis: Fortress, 1993.

————. "Messiahship in Galatians?" In *Galatians and Christian Theology: Jus-*

tification, the Gospel, and Ethics in Paul's Letter, edited by Mark W. Elliott et al., 3–23. Grand Rapids: Baker Academic, 2014.

Zahl, Simeon. "The Drama of Agency: Affective Augustinianism and Galatians." In *Galatians and Christian Theology: Justification, the Gospel, and Ethics in Paul's Letter*, edited by Mark W. Elliott et al., 335–52. Grand Rapids: Baker Academic, 2014.

Index of Names and Subjects

Index of Scripture and Other Ancient Sources